ONTOLOGY AND ALTERITY
IN MERLEAU-PONTY

Northwestern University
Studies in Phenomenology
and
Existential Philosophy

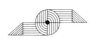

ONTOLOGY AND ALTERITY IN MERLEAU-PONTY

Galen A. Johnson and
Michael B. Smith, Editors

Northwestern University Press
Evanston, Illinois

1990

Northwestern University Press
Evanston, Illinois 60201

Emmanuel Levinas's "De l'intersubjectivite, Notes sur Merleau-Ponty" and
"De la sensibilite" were originally published in his *Hors sujet*, published in
1987 by Fata Morgana, and appear here in English translation by permission
of the publisher.

95 94 93 92 91 90   5 4 3 2 1

The paper used in this publication meets the minimum requirements of American National Standard for Information Sciences—Permanence of Paper for
Printed Library Materials, ANSI Z39. 48-1984

Library of Congress Cataloging-in-Publication Data

Ontology and alterity in Merleau-Ponty / Galen A. Johnson and Michael B.
Smith, editors.
    p. cm. — (Northwestern University studies in phenomenology and existen-
tial philosophy)
    Includes bibliographical references and index.
    ISBN 0-8101-0872-0. — ISBN 0-8101-0873-9 (pbk.)
    1. Merleau-Ponty, Maurice, 1908–1961—Contributions in ontology.
2. Merleau-Ponty, Maurice, 1908–1961—Contributions in concept of difference in philosophy. 3. Ontology. 4. Difference (Philosophy)
I. Johnson, Galen A., 1948– . II. Smith, Michael B. (Michael Bradley),
1940– . III. Series: Northwestern University studies in phenomenology &
existential philosophy.
B2430. M3764067 1990
111'.092—dc20   90-38391
                                                                      CIP

To the memory of
Joan Johnson

Contents

Acknowledgments

We extend our thanks, first of all, to our authors who have given so generously of their time and scholarship to make this collection possible. In particular, we are grateful to Professor Claude Lefort, originally for his Distinguished Lecture at the 1987 meetings of the Merleau-Ponty Circle held at the University of Rhode Island, subsequently for his attention to editing and revising the transcript, and for his permission to publish it here.

We also express our thanks to Emmanuel Levinas and Bruno Roy, editor of Editions Fata Morgana in Montpellier, France, for the translation rights to Professor Levinas's essays.

For their financial support of the 1987 conference of the Merleau-Ponty Circle, we are grateful to the University of Rhode Island offices of the President, the Vice-President for Academic Affairs (Provost), the Dean of the College of Arts and Sciences, the Council on the Humanities, and the Honors Program and Visiting Scholars Committee.

We also gratefully acknowledge the professional assistance of Kathy Cromer, of the Berry College Research Department, in final manuscript preparation.

Abbreviations

Abbreviations of titles of English works are given in Roman print; non-English in italic.

Works of Merleau-Ponty

A.D. *Adventures of the Dialectic,* trans. Joseph Bien (Evanston: Northwestern University Press, 1973).

A.D. Les aventures de la dialectique (Paris: Gallimard, 1955).

C.R.O. "The Child's Relations with Others," trans. William Cobb, in Pr.P.

R.A.E. "Les relations avec autrui chez l'enfant," *Cours de Sorbonne* (Paris, 1960).

E.M. "Eye and Mind," trans. C. Dallery, in Pr.P.

Œ. L'Oeil et l'esprit (Paris: Gallimard, 1964).

H.T. *Humanism and Terror,* trans. John O'Neill (Boston: Beacon Press, 1969).

H.T. Humanisme et terreur (Paris: Gallimard, 1947).

P.H. "Phenomenology and Psychoanalysis," Preface to Hesnard's *L'Oeuvre de Freud,* trans. Alden L. Fisher, *Review of Existential Psychology and Psychiatry,* 18 (1982–83), 67–81.

Ph.P. *The Phenomenology of Perception,* trans. Colin Smith (London: Routledge & Kegan Paul, 1962).

P.P. Phénoménologie de la perception (Paris: Gallimard, 1945).

Pr.P. *The Primacy of Perception and Other Essays,* ed. James E. Edie (Evanston: Northwestern University Press, 1964).

P.W. *Prose of the World,* trans. John O'Neill (Evanston: Northwestern University Press, 1973).

R.M.M. "Un inédit de Maurice Merleau-Ponty," *Revue de Métaphysique et de Morale,* 67/4 (1962), 400–409.

S. *Signs,* trans. Richard C. McCleary (Evanston: Northwestern University Press), 1964.

S. *Signes* (Paris: Gallimard, 1960).

S.B. *The Structure of Behavior,* trans. Alden L. Fisher (Boston: Beacon Press, 1963).

S.N.S. *Sense and Non-Sense,* trans. Hubert L. Dreyfus and Patricia Allen Dreyfus (Evanston: Northwestern University Press, 1964).

S.N.S. *Sens et non-sens* (Paris: Éditions Nagel, 1948; 4th ed., 1963).

T.E.O. "The Experience of Others," trans. Fred Evans and Hugh J. Silverman, *Review of Existential Psychology and Psychiatry,* 28/1–3 (1982–83).

T.L.C.F. *Themes from the Lectures at the Collège de France 1952–1960,* trans. John O'Neill (Evanston: Northwestern University Press, 1970).

R.C.C.F. *Résumés de cours, Collège de France 1952–1960* (Paris: Gallimard, 1968).

V.I. *The Visible and the Invisible,* trans. Alphonso Lingis (Evanston: Northwestern University Press, 1968).

V.I. *Le Visible et l'invisible* (Paris: Gallimard, 1964).

Works of Levinas

A.Q. *Autrement qu'être ou au-delà de l'essence* (The Hague: Martinus Nijhoff, 1974).

O.B. *Otherwise than being or beyond essence,* trans. Alphonso Lingis (The Hague: Martinus Nijhoff, 1981).

C.P. *Collected Philosophical Papers,* trans. Alphonso Lingis (Dordrecht: Martinus Nijhoff, 1987).

D.P.I.C. "Détermination philosophique de l'idée de culture," in *Philosophy and Culture. Proceedings of the XVIIth World Congress of Philosophy* (Montreal: Editions de Beffroi, 1986), 73–82.

D.L. *Difficile liberté* (Paris: Albin Michel, 1976).

H.H. *Humanisme de l'autre homme* (Montpellier: Fata Morgana, 1972).

D.C.P. *"Il y a," Deucallion, Cahiers de Philosophie,* Jean Wahl, ed., vol. 1 Paris: Editions de la Revue Fontaine, 1946).

R.P. "Signature," Adriaan Peperzak, ed.; trans. Mary Ellen Petrisko, *Research in Phenomenology,* 8 (1978), 175–89.

T.I. *Totality and Infinity,* trans. Alphonso Lingis (Pittsburgh: Duquesne University Press, 1969).

T.I. *Totalité et infini* (The Hague: Martinus Nijhoff, 1961).

Works of Husserl

C. *The Crisis of European Sciences and Transcendental Phenomenology,* trans. David Carr (Evanston: Northwestern University Press, 1970).

K. *Die Krisis europäischen Wissenschaften und die transcendentalen Phänomenologie,* Husserliana VI, hrsg. Walter Biemel (The Hague: Martinus Nijhoff, 1962).

Others

R.E.P.P. *Review of Existential Psychology and Psychiatry,* 18 (1982–83), "Merleau-Ponty and Psychology."

Introduction

Alterity

as a

Reversibility

Galen A. Johnson

This book is a thematic study of the question of alterity in Merleau-Ponty's ontology. What account of our relations with others does that ontology offer us? Is the account adequate to our concerns regarding genuine difference and a sense of justice suspicious of totalizations, whether they be philosophic or practical? Our relations with others refer here primarily to relations with other human beings, but because an ontology is at stake, we must also refer to our relations with nature and with things. And because our relation to ourselves is not one of sheer coincidence but includes otherness, we must also speak of personal identity and difference. Ultimately we will find ourselves confronting the ontological differentiation of Being from beings, and the methodological strictures the ontological difference brings to light.

It should be apparent that these questions we now put to Merleau-Ponty's ontology retrospectively come largely from elsewhere than his own thought. They are given to us by the clamor of contemporary philosophies of difference that count the Western philosophic tradition among the totalizing tendencies of our civilization, that contend for the end of metaphysics in the name of respect for plurality and genuine otherness. They are given to us by Derrida, Lyotard, Levinas, even Lefort, and their antecedents, certainly Nietzsche, perhaps Freud and Heidegger. Nothing less than the very project of philosophical ontology is at stake. Is it even possible to address our fundamental ontological concerns regarding being and nothingness without violating the alterity we encounter in the eyes of oppressed peoples, in the embraces of children, or in the resistance of nature? Do these representatives of otherness necessarily withdraw from systematic thought, rendering ontology and alterity an irresolvable dispute? Thus it has seemed to us reasonable to address an interrogation regarding alterity to what is for many of us the most creative recent ontology available, that of Merleau-Ponty.

The occasion for this volume was given us by its opening chapter, originally Claude Lefort's Distinguished Lecture at the 1987 annual meetings of the Merleau-Ponty Circle, now considerably edited and revised. Into the domain of Merleau-Ponty scholars and authors came Lefort, Merleau-Ponty's student, colleague, posthumous editor, and commentator, to challenge Merleau-Ponty's ontology. It is misleading, Lefort contended, to take the experience of sensible reversibility as the ultimate ontological truth, for to do so fails to recognize the irreducibility of otherness. Regardless of the force of Lefort's arguments, which we will briefly state in a moment, the force of the occasion was not lost on those in attendance.

We also publish here for the first time in English translation two complementary recent essays by Emmanuel Levinas that are parallel assessments of Merleau-Ponty's ontology on the question concerning alterity.

The term "alterity" is nearly a foreign word in English, and the reader may well wonder why a more graceful English word has not been chosen. The term derives from the Latin *alteritas*, meaning "the state of being other or different; diversity, otherness." It does have its English derivatives: alternate, alternative, alternation, and alter ego. The term *alterité* is more common in French, and has as its antonym *identité*.[1]

But a few years ago we would have been content to designate our thematic by a phrase such as "the question of intersubjectivity" or even "the problem of other minds." However, names have their histories. To speak of intersubjectivity or other minds has been associated with the modern tradition in Western philosophy beginning with Descartes. From him through Husserl, individual consciousness has, for the most part, been taken as the privileged starting point for knowledge. This had drastic repercussions for the philosophy of otherness. It is not only that the central position to be defeated was solipsism; it is more deeply that "the other" appears in these philosophies as a reduced "other," as an epistemological question. How can I know that the other exists, in the first place, and how can I understand the other's inner mental life? The term "alterity" shifts the focus of philosophic concern away from the "epistemic other" to the concrete "moral other" of practices—political, cultural, linguistic, artistic, and religious. This is consistent with the movement from the concerns of modern philosophy of knowledge and of the subject to the more decentered philosophies of postmodernism.

Merleau-Ponty seems to us a transitional figure in this regard. On the one hand, he was a critic of the philosophy of consciousness and individualism; yet on the other, as a phenomenologist indebted to Husserl, he was committed until the end to the primacy of bodily perception as the starting point for ontology. Thus the question of solipsism is not our principal address to Merleau-Ponty's ontology, but questions pertaining to moral goodness and political justice, psychological and cultural growth, and the interpretation of spoken and written expression. Of course, the question of solipsism does not disappear, as Merleau-Ponty's own texts amply testify, for if human beings, or nature and things, are assigned an irreducible difference and otherness, one immediately wonders how they may come to be known and understood.

The textual locus of our interrogation is Merleau-Ponty's work published posthumously in 1964 under the title *The Visible and the Invisible*, edited by Claude Lefort. In the remarkable chapter entitled "The Intertwining—

The Chiasm," Merleau-Ponty articulated the fundamental model for understanding the subject-object relation in perception as the reversibility relation. My left hand touches my right even as it is touched by the right, and this relation of touching–being touched can be, in the next instant, reversed. What does it mean to say that vision is similarly reversible? It does not mean the absurdity that the trees and things I see also see me in return. Rather, as I see objects, they reflect back to me an image of myself. Inanimate things do so only feebly; thus the confrontation with living beings, finally with other persons, is decisive advent for the reversibility of seeing–being seen. As Merleau-Ponty wrote, "The visible can fill me and occupy me only because I who see it do not see it from the depths of nothingness, but from the midst of itself; I the seer am also visible" (V.I., 113; *V.I.,* 152–53). Yet even within this reversibility of subject and object, for-itself and in-itself, my differentiation from things is preserved, the things—the others—escape me. "There is no coinciding of the seer with the visible. But each borrows from the other, takes from or encroaches upon the other, intersects with the other, is in chiasm with the other" (V.I., 261; *V.I.,* 314).

Perception is contact with differentiation. In touching, my hand is touched, but the touching is not coincident with being touched. In seeing, I am or at least can be seen, but the seeing is differentiated from being seen. There is contact because there is reversibility, but there is difference. When the difference is removed, as when my eye grows too close to the object, there is blurring, then blindness. With my eyes too close, there is loss of the visual field, loss of a horizon to ground a figure. Vision is contact that includes differentiation; loss of vision is contact without differentiation.

Merleau-Ponty had already introduced the perceptual reversibility of subject and object in *Phenomenology of Perception* (1945). He now sought to delineate its ontological import, deploying the phenomenology of perception as the parameters for a new ontology that would move beyond the hiatus of idealism or materialism, giving due weight to subject and object. Visibility requires contact of seer and seen. Thus they must be of one tissue, one flesh, and Merleau-Ponty's ontology may be cast as a monism, yet only if it be elaborated as a strangely turned, even paradoxical, monism capable of preserving divergence within the sensible and between the sensible and the intelligible. Flesh as prototype of Being is the opening to self-other communion and solidarity, just as it is the opening to self-other divergence and alterity. This is the genius of Merleau-Ponty's ontology, no doubt also its point of most severe tension. My own body that is flesh, as well as the flesh of language, the flesh of history, and the flesh of the world, are in every instance, both subject and object, both for-itself and in-itself. My own body prefigures its contact with and divergence from the other, for when one hand touches the other, the subject is for itself *already an other*. The self is not entirely coincident with itself, but includes otherness within its heart of hearts. All Merleau-Ponty's metaphors and images for the one element that he named "flesh" are cases of doubling: inside and outside, obverse and reverse, left and right, a hand in a glove, two leaves, two laps overlapping, a two-sided strait.

The authors in this collection elaborate the details of Merleau-Ponty's ontology and offer varying and conflicting interpretations of its complexities. Yet from this brief and introductory sketch, two fundamental issues surface in Merleau-Ponty's movement from a philosophy of visibility founded on contact and differentiation to an ontology of flesh and divergence, identity and difference. First is Merleau-Ponty's ontological starting point with bodily sensibilities such as touching and seeing. The phenomenological thesis of the primacy of perception is still present in *The Visible and the Invisible*, even though in a drastically revised form compared with Husserl's privileging of phenomenologically reduced consciousness. Therefore, the limits of phenomenology are at stake in this discussion. Second is Merleau-Ponty's effort to extend the reversibility relation within my own bodily sensibilities to all subject-object relations. The reversibility of touching–being touched as my right hand touches my left provides a pattern for approaching an understanding of our contacts with other persons, and with nature and things. For example, the same reversibility of touching and being touched seems present in a handshake with another person, or in an embrace, or in a look.

In *Phenomenology of Perception* Merleau-Ponty had put the thesis this way: "As the parts of my body together comprise a system, so my body and the other person's are one whole, inside and outside of one and the same phenomenon, and the anonymous existence of which my body is the ever-renewed trace henceforth inhabits both bodies simultaneously" (Ph.P., 354; *P.P.,* 406). Thus he could write that "the experience of an *alter ego* . . . presupposes that already my view of myself is halfway to having the quality of a possible 'other' " (Ph.P., 448; *P.P.,* 511). By the time of *The Visible and the Invisible,* this "halfway" had grown stronger: "Why would this generality which constitutes the unity of my body, not open it to other bodies? The handshake too is reversible. . . . Why would not the synergy exist among different organisms, if it is possible within each? Their landscapes interweave, their actions and their passions fit together exactly" (V.I., 142; *V.I.,* 187).

To combine these two fundamental issues, we may say that this book addresses this overarching concern: Is the reversible alterity of sensing-sensed that we discover within our own bodies sufficient for understanding the alterity of other persons and of nature, or are we confronted in these cases with an alterity of a wholly different kind?

Merleau-Ponty and Lefort on Alterity

Lefort's challenge to Merleau-Ponty's account of alterity is grounded in an interpretation of his ontology that stresses flesh as an account of genesis or origins—in short, birth. From this point of view, he argues there are three main deficiencies. First, the ontology of reversibility ignores infantile experience. For the infant, the other is not originally an *alter ego,* such that the perspective of the infant is reversible with that of the adult. Merleau-Ponty erred in imagining that for the infant, let alone the adult, "nature is always for us as at the first day," because between the infant's eyes and the things there is a mediator who does not stand on the same level as the infant. There is "the third one" who gives names to things, who indeed names the child, thus introducing the infant into the sphere of law.

This means that, second, vision is not the original openness to the sensible. All the contacts with the maternal body come before seeing, and at the first moment there is no separation between outside and inside. Here then are two asymmetries, therefore irreversibilities, in the alterity of children, an irreversibility of name and law due to the mediation of "the third," and an irreversibility of desire because between mother and infant there is no differentiation of perspectives. The second irreversibility is a challenge to the phenomenological thesis of the primacy of perception. As Lefort writes, the adult-child alterity "is not a question of perspectives" (Lefort, "Flesh and Otherness," 9).

Lefort states a third challenge, again beginning from the experience of children. Referring to the research of Melanie Klein, as well as Freud, Lefort contends that there is an asymmetrical split between the good and the bad object. The infant is called to respond to things mediated by the desires and needs of others that assign values to things. These desires and needs mediating the infant's relation to things emerged from an archaic history of wishes, expectations, and fears that are in principle unrepresentable to the child because they are unrepresentable to ourselves.

In general, what is not taken into account by Merleau-Ponty, Lefort believes, is "the third one" who mediates the child's relation to the world and who is the true representative of irreducible and irreversible otherness. Lefort contends that this general omission enlightens the difficulties Merleau-Ponty encountered in his political analyses. The evolution from the Marxist sympathies of *Humanism and Terror* (1947) to the disavowal of Marxism in *Adventures of the Dialectic* (1955) is in part theoretically grounded in Merleau-Ponty's failure to admit an asymmetrical and irreversible separation between political forms of society, especially between modern democracy and totalitarianism. Thus Merleau-Ponty did not overcome relativism in his account of political justice.

Since Lefort's lecture, a transcript was prepared and has circulated among members of the Merleau-Ponty Circle. We publish here four replies, three of which defend

Merleau-Ponty each from a different point of view, and one of which is in substantial agreement with Lefort's criticisms. M. C. Dillon has taken up the challenge that Merleau-Ponty's account of alterity ignores the experience of children. After all, it is somewhat odd to state such a challenge to Merleau-Ponty who held the chair of child psychology and pedagogy for three years at the Sorbonne (1949–52), succeeded in that chair by Jean Piaget, and who devoted a 1951 lecture course to the topic "The Child's Relations with Others" that reflected on Lacan's research regarding the mirror stage. Dillon returns to the 1951 Merleau-Ponty course at the Sorbonne, as well as to texts from *The Visible and the Invisible,* to argue that Merleau-Ponty's ontology of the reversibility of flesh is uniquely capable of disclosing the kind of transcendence known as alterity, including the alterity of the child. He also argues, however, that Merleau-Ponty's study of child development was overlaid with the influence of Husserl's transcendentalism, such that Merleau-Ponty erred in his presentation of the doctrine of alterity. Flesh is not a substance or, in the language of Aristotle, the *hypokeimenon* (underlying being), Dillon argues, and Merleau-Ponty's ontology was not a monism. Flesh is a relational term only, to be understood adverbially rather than substantially, and is fully compatible with the kind of empirical realism Lefort takes as irrelevant for understanding Merleau-Ponty.

Gary Brent Madison has defended Merleau-Ponty against Lefort, and somewhat against Dillon's reading of Merleau-Ponty, by situating Merleau-Ponty's ontology of flesh within the history of philosophic attempts to deal with that most basic problem of identity and difference, *ipseity* and *alterity.* He argues that Merleau-Ponty's "postmodern" solution to the problem of selfhood returns us to the premodern thought of St. Augustine. The term "flesh" is not really a genetic concept at all for Merleau-Ponty, and genetic interpretation of it too easily falls prey to the kind of causal, empirical realism that is completely incompatible with the whole basic thrust of phenomenology. The function of "flesh" is twofold: it offers Merleau-Ponty a definitive overcoming of modern subjectivism and solipsism, and at the same time introduces alterity into the very definition of subjective "self-sameness." Merleau-Ponty undertook a postmodern decentering of subjectivity in *The Visible and the Invisible,* but with no desire to rid philosophy of the notion of subjectivity itself. Though he undertook a pitiless critique of Husserlianism and sought to realize a "hyper-reflection" that is "the perceptual faith questioning itself about itself," Merleau-Ponty never abandoned phenomenology as a form of reflective or "transcendental" philosophy. Lefort is wrong to set up a dispute between "flesh as reversibility" and "flesh as alterity," for the meaning of the term flesh—a term without equivalent in the history of philosophy, as Merleau-Ponty said—is nothing other than the presence of the other in the same. The flesh is the trace of the other, the inscription of the other, in the subject's own selfhood. What "flesh" means is that the subject is for itself an other.

In his reply to Lefort called "Justice in the Flesh," David Michael Levin takes up Lefort's challenge regarding political justice. Against Lefort's claim that reversibility ignores the asymmetry between the good and bad object, the good and evil political regime, Levin argues that perceptual reversibilities embedded in infant bodies are a primordial sociality that make us ready for the mutual recognitions and reciprocities necessary to a more mature social, moral, and political community. Perceptual reversibility is not identical with political reciprocity, but is its originating ground. Merleau-Ponty's phenomenology of narcissism shows that the flesh plays with infantile narcissism in order to "double-cross and reverse" it. By the grace of the flesh, the sociality that is potential in our bodies can be drawn out and educated. In order to establish this account of bodily reversibility as ground for the communicative praxis of moral community, Levin contests both the historicist view that the only order in the human body is an order totally imposed by society, as well as the biologism sponsored by Nietzsche, Freud, and their descendants that reduces the body to a chaos of disorganized drives. It is also necessary to disavow the historic alliance between the ego-centered, gratification-seeking body and the capitalist social system that privileges it, splitting us off from the reversibilities of the flesh and the communicative reciprocity requisite to our bodily sense of justice. Levin also contests Dillon's use of the language of encroachment, transgression, and alienation in defending Merleau-

Ponty against the criticisms of Lefort, language Levin admits was Merleau-Ponty's own in describing the socialization of children, but was taken over by him under the undue influence of Lacan. Nevertheless, Merleau-Ponty's best insights illuminate the intertwinings and reversibilities in the intercorporeal body of our experience that are the natural, inaugural, and most radical grounding of the ideal of justice in the body politic.

Finally, it is in Stephen Watson's essay that we find the boldest agreement with Lefort's charges against Merleau-Ponty, and an assessment of their implications for post-transcendental philosophy. Watson argues that the play of the signifier in Merleau-Ponty's own texts has come home to haunt him, even now in Lefort's deviation from his earlier precise explications of Merleau-Ponty's thought. With "structuralist" hindsight, we can see that neither the Lacanian challenge of desire nor the discourse of the name can be handled without remainder by Merleau-Ponty's ontology of flesh and divergence committed to the single speaking subject. Moreover, Merleau-Ponty cannot be defended by either a transcendentalism of the lived-body or by a return to Husserl reinvoking the pure forms of grammar. Watson interprets Lefort's emphasis upon "the third" as the genuine source of ethical and political alterity in relationship to Levinas's emphasis upon the primacy of the moral other. Nevertheless, Levinas with Lefort has less bridged the abyss from which Merleau-Ponty spoke, Watson argues, than simply overlooked it in favor of the primacy of the practical. Thus, if Merleau-Ponty's failure to handle alterity as a theoretical question points to the end of transcendental philosophy, postmodern philosophy cannot simply ignore theoretical reason in favor of practice, and no one recognized this better than Merleau-Ponty.

Merleau-Ponty and Levinas on Alterity

Watson's detection of the Levinasian primacy of practical reason in Lefort's invocation of "the third," as well as references to Levinas in the essays by Dillon and Madison, indicate the benefit to be gained by introducing into our discussion Levinas's critical analyses of Merleau-Ponty's ontology. It is correct that Levinas's philosophy of alterity raises issues regarding Merleau-Ponty similar to those found in Lefort's analysis, but without the genetic context. The two essays we publish here for the first time in English, translated and introduced by Michael Smith, appeared originally in French in 1984, and were reprinted in the collection *Hors Sujet* (1987). In both, Levinas frames his confrontation with Merleau-Ponty through an examination of Merleau-Ponty's late essay on Husserl called "The Philosopher and His Shadow." In Merleau-Ponty and Levinas we have two of our most able interpreters of Husserl directing their attention to the same Husserlian text, *Ideas II*, arriving at conflicting results, and the confrontation is exciting to follow.

The density and subtlety of Levinas's analyses defy summary, for they emerge from themes now applied to Merleau-Ponty that have grown out of Levinas's earlier work, especially *Time and the Other* (1947), *Totality and Infinity* (1961), and *Otherwise than Being, or Beyond Essence* (1974). Levinas argues that the alterity of other human beings cannot be accommodated within Merleau-Ponty's framework of the primacy of perception, for in spite of all Merleau-Ponty's adjustments in the meaning of perception pertaining to embodiment, social, cultural, and linguistic situation, he still continues the Husserlian approach to others as a problem of knowledge. The approach to the other must be through *sentiment* (feeling) rather than *sensation*. Levinas writes that the handshake is not simply the notification of cognitive agreement, but prior to that notification the extraordinary event itself of peace, just as the caress is already affection and not information. In the touch itself is presupposed the possibility of a helping hand. I lend myself to the other by the generosity and ethical value of the gift, and such feeling (*sentiment*), which points ultimately to love and the love of God, is prior to the sensations of "double touching." Alterity is therefore not a modality of sensation, but of sentiment.

Though it would be wrong to reduce the disagreement among Merleau-Ponty, Lefort, and Levinas to one dimension, the discussion does focus attention on the hermeneutic overdetermination surrounding Merleau-Ponty's term "reversibility," and its conceptual relation to symmetry and reciprocity. Merleau-Ponty is no doubt in some part responsible for this. His critics (and some of his defenders) assume, naturally enough, that Merleau-Ponty's guiding ontological insight into subject-object reversibility implies the symmetry of subject and object, and therefore implies their reciprocity and substitutability. After all, the weight of logical reversibility is carried by the biconditional. Thus ontological difference between subject and object is excluded. However, if reversibility is not taken as a strictly logical term associated with the biconditional, it might be possible to speak of reversibility without the implication of symmetry, reciprocity, or substitutability. For example, reversibility might be construed dialectically, or most likely, aesthetically, as in mirror images where there is reversibility with difference. In the mirror, the right hand is transposed as the left hand. Lefort and Levinas trade on showing that self-other relationships are so often asymmetrical, then conclude against the reversibility thesis. The conclusion, however, need not follow. All this needs to be developed carefully, but in this way the dispute between Merleau-Ponty on the one side with Lefort and Levinas on the other might be considerably eased.

With the support of Robert Bernasconi's careful scholarship regarding the relation of Merleau-Ponty to Levinas, we begin to see that the distance between these two thinkers might indeed not be as great as first approach would suggest. For one thing, we are led to wonder if Merleau-Ponty's account of touching–being touched, seeing–being seen was meant purely as a modality of sensation, or if it was not already imbued with the modality of sentiment and thereby charged with ethical significance. For another thing, Levinas wrote an earlier essay on Merleau-Ponty in 1961, the year of Merleau-Ponty's death and of the publication of Levinas's *Totality and Infinity*. It is entitled "Meaning and Sense" and is the subject of Bernasconi's attention in "One-Way Traffic: The Ontology of Decolonization and its Ethics." Because in "Meaning and Sense" Levinas associates Merleau-Ponty with the phrase "fundamental historicity," and because for Levinas the origin of meaning is beyond history located in the ethics of the face of the Other, we begin from the appearance of a dispute. Nevertheless, Merleau-Ponty's reason for standing by the historicity of cultural expression as fundamental for meaning (*sens*) was to break Western thought's nostalgia for a culture capable of encompassing all historical cultures, and this ethic and politics of decolonization Merleau-Ponty shares with Levinas. In addition, both thinkers find the generosity of comprehension in approaching non-Western cultures to be the most praiseworthy feature of occidental thought. Such shared ethical attitudes lead Bernasconi to explore Levinas's trajectory with respect to "ethical culture" in relation to meaning and sense, and to the conclusion that Merleau-Ponty's "humanism in extension" corresponds with the asymmetrical relation in favor of the Other evoked by the ethical weight of Levinas's phrase *sens unique,* one-way traffic.

In Patrick Burke's essay, "Listening at the Abyss," we have an exposition of Merleau-Ponty's interrogative methodology and examination of its implications for the revision of ontology in terms of the "there is" (*il y a*) of abyssal or wild Being. Burke succeeds in bringing us as close as we might come to feeling the spirit and hearing the voice of Merleau-Ponty at work on *The Visible and the Invisible* as he guides us through the philosopher's critique of reflection, dialectic, and intuition, bringing us to a consideration of the seriousness and import of the idea of divergence (*écart*) in Merleau-Ponty's ontology. If the account of Being includes difference as well as sameness, emptiness and distance as well as fullness, we are led to inquire about the ontological status of this porosity, these hollows in Being. Is *écart* a nothingness? Is it an abyss? Merleau-Ponty's own statement in the preface to *Signs* calls for our meditation: "As a matter of principle, fundamental thought is bottomless. It is, if you wish, an abyss" (S., 21; S., 29). What is the meaning of this abyss, and how is it to be thought?

Burke argues that Merleau-Ponty understood the meaning of Being in terms of astonishment at presence, a wonder prior to the subject-object distinction. More than an act or attitude of the perceiving subject, wonder is the meaning of the "there is," and Being is an abyssal and eternal bursting open of wonder that is essentially narcissistic. This explains why the self-differentiations of Being, for-itself and in-itself, are reversible. Here we have an account of the ontological difference between Being and beings that offers us the best and most fundamental defense of ontological reversibility. Burke contrasts Merleau-Ponty's description of the "there is" as wonder with that of Levinas, for whom the experience of *il y a* does not blend into and become reversible with brute Being itself because this experience is one of horror or repulsion at the eternity of Being, the horror of not being able to die. Burke's profound and poignant meditation concludes with a reflection on whether Merleau-Ponty's account of Being escapes the methodological strictures he himself set out for ontology, and leaves us with an indirect reflection upon Merleau-Ponty's name, the blackbird posed on a bridge over an abyss, listening in wonder for the sublime Silence.

Wayne Froman offers us a reading of reversibility that also draws our attention to listening and may bring us closer to Levinas's concerns regarding sentiment. He begins from Derrida's essay, "Violence and Metaphysics," comparing Husserl and Levinas on the question of alterity, in order to raise the issue of whether Merleau-Ponty's account of alterity is guilty of "transcendental violence." Froman argues that we find in *The Visible and the Invisible* an account of alterity that is beyond the circle of visibility—namely, the reversibility of hearing—phonation. If I am close enough to the other who speaks to hear his breath and feel his effervescence and fatigue, Merleau-Ponty wrote, I almost witness in him as in myself, the awesome birth of vociferation. The motor echoes awakened by movements of phonation have their sonorous inscription in me, they "resound" in me. Froman argues that in hearing–being heard, in genuine listening, there is a reversibility anterior to the zone of transcendental violence such as it may always lurk in "the look."

Other Explorations of Alterity in Merleau-Ponty: Philosophy of Nature, Derrida, and Hegel

In Merleau-Ponty's meditations on the alterity within selfhood and between self and other persons, the challenge was to frame an ontology of identity, communion, and soli-

darity that would not absorb and nullify the force of self-
deception, divergence, difference, and strangeness. If we
turn to a consideration of the alterity of things and nature,
the challenge seems to be reversed, to draw nature toward
ourselves (or ourselves toward nature) and restore communion and solidarity where difference and alienation
have been assumed. In her essay "Merleau-Ponty and
Deep Ecology," Monika Langer reminds us of what Husserl taught us in *Crisis of European Sciences,* that Galileo and
Descartes bequeathed to us an alienated view of nature
that regards the nonhuman world as a realm of quantifiable facts devoid of meaning. This worldview restricts
value to rationality and consciousness, resulting in a fact/
value dichotomy and legitimating the anthropocentrism
that relegates nature to the status of "resources." Langer
argues that world alienation is now embedded not only in
our philosophy and science, but in our technicized everyday existence. For ecological philosophers, at issue is not
merely the protection and reparation of things, but the
restoration of reciprocity and interrelatedness between
humans and nature.

Langer contends that nothing less than a new ontology
is required that can challenge the Cartesian paradigm. The
resources for this ontology may be found not only in Heidegger, as often has been presumed, but in Merleau-
Ponty, who was at work on a new philosophy of nature in
his last lectures and writings. In "The Philosopher and His
Shadow" Merleau-Ponty followed the lead found in Husserl's fragment "Overthrow of the Copernican Theory,"
and began to elaborate an account of Earth as an intertwining (*Ineinander*), an enfolding of humans within nature
that is an "embrace." Because many of the ecological sciences that focus on structures, systems, processes, organisms, and wholes have also adopted the mechanistic
assumptions of Newtonian physics and the general concern with prediction, control, and management, Langer
argues that Merleau-Ponty was also correct in "Eye and
Mind" to turn to painting for an interrogation of the visible that allows the meanings and norms within nature to
come to expression.

This volume on the dimensions of alterity in Merleau-
Ponty's later philosophy could not approach completion

without introducing into the discussion Derrida and *différ-ance,* and the relation of Derrida to Merleau-Ponty. In his middle period, when he most privileged the question of language within philosophy and worked on *The Prose of the World,* Merleau-Ponty wrote that a phenomenology of language seeks a "return to the speaking subject" (S., 85; *S.,* 106). In this single phrase Merleau-Ponty seems to have set himself at odds with subsequent French philosophy, even to an extent with Ricoeur's hermeneutics, but certainly with the postmodernism of Lyotard and the deconstruction of Derrida. Merleau-Ponty brought language to the forefront, but his attention to style, expression, and signification appeared to many a "subjective" approach to language that excluded contact with the sciences of language, as well as with Derrida's polar opposite attention to inscription, signature, and trace. Deconstruction insinuates itself between the "speaking subject" and his or her word, disarming all pretensions to univocity, disarming even an unsayable or silent univocal thrust carried by the "significative intention." The colonial emperor of reason and order has no clothes.

In his essay "Merleau-Ponty and Derrida: Writing on Writing" Hugh Silverman casts doubt on this picture of opposition between the two philosophers. Derrida's writing, he argues, is a new language that cannot yet dissociate itself entirely from Merleau-Ponty's writings. It is true that in Derrida, writing is not simply the product or the correlate of speech, but the inscription of difference, of spacing between text and context, between what is one's own and what is not one's own. It is true that style for Merleau-Ponty is a way of being in the world, and that for Derrida style is also the stylus, the pointed thing, the writing tool, the male instrument. Nevertheless, already for Merleau-Ponty the style of writing was said to be an indirect language that precedes formulation and makes it possible, that is not entirely one's own, that is shaped out of its past, and that awaits the present of its readership. Thus there is a distinct juxtapositional contact between the Merleau-Pontean account of style and the Derridean formulation of writing. In this and similar probing ways, Silverman argues for rapprochement between these two theories of writing. Indeed, Merleau-Ponty's account of writing, he contends, seems to have prepared the way for the looming presence of alterity that marks the difference in which Derridean writing operates.

No doubt Hegel's account of "unhappy consciousness" in *Phenomenology of Spirit* is the clearest historical precedent in modern times for finding alterity within the structure of selfhood. Therefore we also include here two reflections on Merleau-Ponty's thought by Hegel scholars. Joseph Flay gives us an explication of the mature Hegel's doctrine of essence in the *Encyclopedia* that he argues supports Merleau-Ponty's ontology of being. Hegel's essentialism contains a notion of radical otherness that undergirds his thought about necessity and contingency, truth and ambiguity, as well as the gap between philosophy and nonphilosophy, especially between philosophy on the one hand, and politics and history on the other. Merleau-Ponty need not have joined Hyppolite, overinfluenced as well by the anthropological reading of Hegel offered in Kojève's lectures, in defending a split between the "existentialist" Hegel of the *Phenomenology of Spirit* in opposition to Hegel the "system-builder" of the *Encyclopedia*. In both places, Flay argues, Hegel defended a view of reality as the upsurge of being in which the nature of what comes to be is not predeterminable, is thus a matter of contingency and otherness. In Hegel we find a persistent and fundamental asymmetry between past and future that is nowhere overridden by his concept of the "end of history." Any temporal end is a qualified end, and any talk of essence is restricted to a discussion of what has happened, and not what will happen or what happens eternally. All necessity is post hoc. Hegel's critique of the traditional doctrine of essence shows that the attempt to grant stability to Being itself fails, and that any such attempt gives in to the Socratic anxiety to tame being by imposing a stable, consistent, and unchanging measure upon the cosmos. Had Merleau-Ponty realized this, he might have found in Hegel the resources for extending his own nonabsolutist, situational philosophy of freedom, action, and politics.

Merold Westphal undertakes an examination of the apparent gap between Merleau-Ponty's phenomenology of perception and philosophical ontology on the one side and his political writings on the other. The best in Merleau-

Ponty's politics, Westphal contends, encompassing both the Marxist sympathies of *Humanism and Terror* and the anti-Marxist liberalism of *Adventures of the Dialectic,* was a hermeneutics of suspicion interested in exposing the self-deceptive mythology found in communism as well as in capitalism. However, neither Merleau-Ponty's phenomenology of perception nor his ontology of the visible and invisible provides a philosophical rationale for a hermeneutics of suspicion. They do not, because both are grounded in a commitment to the primacy of perception; interpretation theory suspicious of political mythology must be grounded in a phenomenology of desire and will. The self-deception at the heart of politics is a phenomenon of desire, repression, and ambivalence as described by Kierkegaard, Nietzsche, and Freud, and is not a phenomenon of sense-experience, situation, and ambiguity, as the limits of Merleau-Ponty's philosophy dictated. Merleau-Ponty's break with Husserlian idealism in *The Visible and the Invisible* remained too Heideggerian and too little Hegelian, for it was Hegel in *Phenomenology of Spirit* who taught us that the opening moment in the development of intersubjectivity is desire and its culminating moment is self-divided unhappy consciousness. In this way, Westphal brings us full circle by implicitly restating Lefort's claim that the aporias in Merleau-Ponty's phenomenology and ontology of self and other explain his difficulties in political theory, as well as seconding Levinas's opinion that the reversibility of sense experience found in touching and being touched cannot adequately illuminate our radical confrontation with the other.

This collection marks an interreferential dialogue and debate, rare in contemporary philosophy, on one of the most pressing philosophical issues of our age. Nothing less is at stake than the limits of phenomenology and the possibility of philosophical ontology in an age in which difference and alterity are woven into our consciousness and require philosophical illumination. This collection also marks the progress of Merleau-Ponty scholarship from an initial period of silence and neglect, to devoted translation and exposition, and now to sober, critical assessment.

PART 1

MERLEAU-PONTY AND LEFORT ON ALTERITY

1

Flesh and Otherness

Claude Lefort

A ddressing an audience of philosophers who are intimately acquainted with Merleau-Ponty's works, I will suppose that his philosophical itinerary is well known and permit myself a short investigation at the frontiers of his last writings.[1]

First of all, my purpose is to bring to light the ambiguities of the concept of flesh, such as it was defined in *The Visible and the Invisible*, by referring particularly to the chapter "The Intertwining—The Chiasm." In that chapter, as you know, Merleau-Ponty goes so far as to present the flesh as a prototype of Being. In the "working notes" joined to the manuscript of *The Visible and the Invisible*, and earlier in different essays, he speaks of the flesh of language, the flesh of history, and the flesh of the World. Moreover, he says that thought itself is a "sublimation of flesh" (V.I., 145; *V.I.*, 191). Nonetheless, in accordance with the analyses of the *Phenomenology of Perception*, the characteristics of one's own body and its insertion in the sensible apparently continue to provide the original pattern. I should like to point out the tensions between an interpretation principally founded upon the experience of reversibility and an interpretation that makes us admit the irreducibility of Otherness. From this point of view, the last sentence of *The Visible and the Invisible*, saying that reversibility constitutes the ultimate truth, could be misleading, although it corresponds to Merleau-Ponty's previous characterization of flesh as the "ultimate notion" (V.I., p. 140; *V.I.*, 185).

In a second moment, I will attempt to put a few questions of my own, in order to emphasize the new difficulties we encounter as soon as we take into account the relation to the other, or the others. Finally, I will suggest that these last questions draw our attention to the oscillations of Merleau-Ponty's thought in the field of politics and history.

I certainly do not intend to comment in detail on the texts to which I will refer. Nonetheless, it seems to me useful to take as a starting point three particularly meaningful texts in order to scrutinize the primary image introduced in the first outline of flesh as prototype of Being. My first quotation is borrowed from the chapter "Interrogation and Intuition." Merleau-Ponty said:

> The visible can fill me and occupy me only because I who see it do not see it from the depths of nothingness, but from the midst of itself; I the seer am also visible. What makes the weight, the thickness, the flesh of each color, of each sound, of each tactile texture, of the present and of the world is the fact that he who grasps them feels himself emerge from them by a sort of coiling up or redoubling, fundamentally homogeneous with them; he feels that he is the sensible itself coming to itself and that in return the sensible is in his eyes as it were his double or an extension of his own flesh. [V.I., 113–14; *V.I.*, 152–53]

The second passage is extracted from the chapter "The Intertwining—The Chiasm":

> It suffices for us for the moment to note that he who sees cannot possess the visible unless he is possessed by it, unless he is of it, unless in principle, according to what is required by the articulation of the look with the things, he is one of the visibles, capable, by a singular reversal, of seeing them—he who is one of them. [V.I., 134–35; *V.I.*, 177–78]

And later, saying that body is a "sensible for itself, which means, not that absurdity: color that sees itself, surface that touches itself," Merleau-Ponty notices:

> [It is] an exemplar sensible, which offers to him who inhabits it and senses it the wherewithal to sense everything that resembles himself on the outside, such that, caught up in the tissue of things, it draws it entirely to itself, incorporates it, and, with the same movement, communicates to the things upon which it

closes over that identity without superposition, that difference
without contradiction, that divergence (*écart*) between the
within and the without that constitutes its natal secret. [V.I.,
135–36; *V.I.*, 179]

Emergence, coming of itself to itself, coiling up, reversal, homogeneity, resemblance, doubling, divergence from the inside to the outside: each of these images is bound to clarify the description of Flesh.
And such a description tends to be that of a *genesis*.

In another place, as you know, flesh appears as an element of
Being, in the sense that this word has when we are speaking, Merleau-
Ponty says, of air, earth, fire, and water. Nonetheless, this last assertion
leaves aside something essential. To think flesh, we have to think a genesis that is a self-genesis, more precisely, to think something as a movement of self-begetting. No doubt, we are confronted with the image of
birth. Later, in the same chapter, Merleau-Ponty uses this image explicitly by speaking of "the current making of an embryo a newborn infant,
of a visible a seer, and of a body a mind, or at least a flesh" (V.I., 147; *V.I.*,
193). And on the same page, he enunciates this final sentence: "What we
are calling flesh, this interiorly worked-over mass (*cette masse intérieure-
ment travaillée*) has no name in philosophy" (V.I., 147; *V.I.*, 193). Indeed
this word *travaillée* has a singular connotation in French, for it is employed to indicate the moment when the mother is about to be delivered.
Later we will return to this relation between flesh and the mother, which
is mentioned again from another point of view in a working note.

Now let us observe that it is a question of a bizarre begetting. A
singular sensible emerges from the mass of the sensible by a sort of coiling up, and through redoubling, turns back upon itself—that is to say, at
the same time, upon the whole sensible—so that a double doubling occurs, the body becoming at once sentient and sensible and distinct from
the external world that it continues to belong to, to adhere to. These
sentences themselves are strangely turned. The seer grasps the visible
from the midst of it, Merleau-Ponty says. So it is caught up in it because
the sensible is already thick, in a certain sense, already flesh. Simultaneously, what makes its thickness, its flesh, is the fact that the body communicates to the things its own divergence. The description makes
irrelevant any attempt to elucidate the phenomenon from a positive, realistic point of view.

Paradoxically, everything comes to pass as though simultaneously
the body emerged from the flesh of things and transported into the
things the flesh of its own body. Merleau-Ponty was fully aware of this
paradox. Indeed, it is "a paradox of Being," he says, "not a paradox of

man, that we are dealing with here" (V.I., 136; *V.I.*, 180). However, as he fully admits, we could no longer be satisfied with the assertion that the body is simply an "exemplar sensible" (V.I., 135; *V.I.*, 179), or as he says anew, "a very remarkable variant whose constitutive paradox lies in every visible" (V.I.,136; *V.I.*, 179). It does not suffice to say that the human body is a body that unites us directly with things through its own genesis. We should rather recognize that Being means *coming to being*, that not only the body but already everything outlines a coiling up, a redoubling, that the body, the human body, sensible to itself, is required to exist, is premeditated, or in gestation within the sensible itself. We should also admit that the doubling concerns time as much as space. The body connects not only the outside and the inside, but the before and the after, such that self-genesis cancels the image of a singular origin.

Merleau-Ponty insists on the ontological meaning of his description. The flesh of the body is not separated from the sensible. He says: "When we speak of the flesh of the visible, we do not mean to do anthropology, to describe a world covered over with all our own projections leaving aside what it can be under the human mask" (V.I., 136; *V.I.*, 179). So later, his particular exploration of the visible, of the sensible, does not allow us to forget its connection with the seer, the sentient who grasps it. I remind you in passing of his beautiful analysis of the color of redness. Indeed, we find the same working concepts in the analysis of the human body: depth, interior differentiation, latency, origins, straits, field.

I should like to bring to light only two points in the exploration of the human body that seem to me particularly relevant for my purpose. I am referring to the problem of duality—the problem of "the two"—and the problem of laterality. Perhaps duality is not the right word, for "the two" is not thinkable unless we keep in mind that body remains the same throughout the doubling itself. In the first moment, Merleau-Ponty starts by speaking of two laps, two leaves, two sides. The internal divergence of the body provides the means for it to be sensible to itself and by the same token to be opened upon the whole of the sensible. Through this openness, a double incorporation occurs, incorporation of the external sensible and incorporation into it. But in the second moment, this image of two laps or two leaves turns out to be unsatisfactory. Externality seems too much emphasized. Indeed, there are not on one side the seer and on the other side the visible as far from each other as pure activity and pure passivity. Merleau-Ponty notices: "If one wants metaphors, it would be better to say that the body sensed and the body sentient are as the obverse and the reverse, or again, as two segments of one circular course which goes above from left to right and below from right to left, but which is but one sole movement in its two phases" (V.I., 138; *V.I.*,

182). We know that the glove that turns back upon itself will provide another metaphor in a working note.

First of all, what Merleau-Ponty intends to underline is the adherence of vision to the visible. The body is capable of seeing itself, touching itself, hearing itself, because it keeps on being the same in this double experience. There is, for instance, an imperceptible shift from the touching to the touched when the right hand touches the left hand that is touching something else outside, a shift that reveals the reversibility of the sentient-sensible. This beautiful description is too well known to dwell on this point. But if the fact that I can see myself in the mirror does not lead us very far into quasi coincidence, it teaches us something more. The vision the seer exercises he also undergoes from the things. Merleau-Ponty goes so far as to say that "there is a fundamental narcissism of all vision" (V.I., 139; V.I., 183). Inasmuch as the more profound meaning of narcissism is not to see oneself in the outside but to be seen by the outside, to emigrate into it, the gaze that is fixing the things is caught up in them, its movement is guided by what it sees in such a way that it is doubled by an inverse movement. In that sense we should not limit ourselves to saying that the body at once sees and is visible, but we have to recognize that reversibility inhabits the seer itself. In fact, the gaze can detach from the subject and turn back upon itself as though it emerged from the things. Merleau-Ponty does not mention Freud in this place, but we can suppose he had in mind the example of the wolf-man, the example of the child terrified by the wolves whose looks are but his own look reversed. We can also suppose he remembered what Freud said about voyeurism and exhibitionism defined as two sides of the same impulse.

At a certain moment Merleau-Ponty, as you know, rectifies his description of the flesh: "To begin with, we spoke summarily of reversibility, of the seeing and the visible, of the touching and touched. It is time to emphasize that this is reversibility always imminent and never realized in fact" (V.I., 147; V.I., 194). However, we should ask ourselves if this sentence brings to us anything new. Indeed, we had already understood that there is no coincidence between the sentient and the sensible within the body, nor between the several tactile experiences and visual experiences, and we already knew that these experiences never exactly overlap, that they slip away at the very moment they are about to rejoin. This is, he repeated, the very condition of the incorporation of the sensible and the incorporation into the sensible.

It seems to me that under its apparent meaning the rectification ends by illuminating what did not appear, the fact that the divergence goes along with a split. The human body is not only sensible to itself, it is outside itself, it is a stranger to itself. Merleau-Ponty attempts to say that in both the body and the visible the opaque zones indicate nothing but articulations or hinges that remain hidden. However, his language testifies to a certain tension in the notion of flesh. On the one hand, Merleau-Ponty speaks of hinges. Even though they are hidden, they participate in the natural world, they are localized in the structures of the sentient-sensible, and in a certain sense they are fully thinkable. On the other hand, he speaks of "interior horizons," of "straits," and says that we have to conceive of "a new type of being, a being by porosity, pregnancy, or generality" (V.I., 149; *V.I.*, 195), whereas in his working notes he stresses more and more the phenomenon of "dehiscence." Thus, what was first announced in terms of overlapping, homogeneity, and reversibility seems later to have to be qualified in terms of segregation, fission, and alterity. Finally, the original incorporation of the sensible and the incorporation into the sensible comes to be connected with an original "depossession."

At this point I should like to put a few questions of my own in the wake of Merleau-Ponty's analyses. Can one go as far as Merleau-Ponty hoped with the conception of flesh, staying within the limits of the relationships between the sentient and the sensible? Can one even temporarily avoid taking into account the question of the other, the others? When we encounter this question, is there not a danger of dealing with it in an already determined theoretical frame? I certainly do not forget that Merleau-Ponty mentions the connections of one's own body with the bodies of others in the chapter to which I am referring. But all the more remarkable is the fact that he does so at the very moment he is speaking of the synergic body. Let us turn back to this passage briefly. After noticing that there is a *lateral, transversal* operation through which the body comes into relation to itself, he pursues the question: "Now why would this generality, which constitutes the unity of my body, not open it to other bodies? The handshake too is reversible. . . . Why would not the synergy exist among different organisms, if it is possible within each? Their landscapes interweave, their actions and their passions fit together exactly" (V.I., 142; *V.I.*, 187). Moreover, speaking of a circle of the sentient-sensible and of a transfer of each experience into another within the body, Merleau-Ponty says that "there is finally a propagation of these exchanges to all the bodies of the same type and of the same style which I see and touch—and this by virtue of the fundamental fission or segregation of the sentient and the sensible which, laterally, makes the organs of my body communicate and founds transitivity from one body to another" (V.I., 143; *V.I.*, 188).

It is worth scrutinizing the notion of laterality. We find again the same notion in the "working notes." In one of them, rejecting the cleavage of for-itself from for-the-other, Merleau-Ponty connects the chiasm between my eyes and the eyes of the other with the chiasm of my two eyes, and he says specifically, "we function as one unique body." In another note, he insists on the similarity of the relation with things and with others: "There is an unfolding and a *lateral* relation with the things no less than with the others."

First of all, how is it possible to ignore infantile experience? Merleau-Ponty himself calls us to take it into account in a passage of the first chapter of *The Visible and the Invisible*:

> That a child perceives before he thinks, that he begins by putting his dreams into things, his thoughts in the others, forming with them, as it were, one block of common life wherein the perspectives of each are not yet distinguished—these genetic facts cannot be simply ignored by philosophy in the name of the exigencies of the intrinsic analysis. Thought cannot ignore its apparent history. [V.I., 11–12; *V.I.*,27–28]

However, these short reflections on the child's perception are disappointing. The genetic facts do not confirm the image of a lateral exchange. Indeed, it does not suffice to say that the child puts its dreams or its thoughts in others and confounds its own perspective with that of others. It is not a question of perspectives at that moment. The child, the infant, begins by coming into a world that the other sees, whereas it does not see it as one world. What we should bring to light is the original asymmetry between the experience of the infant and that of the adult. For the infant, the other is not originally an alter ego. It is true that the human organism is prepared to see; the seer, as Merleau-Ponty says, is premeditated in counterpoint in the embryo. Nonetheless, before he sees distinct, single things, before space unfolds itself before him and tends to be deep and differentiated, before the object appears as distinct and identified, the infant does not feel the distinction between the within and the without. The look of the other opens the world to him.

I remember a passage of *Phenomenology of Perception* wherein Merleau-Ponty emphasized the capacity of the infant to transfer its look from the finger that points something out to him to the object pointed at. Consequently, he noticed that vision already made us enter into the symbolic order. However, we should not ignore the finger itself, the movement of the hand that gives something to see. Between the infant's eyes and the things there is a mediator, and to use a metaphor, this mediator, the other, does not stand on the same level as the infant. He gives something to be seen *from above*. This is not a contingent fact. Quoting Lucien Herr, an interpreter of Hegel, Merleau-Ponty notes in a lecture that nature is always for us as at the first day (T.L.C.F., 65; *R.C.C.F.*, 94). We should rather say that nature is always seen as having already been seen by another. The reversibility between the thing and the seer masks the eye that already had seen before what we are seeing now, and that saw us.

Furthermore, we cannot deal with vision as the original openness to the sensible. All the contacts with the maternal body and the first relation to the breast come before seeing; and at the first moment there is no cleavage between the outside and the inside. At that moment there is neither perception of an external body nor perception of one's own body. The perception of the latter as unity is not originally given, but constitutes itself from the experience of a primitive dispersion. As Freud has taught us, the whole of the relations to the other are condensed into the functioning of an organ that is not only physiologically regulated but bears the working of impulse. It is needless to insist on this point. In particular, eating supports the impulse to swallow up external being, and this impulse goes along with the feeling of being at risk of being swallowed up.

You could say that this example testifies to reversibility. In a certain sense, that is right. Nevertheless, to refer to Melanie Klein's conception of the introjected object as good and bad object, we cannot say that the latter is simply the reverse and the former the obverse of one unique experience. There is a split between the good and the bad object, because one is the mark of the consistency of the substantial identity of the body itself and the other bears the threat of disintegration coming from the inside, the loss of the body. Upon the vicissitudes of the oral, anal, and phallic phases an individual history is built up, through which the first impasses are normally overcome. I should say that the development of perception, language, and thought keeps as a mark an experience of loss from which later a new sort of sense, the sense of lack, constitutes itself—*un sens du manque*, or as the poet Henri Michaux said, that is intermittently reactivated. Michaux notes, "je la sens comme du bois." Now I do not believe that we can account for such an experience by referring only to the concept of *horizons* or *straits* borrowed from the domain of perception.

Permit me a last remark on this same issue. We have to recognize that the infant is originally called to respond to the desire and the needs of others, desire and needs that emerged from their own archaic past. So the infant is immediately, and even before coming into the world, taken into a web of wishes, expectations, and fears of which he will never possess the meaning. So it is too little to say that the passions adjust themselves like landscapes. In fact they are rooted in what is for each one unrepresentable—unrepresentable, that is to say, deeper than any representation of which we are able to become aware. We have to wonder whether the world that Merleau-Ponty attempted to explore was not an already tamed world rather than that wild experience to which he hoped to give expression.

On another side, as we take into account the original relation to the other, we should also ask ourselves if it is possible to separate the perceptive life from speech. Merleau-Ponty did not deny that relation, but he apparently thought that it was possible to postpone the point in order to introduce the analysis of the sentient-sensible. However, things in the outside tend to be distinct, consistent, and identifiable through the speech that gives them a name.

We certainly do not exchange our perspectives before a common landscape in the same way that we communicate by talking of it. Mutual understanding implies that we belong to the same linguistic community. Nonetheless, within a single community names and things are, as it were, wedded. For the child the name is quasi-natural. Moreover, the child tends to deal with names and words like things. The sound offers a materiality closer to that of the image, as its dreams testify, but no less those of the adult who comes back to the time of childhood each night. Then, how would it be possible to mask the function of the other in the initiation to the world of named things? The other gives names, and in a certain sense, introduces the child into the sphere of law whenever he says "this is red, and not yellow," or "this is a house, and not a boat." So he makes it clear that things have an identity on the outside. They are closed upon themselves, as it were, sealed with their names.

Yet more relevant for my purpose is the fact that from the beginning of its appearance in the world, the child itself is named. To be named—whatever the character of the affiliation (through the father or the brother or the mother)—testifies to an original and irreducible transcendence. It is true that one can change one's name. In a sense, the name is contingent. But we cannot escape from having been named and from bearing the mark of some heritage, the mark of debt and law. Now the relation to one's own name is of another kind than the relation to one's own body. I can declare my name, "This is Claude." This is certainly not the same thing as giving my address, or seeing myself in the mirror, or hearing myself speaking. The divergence (*écart*) between my name and myself does not coincide with the divergence between me seer and me visible. The name was imprinted on me and at the same time bound to remain outside me, above me.

As you know, Lacan talked of the mirror stage as the moment when the child is discovering its bodily unity. But before this, the child is captivated by its name. The name is a sign of the irreversible, and of otherness in myself. If we question the relation to one's own name, it seems to me that we can no longer stay within the limits of the milieu of the flesh. Let us recall a curious sentence from a working note of November 1960. This is the note that begins: "Nature is at the first day." Merleau-Ponty says: "Do a psychoanalysis of Nature: it is the flesh, the mother" (V.I., 267; *V.I.*, 320–21). Without seeking to do a psychoanalysis of Merleau-Ponty's ontology, I could not help noting that the identification between flesh and mother enlightens Merleau-Ponty's description of the relation sentient-sensible within the body as well as between the body and the outside. This relation always corresponds to the pattern of a dual relation. So what in general is not taken into account is the other, the third one, the representative of otherness.

These last remarks could help us enlighten the difficulties Merleau-Ponty encountered in his political analyses. I have no time to insist on this point, and I will limit myself to indicating a direction. As you know very well, there is a singular shift, a displacement, from the first thesis of *Humanism and Terror* on. My hypothesis is the following: the political events do not entirely account for the theoretical change. To my mind, at the beginning, the proletariat occupied a place in Merleau-Ponty's theory of history similar to that which the human body had in *Phenomenology of Perception*. The proletariat was supposed to interpret itself and transform itself by interpreting and transforming human history. It emerged from history and, as it were, gave to it meaning from within. Like the body, it was the bearer of the "as yet dumb experience" (the famous Husserlian phrase), or the bearer of the *tacit cogito*. Later the idea of a privileged class that would be both particular and universal was abandoned. At the same time, Merleau-Ponty criticized the conception of history as following one sole course, bound to institute radically new social relations transparent to themselves.

Merleau-Ponty began to speak of the reversibility of history and of flesh in the Epilogue of *Adventures of the Dialectic*.[2] Nonetheless, in my opinion, he did not succeed in leaving the frame of sociological analysis. What he considered essential was the web of purely social relations, so he did not get rid of relativism by comparing the different types of social structures. He did not admit that there was a cleavage between political forms of society, the *régime* as is said in French, especially between modern democracy and totalitarianism. In fact, he abstained from speaking of the totalitarian state. What characterizes this regime is the phantasmatic attempt to give to people the certainty that society is closed upon itself, to present the state-power as the organ that incorporates the whole of the social, and to reduce law to the expression of an internal necessity, in fact an attempt to submit law to the will of the rulers. There is no place, in this case, for reference to the third one, the representative of justice or truth, no sense of otherness. Conversely, modern democracy, no matter its deficiencies, tacitly accepts that it does not possess the meaning of its own genesis and its own ends. So the ambiguities of *Adventures of the Dialectic* seem to me of a philosophical character no less than political.

To sum up these short critical reflections, I can say only this: once the remarkable contributions of Merleau-Ponty's last writings to research in the direction of a new ontology are admitted, perhaps we will have to pursue the exploration beyond the limits of flesh, I dare say, beneath and above this domain.

2

Écart: Reply to Claude Lefort's "Flesh and Otherness"

M. C. Dillon

f ideas transcend the philosophers who express them—as they must
to vindicate the project of reading philosophy—then it is possible for
a thinker to err in the expression of an idea that, for convenience, we
regard as his own. I read the work of Merleau-Ponty, not because it
was written by Merleau-Ponty, but because I think he, more than any
other, provides access to the idea seeking expression in our time. My
allegiance is to the idea; to its frail bearers I give only profound respect
and thanks.

In his paper "Flesh and Otherness," Lefort suggests that the limits of "a philosophy of Flesh" cannot adequately accommodate "the
other, the third one, the representative of otherness" (12).[1] I will argue
that the idea that expresses itself through Merleau-Ponty's doctrine of
the reversibility of Flesh articulates an ontology uniquely capable of disclosing the kind of transcendence known as alterity, but that Merleau-
Ponty erred in the presentation of that doctrine.

I

First, Lefort's argument, or rather, my interpretation of his argument:
Lefort sees reversibility as a relationship of two terms—sensible and sen-

tience, visibility and vision, outside and inside, and so forth—that doubles back on itself, and he sees otherness as requiring a third term. To understand Lefort's criticism, we have to understand the third term. Lefort gives us three examples, all of which center around "the original asymmetry between the experience of the infant and that of the adult" (9): (a) the asymmetry of the contact between the infantile body and the maternal body, including "the first relation to the breast" (10); (b) the relation of the infant's experience to the world of nature, which "is always seen as having already been seen by another" (10); and (c) the relation of the infant to the world of things "closed upon themselves . . . by their names" (11), which includes the relation of the child to its own named identity (which is estranged by the desire and needs of others). The general point, I gather, is that the doubling back on itself of the same (which is Lefort's understanding of reversibility) sets a limit to experience on the other side of which is a third term, which cannot be assimilated within the reversibility model. Beyond the limit of the dual relation between the outside of the inside and the inside of the outside, there is wild otherness, the other "beneath and above" (13) the divergent relation to itself of Flesh.

Why do these instances of otherness elude the reversibility relation? Lefort does not set forth a general statement of his thesis, but there is a portion of his text that might provide the basis for an extrapolation. In this text Lefort comments on the working note from *The Visible and the Invisible* in which Merleau-Ponty says: "Do a psychoanalysis of nature: it is the flesh, the mother" (V.I., 267). Lefort's comment:

> Without seeking to do a psychoanalysis of Merleau-Ponty's ontology, I could not help noting that the identification between flesh and mother enlightens Merleau-Ponty's description of the relation sentient-sensible within the body as well as between the body and the outside. This relation always corresponds to the pattern of a dual relation. So what in general is not taken into account is the other, the third one, the representative of otherness. (12)

My extrapolation. Here Lefort delimits the reversibility relation to (a) relations of the body to itself and (b) relations between body and the outside. But the body, as flesh, is the inside of the outside; that is, the Flesh of the world is the same as the flesh of the body, it is the outside of the inside: the circuit is closed within Flesh, within the relation of Flesh to itself, within its selfsameness. The one Flesh incorporates the duality of its fission, its dehiscence, its folding back upon itself.

Merleau-Ponty says the flesh is mother. Lefort says there is a *tertium quid* to be found beneath and above this flesh, and names it as "infantile experience" (9). The difference that constitutes this otherness lies in the fact that "the infant does not feel the distinction between the within and the without" (9) characteristic of adult relations with the world and other people. Here, then, is an experience that cannot be accommodated within the ontology of flesh because it does not participate in the dialectic of the reversibility between within and without that defines flesh.

II

Now, my response. There are three interrelated points to be made. First, any viable account of alterity has to include both identity and difference, or immanence and transcendence: difference or transcendence because the other has to be genuinely other, and identity or immanence because the other has to be disclosed, and disclosed as an other who is the same as I. Here the doctrine of ambiguity is in full force—as it must be to allow for both the fact of communication and the fact that communication is never adequate—there must be a common ground on which the other and I can reach each other, but still remain in some degree opaque to each other. The other's world and mine are ambiguously the same and different.

Lefort stresses the sameness. In his account, the reversibility of the flesh is the doubling back on itself of the same. This sameness or identity of the flesh is expressed clearly by Merleau-Ponty when he describes flesh as elemental. Lefort initially depicts this oneness in terms of homogeneity, but then, taking up the theme of divergence or fission (*écart*), amends the depiction to include difference. Lefort's account of difference comes in the context of a discussion of the body as exemplar of flesh in its dual role as sensed and sensing:

> The internal divergence of the body provides the means for it
> to be sensible to itself and by the same token to be opened
> upon the whole of the sensible (6). . . . The human body is not
> only sensible to itself, it is outside itself, it is a stranger to itself
> (7). . . . in his working notes [Merleau-Ponty] stresses more
> and more the phenomenon of "dehiscence." Thus, what was
> first announced in terms of overlapping, homogeneity, and re-
> versibility seems later to have to be qualified in terms of segre-
> gation, fission, and alterity. (8)

Immediately the question arises: Why is this difference not strong enough to account for otherness? Why does Lefort argue that we must look beyond the ontology of flesh to do justice to alterity if that alterity is built into the ontology?

Second, as we learned from Husserl, it is impossible to do justice to the phenomenon of alterity from within the ontology of transcendental idealism. If otherness is but a meaning or significance projected upon some immanent object, then that object is not transcendent, not truly other: otherness must be found; the constitution of the other as other must be motivated. This is the insight that inspires Levinas. But it is also the insight that inspires Merleau-Ponty, and, although Lefort seems to have found it in Levinas, apparently he does not see it in Merleau-Ponty.

Two passages in Lefort's paper lead me to this interpretation. Here is the first:

> The seer grasps the visible from the midst of it, Merleau-Ponty says. So it [the seer] is caught up in it [the visible] because the sensible is already thick, in a certain sense, already flesh. Simultaneously, what makes its thickness, its flesh, is the fact that *the body communicates to the things its own divergence*. The description makes irrelevant any attempt to elucidate the phenomenon from a positive, realistic point of view. (5, emphasis added)

The body's own divergence is projected into the world. That is, the difference, the otherness, is a meaning attributed to things by the body. The body here performs the transcendental function of constitution as the transcendental ego does for Husserl. And the result is the same: an ontology that, in denying transcendence to things, cannot account for alterity; an ontology in which phenomena have no positive content apart from that attributed to them by the agency of constitution. It is true that, given this interpretation of the role of the body in the constitution of flesh, flesh cannot be conceived within the ontology of realism. But it is not true that the denial of realism entails idealism.

This interpretation, I think, is based on a fundamental misconception of Merleau-Ponty's understanding of the lived body, which appears regularly in secondary literature where critics explicitly equate Kant's transcendental unity of apperception with Merleau-Ponty's lived body and interpret both as serving the function of unifying the manifold of sensation by synthesizing its data under immanent constellations of meaning (categories, significations, noemata, etc.). This interpretation ignores such fundamental tenets of Merleau-Ponty's ontology as autochthonous organization and the doctrine of matter pregnant with form. It opens Merleau-Ponty to all the criticism he levels against intellectualism under the heading of the problem of organization: that is, the problem of explaining how the agency of constitution determines which meaning to impose upon which congeries of experience. If there is no meaning transcending the agency of constitution, if phenomena have no positive content of their own, then any projection of meaning must be arbitrary, because the agency of projection has no ground for projecting one meaning rather than another. The problem of organization is not solved by shifting the agency of constitution from transcendental ego to lived body. I think Merleau-Ponty was fully aware of this and, hence, did not espouse the doctrine attributed to him by Lefort.

Let us examine the second text. The context, again, is the problem of otherness to which Lefort occasionally refers as the problem of laterality:

> I should like to bring to light only two points in [Merleau-Ponty's] exploration of the human body that seem to me particularly relevant for my purpose. I am referring to the problem of duality—the problem of "the two"—and the problem of laterality. Perhaps duality is not the right word, for "the two" is not thinkable unless we keep in mind that *[the] body remains the same throughout the doubling itself.* (5, emphasis added)

The problem of duality is the problem of the sensed and the sensing, the visible and the vision, the seen and the seeing. It is a problem because the sensed has to be both different from the sensing and the same. The visible transcends the vision, but they must also be one flesh to allow for the reversibility of roles from seer to seen and back.

This is also the problem of laterality or the problem of otherness because the transcendence of the visible precludes it from being the same as or identical with the vision.

As I have argued earlier, both problems remain insoluble if there is not both sameness and difference. They are insoluble for Lefort (a) because he grants a primacy to the sameness—"the body remains the same throughout the doubling"—and (b) because he reduces the difference or transcendence of things seen to a meaning the body projects or constitutes—"the body communicates to the things its own divergence." Otherness becomes a meaning constituted by the body, and genuine alterity is lost in the selfsameness of the flesh. Reversibility becomes a structure immanent within the monolith of flesh. *Écart* (divergence, fission, dehiscence, etc.) is reduced to an illusion the flesh engenders within itself by projecting its own immanent reflexivity into the world it constitutes.

Under this interpretation, the experience of the infant is, indeed, a *tertium quid* irreducible to the internal dyad of flesh. From within the infant's experience, as Lefort understands it, there is no dyadic structure of reversibility, no dialectic of inside and outside: "the infant does not feel the distinction between the within and the without" (9). This is "the original asymmetry between the experience of the infant and that of the adult" (9). Here is the core of Lefort's argument: because the infant does not project its own otherness into the world, because the infant's world is undifferentiated with regard to within and without, the adult is mistaken in projecting the reversibility constitutive of adult experience into the domain of the infant; the infant's domain is different in kind and constitutes a genuine other for the adult.

The question that comes to the fore here is this: How does the infant enter the adult world? How, in the process of growth and maturation, does the difference in kind between infantile experience and adult experience give way to alienated sameness? How does the infant enter the circuit of reversibility and become flesh?

Third, according to Lefort, "the look of the other opens the [adult] world to [the infant]" (9). *How* the look of the other opens the adult world is a question that Lefort does not pose. Had he posed it, he might have seen that it is impossible to answer this question within the framework he has established, the framework of flesh and its other. If infantile experience is completely undifferentiated with regard to "the within and the without," then, according to that very hypothesis, nothing impinging from without can be registered as such from within. The progression from infant to adult presupposes a continuity of experience that allows differences to be recognized as such and mediated in the development of communication. But Lefort denies this continuity in identifying infantile experience as other, as different in kind.

The question that remains here is the question of a positive account of otherness and flesh. If Lefort's interpretation of the reversibility of flesh leads to an understanding of otherness modeled on infantile experience in which the development of communication is rendered inconceivable, how must that understanding be altered to allow us to conceive the everyday occurrence of maturation in which infants learn to enter the adult world? And, finally, how does this modification of the understanding of otherness bear on Lefort's interpretation of the reversibility thesis?

III

Merleau-Ponty's account of the emergence of the self-other distinction in infantile experience is set forth in "The Child's Relations with Others," a compilation of lecture notes from a course he gave at the Sorbonne in 1950–51.[2] In it, he traces the genesis of the self-other distinction to origins in the experience of self-alienation based on the phenomenon of the specular image. As I have argued elsewhere,[3] Merleau-Ponty's account is flawed insofar as he regards self-alienation as a condition for alienation from others (i.e., recognition of others as other).[4]

The influence of Lacan is thematically acknowledged in this text, and, I think, that influence explains in part why Merleau-Ponty overlooks the necessity for a stronger source of alienation than that provided by the objectification of the infant's body in the mirror (which, after all, does not instantly transform the infant's experience, but must be learned to be recognized as a self-objectification). But only in part. The obscuring bias is the residual effect of the thesis of subjectivity, which is central to the transcendental standpoint from which Merleau-Ponty was gradually emerging: if the world for me is only the world as I can experience it (thesis of subjectivity), and if the infant does not have the categories to make the self-other distinction (i.e., if its experience is entirely introceptive),[5] then all otherness actually present in its world will be assimilated to the undifferentiated experience of syncretism.[6] In this view, the other's look/presence/alienating behavior cannot be experienced as such until the infant develops within itself the category of other. Hence, otherness has to be generated within the sphere of the infant's own world. Hence, the emphasis on the mirror stage as an experience that takes place within the introceptive or immanent sphere of the infant.

But this attempt to conceptualize the genesis of the self-other distinction falls under a dilemma. Either the mirror functions as other (in which case, the same difficulty emerges as beset the attempt to explain the experience of otherness by the intrusion of another human); or the mirror does not function as other (in which case, the infant has to generate the otherness category within an immanent sphere defined by its absence, a generation ex nihilo). The point remains: once the infant's experience is defined in terms of sheer immanence in which the otherness of worldly things and other humans cannot be recognized as other, then—by that very definition—no external experience (mirror image or anything else) will be able to account for the genesis of the categorial ability to perceive otherness as such. The mistake here lies in the assumption of the thesis of subjectivity, the incorporation of that thesis into a purely transcendental conception of consciousness, and the correlative reduction of transcendence to a constituted meaning (as opposed to an intrusion on the part of insistent others and a recalcitrant world).

The positive point to be emphasized here is that the difference stressed by Lefort between the infant's experience and the world experienced by the adult educates the infant in the original sense of that term (*e-ducare*): that is, the difference leads the infant out of syncretism and forces upon it an awareness of alien things and perspectives. Little Hans's game of *Fort-Da* responds to the earlier traumas of withdrawal of maternal breast and then mother herself by recapitulating them; these traumas force the infant to accommodate itself to a world that refuses immediately to gratify the latent wishes of the primary process. But, as I have argued, this education, this response, this accommodation is impossible unless the infant is open to otherness from the start. The compulsion to repeat and its project of control, which come to light in Freud's analysis of Little Hans's game, reveals the child's inchoate awareness of a recalcitrant state of affairs and an alien will to be mastered.

How does this impinge upon Lefort's understanding of the reversibility thesis? Here I turn to notes from Merleau-Ponty's course "The Experience of Others" (1951–52), offered the year after his course "The Child's Relations with Others." Note the denial of the doctrine of cenesthesia in the opening sentence:

> My body is not given to me as a sum of sensations but as a whole. A form, which is common to both visual and tactile perceptions, is the link between the other person's body and my own. The two bodies can therefore communicate through the different perceptions. Everything transpires as if the other person's intuitions and motor realizations existed in a sort of relation of internal encroachment, as if my body and the body of the other person together formed a system. [T.E.O., 52]

Later in these notes, Merleau-Ponty asserts that "there is already a kind of presence of other people in me" (T.E.O., 56). Here the conflict of interpretations between Lefort and me comes to its crux. Is the presence of the other an internal phenomenon or an encroachment? Merleau-Ponty uses both terms and puts them together. Under Lefort's interpretation, the otherness of the other is an internal projection: my body imposes its internal fission upon its relation to the other. Under my interpretation, the internal fission is based on an earlier encroachment: through the divergence of the other from myself—and my internalization or introjection of that alien vantage—I discover my own self-alienation.

During the period in question, the early 1950s, both interpreta-tions can be supported with textual evidence.[7] But later, when Merleau-Ponty was working on the manuscript eventually entitled *The Visible and the Invisible*, his critique of the ontology of transcendental subjectivity led him to posit the divergence of my body from the other's as a differ-ence that is discovered rather than projected. I have tried to show above why the fundamental tenets of Merleau-Ponty's emergent ontology re-quire him to acknowledge the genuine (as opposed to the projected) transcendence of the other. Here it remains only to show how this genu-ine transcendence or genuine otherness is expressed in his last text. Among the wealth of passages that could be cited, I have chosen two—one from the chapter "The Intertwining—The Chiasm" and one from the working notes—that strike me as definitive.

In discussing the example of touching one of my hands with the other—the example I have tried elsewhere[8] to show is seminal for the model of reversibility—Merleau-Ponty takes up the similarity of that ex-perience of reversibility with the reversibility that obtains between my own body and the bodies of others. In this text, he argues that just as my touching hand never coincides with the hand touched, even though they are hands of the same body, so is it also the case that I do not experience my body as I experience the body of the other, even though they are both bodies of the same Flesh:

> I do not hear myself as I hear the others, the sonorous exis-tence of my voice is for me as it were poorly exhibited; I have rather an echo of its articulated existence, it vibrates through my head rather than outside. *I am always on the same side of my body;* it presents itself to me in one invariable perspective. [V.I., 148]

"I am always on the same side of my body." From this it follows that the other is always on the far side of my body, that there is a separation between us that has been gestating since my conception and becomes irrevocable at the moment of my birth. This separation is not something projected or constituted; it is a reality that transcends the consciousness of infant and adult alike, a state of affairs to which both must adjust. Yet, as Merleau-Ponty goes on to say, the "hiatus" between the hand that touches and the hand touched "is spanned by the total being of my body" as the separation between my body and the other's is spanned by the total being of the world (V.I., 148). In another context, Merleau-Ponty describes the world in its role as spanning the divergence of self and other in terms that strike me as decisive: the world, he says, is "a world which is *not projective (n'est pas projectif)*, but forms its unity across *incompossibilities (incompossibilités)* such as that of my world and the world of the other'' (V.I., 215, emphasis added). To characterize the divergence of my world from the other's in terms as strong as ''incompossible'' is, I think, to signal that the otherness of the other manifests itself as an insurmountable opacity that thrusts itself upon me.

The second passage is taken from a working note dated September 1959, which I am surprised Lefort does not mention in his paper, for it addresses the central question he raises:

> Do we have the right to comprehend the time, the space of the child as an undifferentiation of *our* time, of *our* space, etc. . . . ? This is to reduce the child's experience to our own, at the very moment one is trying to respect the phenomena. For it is to think it as the *negation* of *our* differentiations. . . .
>
> Solution: recapture the child, the alter ego, the unreflected within myself by a lateral, pre-analytic participation, which is perception, *überschreiten* by definition, intentional transgression. When I perceive the child, he is given precisely in a certain divergence (*écart*) (*originating presentation of the unpresentable*) (*présentation originaire de l'imprésentable*) and the same for my perceptual lived experience for myself, and the same for my alter ego, and the same for the pre-analytic thing. Here is the common tissue of which we are made. The wild[9] Being. [V.I., 203]

Here the notion of divergence or *écart* is defined as a paradoxical ''presentation of the unpresentable.'' The paradox is easily resolved if we understand the phrase to describe the givenness of the transcendent as transcendent. The point here is the same one I have been stressing throughout: there is a perceptual presentation of the other that includes his opacity, his recalcitrance, the recesses of his being that I am finally unable to penetrate, in short, his ineffable transcendence. And, as it is with the other, so is it also with the infant, with my own prereflective being, and with the things of the natural world: in all the cases cited, there is an otherness grounded in an originary difference, which is the *écart* across which the various forms of reversibility operate.

Stated in simpler terms, the differentiations of the world are original differentiations emerging within the perceptual world; they are found*ing* differentiations upon which the constitutions of consciousness or culture or language are found*ed*. Yet these differentiations are differentiations of a unitary world that functions as a common domain to allow the exchanges and transgressions of reversibility to take place. I can take up the space hitherto occupied by the other and see the world from that vantage because we dwell in the same world. This reversibility of position allows us to move toward a common ground, but, ultimately, because I cannot live his body, I can only approximate his experience. Indeed, as is most clearly demonstrated by the case of the infant, the world exerts its own demands on our bodies: we must learn to adjust to its requirements, to orient ourselves according to its gravitational pull, and to orient ourselves to the language, customs, and needs of other worldly inhabitants. If the infant is to survive, its mother must be able to feel its needs, and it must be able to perceive her breast, her warmth, and her smile.[10] The endurance of the species demonstrates the fact that the infant is not excluded from the circuit of reversibility.

IV

Let me conclude by summarizing the two major critical points I have tried to make. The first of these centers around my response to Lefort's interpretation of the reversibility thesis and its bearing on the problem of otherness. I have argued that it is Lefort's misunderstanding of the reversibility thesis and its vicissitudes that leads him to find fault with Merleau-Ponty's account of alterity. Specifically, because Lefort construes the divergence of self from itself and from its other as a difference constituted by the body and projected into its experience, it appears to him that the otherness of other persons, other things, and the self's own other,[11] have been compressed into a closed circuit of relations within the immanent sphere of flesh. He calls for a "third one," which is irreducibly other, for it lies beyond the duality of the relation of flesh to itself. He then cites the experience of the infant as an instance of this *tertium quid*.

I have argued, contrary to Lefort, that otherness is not a projected meaning. Although the primary model of reversibility offered by Merleau-Ponty is that of one of my hands touching another,[12] this self-alienation has an older origin than that of my body to itself. I argued that I discover my own otherness through the traumatic impact of an alien gesture and, further, that the otherness I discover in my relations to things, other persons, and myself is an otherness that cannot be explained by transcendental constitution, for it involves the experience of a difference that transcends my experience (i.e., the other is *given* as opaque and recalcitrant to the categories I project).

The second critical point concerns Merleau-Ponty's responsibility for Lefort's interpretation. I have argued that the key issue is whether transcendence in general and otherness in particular can be understood as a constituted meaning, and I tried to support my claim that it cannot. But, although Merleau-Ponty arrived at this standpoint, he did not begin with it.[13] During his early and middle periods of development, Merleau-Ponty's account of intersubjectivity was not yet free of the thesis of subjectivity and, as I have acknowledged above, he did argue in "The Child's Relations with Others" that self-objectification had to precede recognition of others as other. That mistake was rectified later, but the writings of that period do lend themselves to the interpretation espoused by Lefort.

Along these general lines, I should like to record here my increasing sense that Merleau-Ponty might have chosen a better name than "flesh" for the general rubric under which to array his ontology of reversibility. The word is misleading in several ways. Contrary to Merleau-Ponty's own stated intent, the term invites one to think of flesh in the traditional categories of *substantia* and *hypokeimenon:*

> We must not think the flesh starting from substances . . . but
> we must think it . . . as an element, as the concrete emblem of
> a general manner of being. [V.I., 147]

The description of flesh as an element supports this misconception, despite the correction in the last phrase of the sentence. It is not the case that there is some pervasive stuff out of which all things are carved. It is rather the case that there is "a general manner of being" in which all things participate in the various ways articulated through the vicissitudes of reversibility. As the word "manner" indicates, reversibility must be understood adverbially rather than substantially: reversibility refers to the *how* of the relations among phenomena, and not to their *what.*

The nomination of flesh has led critics to attribute sentience to inorganic things, intentionality to mountains, and vision to things that do not have eyes. In the case at hand, it has led Lefort to think that Merleau-Ponty conceived the entirety of being on the model of the mature human body. The anthropomorphism latent in the term is surely contrary to the basic insight of the philosopher who, more than any other of his time, has worked to decenter philosophy from the traditional standpoint of the transcendental subject.[14]

The world is not made up of flesh. The world is made up of cups and saucers, trees and flowers, rocks and waters, dogs and people. All of which stand in relation. The unifying content is provided by the world articulating itself through people—the species through which the world has reached its present state of self-comprehension. It would be another anthropomorphizing mistake to regard the reversibility that now obtains as ultimate.

3

Flesh as Otherness

Gary Brent Madison

"L'homme est miroir pour l'homme."
—Merleau-Ponty, *L'Œil et l'esprit*

"I have become a question for myself."
—St. Augustine, *Confessions*

W e—the reading-interpreting philosophical community—have been reflecting on the texts of Merleau-Ponty for quite some time now, and never so intensely as when we (I emphasize the first-person plural, for there is no such thing as an isolated reader, a *solus ipse interpres*) attempt to appropriate, to make sense of, that fragmentary, inchoate text, *The Visible and the Invisible*. In this paper I should like to reflect on some of these reflections. This will necessarily involve me in a multilayered reflection where it will be difficult at times to discern clearly what is reflected and what is reflecting—a phenomenon peculiar to human understanding that Merleau-Ponty sometimes referred to as *emboîtement*.[1]

I wish to reflect in the first instance on "Flesh and Otherness," reflections on the later Merleau-Ponty that Claude Lefort presented to the members and friends of the Merleau-Ponty Circle on September 18, 1987. This will necessitate my reflecting indirectly on previous reflections of my own, because Lefort's reflections include, now, sedimented reflections on these reflections, which themselves were reflections on my part of previous ones of his. Similarly, I wish to reflect on Martin Dillon's reflections on Lefort, which must necessarily incorporate the inter-reflexivity that also now exists between his and my reflections on the "same" matter—that is, the later Merleau-Ponty. Matters could be complicated even more were I to bring Levinas explicitly into the picture. Although I shall maintain my own authorial voice throughout what follows, I cannot hope clearly and constantly to demarcate who is saying what about whom. Thus, this piece must be taken for what it historically effectively is: a brief moment in the ongoing, multivocal conversation of "Merleau-Ponty scholarship," which possesses, or has a hold over us, much more than we do over it.

What sets me thinking in this particular instance is a difficulty I experienced with Lefort's text, first as a listener and then as a reader. Lefort appears to find a difficulty in Merleau-Ponty, which he then uses as the basis for criticism ("my purpose is to bring to light the ambiguities of the concept of flesh"). The ambiguity or conceptual tension that Lefort claims to detect is between the flesh as *reversibility* and the flesh as *alterity* (or, more precisely, the relation of the flesh to alterity or otherness).[2] Dillon takes exception to Lefort on this point, and rightly so, I believe. I, too, do not think that there is a textual basis for viewing reversibility as a phenomenon that would be merely *internal* to the incarnate self, such that something "outside" the flesh would then be required in order to account for the phenomenon of otherness—Lefort's "third one."[3]

I hesitate, however, to go along with the way in which Dillon subsequently seeks to deal with the problem of otherness, as I shall attempt to make clear later on. I agree fully with Dillon when he says that "the idea which expresses itself through Merleau-Ponty's doctrine of the reversibility of Flesh articulates an ontology uniquely capable of disclosing the kind of transcendence known as alterity." However, I disagree with Dillon when he goes on to say: "but . . . Merleau-Ponty erred in the presentation of that doctrine" (Dillon, 14). I do not think that Merleau-Ponty erred at all; I think in fact that it is an error to think that he did, and that he therefore stands in need of correction by his interpreters. My intention and hope in this paper is, accordingly, to provide readers with something of an interpretive *tertium quid*, an alternative to both Lefort's and Dillon's reading of Merleau-Ponty.

It is important, I think, to be aware at the outset of the magnitude of the issue at stake. Lefort very appropriately reminds us that for Merleau-Ponty the flesh is "a prototype of Being." Indeed, when Merleau-Ponty speaks about the "flesh," and all the issues that this term subsumes under its designation, he was acutely aware that under this rubric he was confronting afresh some of "the basic problems" of the history of philosophy, of fundamental ontology. The "flesh" is indeed nothing other than a label for that most basic problem running throughout the history of philosophy: the problem of sameness and otherness (*le même et l'autre*), of identity and difference, of the One and its Other, of *ipseity* and *alterity*. For my part, I believe that Merleau-Ponty's approach to this most classic of issues opens up a new, and more promising, approach to the whole issue of ipseity, of *subjectivity*. In order to suggest how this is so, I must pause for a moment to recall some of the principal *étapes* in the unfolding of the problem(atic). This will be no *grand récit* (as Lyotard might say) but the briefest of thumbnail sketches.

The problem for philosophical reflection—for philosophy—is set by Socrates's appropriation of the Delphic injunction: *gnothi seauton*—know thyself! Lacking the concept that for us is now self-evident, that of subjectivity, the Greek philosophers did not respond to this injunction as postancients would: as a call to turn "inward," to explore reflectively, in a search for truth, the depths of the self (*anima*). It was Saint Augustine who creatively appropriated this injunction in such a way as to make it mean what it still tends to mean for us today (and what it most certainly still did mean for Rousseau). *Noli foras ire, in te redi, in interiore homine habitat veritas*. Husserlian phenomenology continued in our own century to let itself be guided by this most un-Greek of precepts.[4] In Augustine there is as yet—nota bene—nothing "subjectivistic" about this turn to subjectivity. For what Augustine discovered by going "inside," into his innermost self, was nothing other than Otherness itself: the truth (the presence) of that which is most real, the reality (presence) of other (human) selves and, above all, the reality of that supremely Other Self, that *Alter Ego* which is "more me than me myself," the *ens realissimum*, God. The Supremely Other (*le Tout Autre*) is discovered in the innermost reaches of the presence of the self to itself: it is, quite simply, *intimior intimo meo* ("deeper than my inmost understanding").[5] Montaigne, sitting at his writing table in the splendid isolation of his stone tower out in the French provinces, pursues, over a thousand years later, the Augustinian line, exploring the "inner self" that is his own very particular self—discovering in the process a world of truths about himself and about others, about the human condition, such that he can exclaim in a kind of genuine astonishment: *Rien d'humain ne m'est étranger*.

With Descartes, Augustine's *cogito* undergoes a radical and momentous metamorphosis. In his attempt to realize philosophy's most metaphysical of goals—a genuine *scientia* of what subsequently would be called "objective" reality or the "external world"—Descartes seeks ruthlessly (methodically) to purify his inherited Augustinian and Montaignesque subjectivity of all traces of what is other than it, such that in a kind of pure self-containedness, self-sufficiency, or self-referentiality, it may serve as an incontestable epistemological ground or *fundamentum inconcussum* of all that is (other than it).[6] Whereas Augustine's *Confessions*, the exuberant outpouring of his soul, were an intimate conversation with that most real of others, God, Descartes's *Méditations* were the soliloquy of a lonely, *désemparé* "mind" (*mens*), the only conversational partner on the horizon being—almost—Descartes's own *malin génie*. Both Descartes and Montaigne pursue their self-reflections in the privacy of their solitary retreats, but what a world of difference! Descartes's monologue comes close to resembling that of a paranoiac. He cannot be sure if there really is a world "out there" or if the others he sees from his window may not, through some grand conspiracy, be merely mechanical automatons dressed up in human clothing.

Subjectivity, as the absolute other of everything that is other than it, subjectivity in the modern sense, as a realm of pure, uncontaminated, transparent interiority (the realm of pure *Selbstgegebenheit [Evidenz]*, as Husserl was later to say) is thereby brought into being (created).[7] The reflecting subject has become *solus ipse*, and philosophical reflection on the self has become a form of thoroughgoing subjectivism. The fate of modern philosophy is thereby sealed. Its history, from Descartes through the empiricists, to Kant and to Husserl, will be the history of the ever-renewed and the ever-unsuccessful attempts to break out of the prison of subjectivity in order to make contact with something "objective," something genuinely *other* (the "real world," "other minds"). In our times, postmodernism (in its poststructualist versions, among others) will—quite rightly—proclaim the inanity of the whole modernist epistemological problematic (as philosophically productive a business as that of the madman banging his head against the padded walls of his cell). But along with the death of modernism will be proclaimed the "death of the subject" (of subjectivity) itself.

Why have I bothered to relate this particular mini-*récit*? I have done so because I think that the real significance of what is going on in *The Visible and the Invisible* and the other late texts can be seen in its true significance only when viewed in this particular narrative context—as I hope that the observations to follow will at least suggest.

What it seems to me that Merleau-Ponty above all is attempting, in an especially rigorous way in his late work, is a thoroughgoing *refonte* or revision of the notion of subjectivity or subjective experience, of, indeed, selfhood. Somewhat like the later Wittgenstein, he is attempting to rid subjectivity, the "inner" self, of all the psychologistic *bric-à-brac* (as he calls it) that modern philosophy managed to clutter it up with. To put it another way, he is attempting a "decentering" of subjectivity, and is thus engaged in a most postmodern kind of endeavor. What makes for the relative uniqueness of Merleau-Ponty's project, however, is that, unlike Heidegger, for instance, and unlike much of postmodern thought in general, he had, in my opinion, absolutely no desire to rid philosophy of the notion of subjectivity itself.[8] This is where the notion of the flesh comes in.

To make the point as briefly as possible, I would say that the function of the "flesh" is basically twofold. It serves as the means whereby Merleau-Ponty seeks to realize the philosophical goal that was always his: a definitive overcoming of modern subjectivism and modern solipsism in general, and of the Husserlian philosophy of consciousness in particular. At the same time, it allows him to hold on to a renewed conception of subjectivity, one that, precisely, introduces *alterity* into the very definition of subjective "selfsameness." For what is the flesh, qua *reversibility*?

Perhaps the most appropriate way to construe the meaning of this term—which, as Merleau-Ponty says, is *sans équivalent* in the history of philosophy—would be to say that it is nothing other than *the presence of the other in the same*. The flesh is the trace of the other, the inscription of the other, in the subject's own selfhood—in its very flesh. What "flesh" "means" is that *the subject is for itself an other*. As Lefort very nicely puts it: "The human body is not only sensible to itself, it is outside itself, it is a stranger to itself" (Lefort, 7). Otherness is that without which the embodied subject would not be a subject; it is constitutive of ipseity itself. This is why, like Dillon, I do not believe that it is necessary to appeal to something beyond the phenomenon of reversibility in order to account for alterity. As a concept, the notion of the flesh does all that needs to be done in this regard.

Unlike Dillon, however, I see no need to buttress up this affirmation with an appeal to childhood experience. Indeed, it seems to me that this route (pursued by both Dillon and Lefort)—that of accounting for adult experience in terms of what things must have been like for us when we were infants—is highly speculative (asking: "What is it like to be a child?" is not all that different from asking: "What is it like to be a bat?"). From a phenomenological as well as a hermeneutical point of view, such a procedure is highly questionable. The "world of the child" can, for us adults, be no more than an interpretive construct, not unlike the various theoretical constructs (e.g., electrons, neurophysiological or unconscious mechanisms) that empirical (or would-be empirical) analysis resorts to. And, as Merleau-Ponty said of Laplace's cosmic-inaugural nebula, an interpretive construct of this sort is not behind us in the "real" world, but before us in the cultural world. "Childhood"—the understanding of which varies from age to age—is an interpretive construct we resort to in order better to understand (or so we think) our present, adult experience. Like reality itself, "the things of childhood," Merleau-Ponty suggests in an allusion to Proust, "take shape only in my memory" (S., 27), only in, as I would say, narrative retrospection. As Freud himself eventually (and reluctantly) realized, childhood experiences can exert an overwhelming influence on us *even when they have never occurred*. Like anything else, childhood is, in the last analysis, what we interpretively make of it.

The point I am trying to make is that the flesh is not really a genetic—that is, an empirical, causal-explanatory—concept for Merleau-Ponty. Whatever genetic-causal explanation one might wish to give of the experience of others (and there are no doubt any number of such explanations, besides those of Lefort and Dillon, to choose among), the simple, undeniable phenomenological fact of the matter, as undeniable as is the *cogito* itself, is that the other is woven into the very fabric of selfhood. There is, moreover, a danger in any appeal to something like "childhood experience": it can easily lead one, as indeed it seems to me that it tends to lead Dillon, into a kind of empiricistic *realism*, which is incompatible with the whole basic thrust of phenomenology. One very important thing to realize when reading Merleau-Ponty is that, despite his pitiless critique of Husserlianism, he never, as I see it, sought to abandon phenomenology itself—that is, a mode of analysis that is basically reflective or "transcendental." Philosophy, Merleau-Ponty says, is "the perceptual faith questioning itself about itself" (V.I., 103)—that is, reflexive analysis.

Merleau-Ponty was seeking not to abandon phenomenological "consciousness," but to probe it to its very depths.[9] He was seeking to realize, as he himself said, a kind of *hyper-reflection*. Dillon seeks to give the impression that Merleau-Ponty abandoned "the thesis of subjectivity," "the transcendental approach" (see Dillon, 20, 25), but I do not believe that this was at all the case. Most certainly, Merleau-Ponty did not resort to any form of causal realism. His approach remained always "phenomenological," although at the end he pushed the method of "intentional analysis" to its extreme, to, indeed, its breaking point. This approach enabled him to circumvent a difficulty that Dillon seems to run into, the classic chicken-and-egg problem: Which comes first, solipsism or openness to the other? Merleau-Ponty's radically reflective approach—the concept of the flesh—enables him to conceive of otherness as a kind of internal phenomenon, rather than, as Dillon in effect says, an encroachment from the outside (Dillon, 21). This "internal phenomenon" is most definitely not, however, an "internal *projection*." What the flesh "means" is that, when I engage in reflection, I am *already* for myself an other. Because of this, otherness is inscribed in my very flesh. It is precisely because the flesh, which introduces otherness into me, is also "my" flesh that there are for me alter *egos*, other *myselves*, such that I am always for myself the other of the other of me.[10] The other, in order to be for me, does not have to "encroach" on me; when I begin to reflect, he or she is already "in" me, as a constitutive dimension of my flesh. I do not "project" the other; the other is what I discover when, in moments of reflexivity, I seek to lay hold of myself.

Lefort and Dillon cite those texts that, in their eyes, are (to use Dillon's term) "decisive." Here is mine, drawn from one of the most important of the later writings, the preface to *Signs*:

> Take *others* at the moment they appear in the world's flesh.
> They would not exist for me, it is said, unless I recognized
> them, deciphering in them some sign of the presence to self
> whose sole model I hold within me. But though my thought is
> indeed only the other side of my times, of my passive and per-
> ceptive being, whenever I try to understand myself the whole
> fabric of the perceptible world comes, too, and with it come
> the others who are caught in it. Before others are or can be
> subjected to my conditions of possibililily and reconstructed in
> my image, they must already exist as outlines, deviations, and
> variants [*relief, écarts, variantes*] of a single Vision in which I too
> participate. For they are not fictions with which I might people
> my desert—offspring of my spirit and forever unactualized
> possibilities—but *my twins or the flesh of my flesh* [emphasis
> added]. Certainly I do not live their life; they are definitely ab-
> sent from me and I from them. But that *distance becomes a
> strange proximity* [emphasis added] as soon as one comes back
> home to the perceptible world [i.e., the flesh of the sensible],
> since the perceptible is precisely that which can haunt more
> than one body without budging from its place. No one will see
> that table which now meets my eye; only I can do that. And yet
> I know that at the same moment it presses upon every glance
> in exactly the same way. [S., 15]

What it seems to me that Merleau-Ponty is describing here is pre-cisely what I have been talking about: *the inscription of the other in the flesh of the same.* Whenever I perceive anything and, a fortiori, whenever I am reflexively aware of perceiving something, the other is already present to me, for as Merleau-Ponty says, I could never see anything were I not myself seeable, were I not visible "from without, such as another would see me, installed in the midst of the visible, occupied in considering it from a certain spot" (V.I., 134). One of Lefort's criticisms of Merleau-Ponty is therefore well taken. We should not say, as Merleau-Ponty once did, that "nature is always for us as at the first day." "We should rather say," Lefort very pertinently observes, "that nature is always seen as having already been seen by another" (Lefort, 10). But that is precisely what the concept of the flesh as reversibility is designed to express.[11]

Also in the preface to *Signs* Merleau-Ponty writes: "In a sense, the highest point of philosophy is perhaps no more than rediscovering these truisms: thought thinks, speech speaks, the gaze gazes [*le regard regarde*]. But, between the two identical words there is each time the whole *écart* one straddles in order to think, speak, and see" (S., 21). This *écart* is of course that marked by the flesh, the spacing of the flesh. It was by means of a phenomenological, transcendental reflection of a radical sort—a hyper-reflection—that Merleau-Ponty sought to discover and vindicate, philosophically, the *Urpraesenz* of the other in the same, the other as inscribed in the text of the same, of the "self," as its reverse side, its own subtext or *arrière-texte*, more intimate to the self than the self itself. The other is inscribed on the very tain of the mirror that we call self-consciousness. Merleau-Ponty sought to overcome modern subjectivism from the "inside" of subjectivity itself, by rendering subjectivity problematic for itself.[12]

Between Merleau-Ponty's postmodern approach to the issue of subjectivity and Augustine's premodern handling of it, there is perhaps something more than just an interesting resemblance. I do not mean to imply that in grappling with the problem of ipseity and alterity Merleau-Ponty merely revives a bygone moment in the history of philosophy. The attempt simply to return to the past is a futile gesture that he himself criticized in Heidegger. For Merleau-Ponty, one can never go back; at the same time, however, history never leaves anything definitely behind. The past, the historically other, is inscribed in our being as is the humanly other. It is something that, like Proust, we can rediscover whenever we plunge beneath the Cartesian surface of self-consciousness and come up against the tain of the mirror. Like Augustine before him, Merleau-Ponty discovers Being and the being of the Other within the innermost recesses of subjectivity itself, in the constitutive folds of its own flesh.

4

Justice
in the Flesh

David Michael Levin

> Words are carried over from bodies and from the properties of
> bodies to signify the institutions of the mind and spirit.
>
> —Giambattista Vico, *The New Science*

In "Flesh and Otherness" Claude Lefort seems to be arguing that Merleau-Ponty's phenomenology of the flesh does not give adequate recognition to the irreducible otherness of the other and that, as a consequence, it cannot contribute to our understanding of the body's role in the formation of our concept of social justice. I want to explain why I do not agree with these criticisms.[1] Thus, in the present chapter, I shall attempt to demonstrate that, on the contrary, Merleau-Ponty's phenomenology of the flesh helps us to appreciate the otherness of the other in all its dialectical subtlety and ambiguity, and that his articulation of the intertwinings, transpositions, and reversibilities taking place in the dimension of our intercorporeality brings to light the body's deeply felt sense of justice—the natural, inaugural, and most radical grounding of the ideal of justice in the body of our experience.[2]

In his essay "Surrealism," Walter Benjamin questions the attempt "to win the energies of intoxication for the revolution." And he concludes, writing, "more concretely, of bodies." For, as he says, the "collective is a body, too." So Benjamin leaves us to reflect on his own vision of things: "Only when in technology body and image so interpenetrate that all revolutionary tension becomes bodily collective innervation, and all the bodily innervations of the collective become revolutionary discharge, has reality transcended itself to the extent demanded by the *Communist Manifesto.*"[3]

Leaving aside Benjamin's peculiarly uncritical consent to technology, I want to question much more skeptically the conception of the body taken for granted here. This conception does not appear only, nor for the first time, in the manifestos of surrealism. It figures in the texts of Nietzsche and Freud—and also in the thinking of those whom these texts have strongly influenced: Marcuse, Lacan, Bataille, Foucault, Lyotard, Deleuze, and Guattari. According to this conception, the body is a chaos of drives: turbulent, frenzied, and without any internal principle of organization. It is conceived in the image of Dionysus, a god of excess, knowing no measure: a body of self-abandonment, intoxication, and wildness. And it is this body, the body conceived in his image and reflecting his narcissism, that Freud wanted to repress, to tame and civilize, and that the others, from Nietzsche through Deleuze and Guattari, have wanted to encourage—to incite, in fact, to riot. This is the body to which they turned for the energies of social revolution.

But while this body may have the brute energy necessary to destroy the old order, an order of repression, it does not have the knowledge and wisdom—not even, it must be said, the empowerments of language—to construct a new order. The body these thinkers celebrate is *eros* without *logos*; without reason, without a sense of measure, without any order of its own. Consequently, it cannot know the difference between reason and domination; nor can it carry within it a concretely felt sense of the difference between justice and injustice. Moreover, this body is monadological, steeped in a madness akin to solipsism; totally self-contained, it neither needs nor has any mature interpersonal relationships. It is a body incapable, therefore, of ethical relationships; without any recognition of the other as other, without any understanding of reciprocity, it cannot carry forward the utopian dream of a genuinely moral community, a body politic governed by the principles of justice.

Against advocates for the disorganized body, I hold the following propositions.

(1) It is not true that the only order in the human body is an order totally imposed by society, and that its order is nothing but the accumulated historical effect of political controls. This is historicism, a position we must reject as both false and self-defeating.

(2) We must also reject biologism, the other extreme. Biologism reduces the body to the causalities of a mass of drives, ignores the phenomenological body of meaningful experience, and assumes that the na-

ture of these primitive drives seals the fate of our experience, our character, our life.

(3) The human body has—is—an order of its own. This order, an immanent *logos* of the flesh, has not been recognized.

(4) This order is *already* geared into the mutual recognitions of social interaction: it is *already* prosocial: the body's prosocial behavior is not, and does not need to be, totally introduced by the work of society.

(5) The body's primal order is not, of course, already completely formed. It is only an order ready for, and in need of, further socialization. Society's work of socialization, and its vision of moral development, should respect, and be responsive to, the primal order of sociality already inherent in the child's body.

(6) This order is the life-affirming order of creatively "carrying forward" (the words in quotes are Eugene Gendlin's). When socialization recognizes that the body is already social, already biologically ordered for social interaction, then its work can carry forward the body's implicate order. This process of "carrying forward" is different from socialization processes, which assume that sociability, civility, and morality must be imposed on, and grafted onto, an essentially wild and amoral body.

(7) Reciprocity is a socially produced discursive order; it is also the only order we know of that adequately carries forward the circuit of reversibilities in which the body's own order is manifest.

(8) All political systems should be at least consistent with the normativity of our biological order; but we have no a priori reason to suppose that there is one and only one political system that could harmoniously fulfill this implicate order, and which would be uniquely fated or prescribed. No political order is given in, or with, the body's biological order the way the oak tree is given in, or with, the chemistry of the acorn. Our biology does not, and cannot, totally determine any specific political arrangements. Nevertheless, given the fact that the order of our bodies *is* an order structured by reversibility, it is clear that *what the implicate order of the body needs for its carrying forward and fulfillment* is a social order governed, at the very least, by forms of reciprocity and an ethics of communicative rationality.

(9) There is a critical function implicit in the concept of the flesh: an implicit critique of society and its body politic. Measured against the justice in the flesh, both capitalism and the ego are questioned and indicted. The dominance of the ego is contested by the communicative infrastructures of an inherently social intercorporeality that *precedes* its individuated formation, while capitalism is indicted insofar as it (a) rein-

forces the rule of the ego, (b) perpetuates the grounds of a subject-centered reason, and (c) does not promote the condition of reciprocity that would realize in a new social order the reversibilities and transpositions—the forms of mutual recognition—already schematized by the flesh.

(10) In a prospectus written shortly before the time of his death, Merleau-Ponty wrote of his dream, his commitment to articulating "a spontaneity which gathers together the plurality of monads, the past and the present, nature and culture into one single whole." And he added that "to establish this wonder would . . . give us the principle of an ethics" (Pr. P., 11). In Merleau-Ponty's hermeneutical phenomenology, and especially in his work on the dialectic of reflection opened up by the *écarts* of the flesh, we can see our awakening to the ethics of reciprocity: we can see it taking shape in the character of the body's primal order. This order is not only prosocial; it is also protomoral.

(11) Working for social justice today calls for "promoting new forms of subjectivity," as Foucault finally argued—and this means collaborating with the inherently prosocial order of our bodies to achieve in society at large a level of moral development in which questions of social justice, and the communicative procedures that reflection on these questions require, are of paramount concern: a possibility we cannot recognize, without understanding that neither the monadic ego (in the discourse of Cartesian metaphysics) nor the disorganized body of drives (in the discourse of Freudian psychoanalysis) should continue to represent for us the distinctive social character of the human self.

(12) Most of all, however, what I want to emphasize in this brief chapter is that justice is not just an abstract ideal, a principle conceived by the mind; it is also a critical measure rooted in the body. By virtue of the body, we carry within us a rudimentary, preconceptually formed, sense of justice. This experiential ground of justice cannot be recognized, however, unless we rescue the body from reification: social practices and cultural discourses that continue to objectify the body and miss its inherent, prosocial organization, denying it the power to mean, to speak, to reason. The body of experience is the subject of this power.

In "The Indirect Language" Merleau-Ponty observes that "it is characteristic of cultural gestures to awaken in all others at least an echo, if not a consonance" (P.W., 94). We live in a social world: we inhabit this world. But the world also inhabits us. "I live in the facial expressions of the other, as I feel him living in mine" (C.R.O., 146). Much of our comportment is choreographed by "postural impregnation": a proximity and intimacy with others through which the gestures, postures, and bodily attitudes of others gradually inhabit my own body, simultaneously shaping me in their image and carrying forward my body's own implicately ordered needs (C.R.O., 118). Why is this so? What is it about the embodiment of human beings that accounts for this phenomenon? The disembodied, monadic subject that appears in the discourse of metaphysics cannot account for the phenomenological truth: it assumes that an absolute solitude comes first, and then sociability. Merleau-Ponty's phenomenology of narcissism, however, takes us into the depths of the flesh in order to show (1) that there is a primordial sociability already shaping and moving the infant's body; (2) that our engagement by (and in) a dialectic of reflections is a seduction that draws us out of ourselves, a seduction that plays with our infantile narcissism only to double-cross and reverse it; and (3) that what socialization does is educate—draw out and develop—the sociality potential already inscribed in the flesh.

In later stages of the process of socialization, stages that involve bodily mirroring and reflecting, the interactional nature of the infantile body is increasingly called forth—and, in favorable circumstances, carried forward. Young children get to see themselves in and through others. This helps them to *become* themselves—helps them to achieve further individuation. Insofar as the mirroring and reflecting involve the mediations of other persons, and not (only) objective mirrors, and to the extent that these mediations are bodily experienced as benevolent and not pathological, they also will show the children that they are already, and from the very beginning, social beings, beings who, by grace of their embodiment, are internally ordered for, internally readied for, social interaction. This self-knowledge will encourage, in turn, further steps of individuation—a process the maturity of which is a function, in part, of the subject's responsiveness to this self-recognition, the disclosure of a primordial, bodily organized sociability.

In his reply to Lefort, Martin Dillon asks whether the presence of the other is internal to the body-self, an "immanent phenomenon," or whether it is, instead, an "encroachment," a kind of "transgression." He argues for the "encroachment," taking the alternative, an immanence that projects the other as transcendent, to perpetuate the problematic of idealism in a transcendentalism—a transcendental narcissism—of the flesh. Although I can see the logic of this argument, my answer is different. First of all, I must contest the use of words such as "encroachment," "transgression," and "alienation." These words come from, and only make sense within, a discourse (such as Husserl's) that posits the metaphysical priority of the subject and conceptualizes it as a self-contained monad. These words, which figured in the work of Husserl, Wallon, and Lacan before they were taken over by Merleau-Ponty, implicitly contradict the very thesis we are presumably trying to establish—namely, that the body (the embodied subject) is *not* an essentially unorganized, autistic, self-contained entity, but is already organized, from the very beginning, for social interaction.

If the body (the embodied subject) is *inherently* interactional, oriented from the very beginning toward the engagement and development of its sociability, then the child's initiation into social relationships cannot be an alienation; nor is the presence of others an encroachment and transgression. These words do not narrate the inherent nature of the situation. In fact, they essentialize pathology. What they describe is possible only as pathology: distortions in the structures of mutual recognition; disruptions and disturbances in the processes of communication within which some very unfortunate children may find themselves bound. Thus I dispute the premises behind the question Dillon asks.

The point that calls for phenomenological work is not the fact that the presence of the other draws me out of my present state, but rather the fact that it enables me to see myself as *always already* social—as having *already been* social, social from the very beginning. This new and deeper self-recognition then enables me to make further steps toward a mature individuation, integrating and balancing strong needs for autonomy and equally strong needs for solidarity.

Rather than being essentially isolated from others, which is how we have understood ourselves in the discourse of consciousness, we are, as bodies, joined inseparably, inseparably bound, to others. What Merleau-Ponty shows us is the fact that *it is by grace of the flesh* that we are gathered with others into a primordial sociality. The body is from the very beginning interactional, not monadic: protosocial, and even protomoral. Individuation is a process of socialization, drawing on the fact—the embodiment—of our primordial sociability to make it possible for the child to achieve a personal identity.

It is essential that we understand the nature and role of the body in this dialectical process. This is the understanding that Merleau-Ponty tries to establish. "My body," he says, "discovers in that other body a miraculous prolongation of my own intentions, a familiar way of dealing with the world. Henceforth, as the parts of my body together comprise a system, so my body and the other person's are one whole, two sides of one and the same phenomenon, and the anonymous existence, of which my body is the ever-renewed trace, henceforth inhabits both bodies simultaneously" (Ph.P., 354).

This prolongation is also our openness: "In reality, there is neither me nor the other as positive subjectivities. There are . . . two opennesses, two stages where something will take place" (V.I., 263). Our bodies hold us open to others from the very beginning—the prepersonal beginning—of our lives. Moreover, our prolongation in the other is a relationship that is always, in principle, open to further extension. The inherent communicativeness of an elemental flesh, a flesh we share even as it keeps us apart, makes this extension possible, and indeed desirable.

According to Merleau-Ponty, we are born into an "initial sympathy," an "initial community," a "syncretic sociability" (C.R.O., 119, 120, 135). We are from the very beginning *individuated* bodies, inhabited by intercorporeal synchronizations, predispositions to acknowledge others and be responsive, to be touched and moved by their presence. We belong to a matrix of flesh; so much so that we can achieve an "interior life" only by grace of our intercorporeality. Being with others, we are drawn into, and take part in, a dialectic of reflections. But "every reflection is after the model of the reflection of the hand touching by the hand touched" (V.I., 204).

When the process of socialization is experienced bodily as benevolent and not pathological, I gradually come to appreciate "the intertwining of my life with the other lives, of my body with the visible things, by the intersection of my perceptual field with that of the others" (V.I., 49). This chiasm, this intertwining of our lives, our bodies, sets in motion a certain reversibility in perspectives—mine in relation to the others: "The chiasm, reversibility, is the idea that every perception is doubled by a counter-perception, . . . one no longer knows who speaks and who listens" (V.I., 264). Lefort thinks of this reversibility as a doubling back on itself of the same. This is true; but it is only half the story. The doubling back is actually made possible by the other: it is possible only because there is a real other, irreducible to the immanence of my own body of experience. Social coexistence is a dialectic of reversibility. In the moment of self-recognition, we see and hear ourselves in a reversibility that could happen only by grace of the presence of others. There could be no circuit, no doubling back, if "the other" were nothing but a *projection* of transcendence originating in the immanence of my own self-contained life. The sameness is therefore a mediated identity: an achievement that requires a passage through otherness, real nonidentity.

Reversibility, which, for Merleau-Ponty, is the "truth" of the flesh, constitutes, in fact, the very ground of reciprocity. As such, its occurrence is of the utmost importance for our ethical and political life. So we should not be surprised to find that, in his *Phenomenology of Perception*, Merleau-Ponty gives some thought to reciprocity: "The communication or comprehension of gestures," he says, "comes about through the reciprocity of my intentions and the gestures of others, of my gestures and intentions discernible in the conduct of other people. It is as if the other person's intentions inhabited my body and mine his" (Ph.P., 85). Here, though, "reciprocity" is used rather uncritically, as if it were, or could be, a synonym for "reversibility": as if the two terms were basically equivalent. This misses an opportunity to make a very important, very consequential, distinction. I submit that it would be better to regard the reversibilities of perception as the rudimentary, inaugural form of reciprocity. According to this interpretation, reciprocity would then be the more mature form, the more fully developed stage. I see reversibility as a primal dialectic of reflection and communication, a perceptual interaction engaging subjectivity in a primordial sociality and making it ready for the mutual recognitions and reciprocities constitutive of a more mature social world, a moral and political community.

In "The Concept of Nature," a lecture in a series of lectures he gave at the Collège de France, Merleau-Ponty spoke of "an ideal community of embodied subjects, an intercorporeality." This needs to be thought in conjunction with something that he says in *The Visible and the Invisible*: "We will have to recognize an ideality that is not alien to the flesh, that gives it its axes, its depth" (152). I want to give a name to this ideality: I want to call it "reversibility," a name for the elementary form of reciprocity our bodies already know about long before they are of an age to be tutored; a name, in short, for the very root of our sense of justice.

In "The Child's Relations with Others" Merleau-Ponty resumes a discussion he began in *The Structure of Behaviour* and *The Phenomenology of Perception*: a discussion focused on the corporeal schema. Now, I submit that reversibility is at work in the corporeal schema—that it is a preliminary enactment of justice encoded in the flesh, an implicate order that anticipates, calls for, and is carried forward to completion only by, the achievement of reciprocity in our social and political life. In brief, the reversibilities of the flesh constitute a rudimentary schematism of reciprocities, relationships that are grounded in primal interactions that prepare us for a dialectic of reversible standpoints and viewpoints, and lay the ground for subsequent discursive engagements aimed at mutual understanding.

In his lecture on child development, Merleau-Ponty asserts:

> To the extent that I can elaborate and extend my corporeal schema, to the extent that I acquire a better organized experience of my own body, to that very extent will my consciousness of my own body cease being a chaos in which I am submerged and lend itself to a transfer to others. [C.R.O., 118]

Although he gave much thought to the body's schematism, Merleau-Ponty did not make what I regard as the next phenomenological step—namely, thinking this schematism in terms of the intertwinings and reversibilities at work in the flesh. This would have been—or anyway should have been—his next major step. Perhaps his untimely death cut off this step.

All interactions are opportunities for the progressive fleshing out of this originary schematism, this implicate order, this hint, in our intercorporeality, of a more *utopian* intercorporeality, concretely structured forms of reciprocity generated from within the shared body of social experience.

Our sense of justice is deeply rooted, firmly grounded in the body of our experience. There is a preliminary sense of justice *already* schematized in and by the flesh: this sense is an original ideality, a *logos*, which gives the flesh its ethical and political axis; this sense is an implicate *logos*, which already lays down, for our intercorporeality, a direction for further exertions, and gathers us into forms of communication by which we can extend its enlightening rule.[4]

The order of the body—the body's own order—needs, and orders, a just society. Only a society really governed by principles and procedures of justice, a society truly structured for the realization of democratic pluralism, can fulfill the needs deeply implicate in the body's nature as a "universal flesh." Foucault asks: "What kind of bodies does our society require?"[5] This is an important question. But it must be coupled with another question, one he never asks: "What kind of society do our *bodies* need and require?" What kind of society do our bodies dream? We can at least, I think, say this much: given the fact that the order of our bodies is an order structured by reversibility, what the body needs for its fulfillment is a social order governed by institutions of reciprocity.

In his Preface to *The History of Sexuality*, vol. 2, Foucault says that he is trying "to analyze the formation of a certain mode of relation to the self in the experience of the flesh." However, instead of analyzing experiences belonging to the past, I am attempting to show how Merleau-Ponty's phenomenology of the flesh opens up not only the possibility of a historically different ontology of ourselves and historically different self-formations, but also the possibility of a radically different framework for conceptualizing the historical subject of praxis. Although the ego-body (the ego-centered body) has appeared in many different societies and cultures, our analysis points to the conclusion that, because the ego-centered body is split off from the reversibilities of the flesh—from experiences of reversibility that lay the ground for reciprocity—to the extent that the capitalist social system privileges the ego-body of bourgeois character and promotes its rule, to that same extent capitalism can only be inimical to the experiential grounding of principles of justice. Thus, our hermeneutical phenomenology works for the cause of justice by developing our experience of the flesh and its reversals, and by contesting the historical alliance between capitalism and the ego-body.

In *Humanism and Terror*, Merleau-Ponty contends that "to understand and judge a society, one has to penetrate its basic structure to the human bond upon which it is built" (p. xiv). I think that Merleau-Ponty has contributed significantly to this very project. So what I have tried to argue in this brief reply to Lefort is that, in his hermeneutical phenomenology of the flesh, Merleau-Ponty has cast a penetrating light on the depths and dimensions of this "human bond," letting it be seen and re-cognized as a justice in the flesh. The rule of justice depends on structures of reciprocity, an ethics of communicative rationality. But reciprocity, in turn, depends on the experience and understanding of reversibility: the reversing of roles and points of view.[6] My reply, then, to Lefort is that, thanks to Merleau-Ponty's work, it is now possible for us to see, in the reversibilities of the flesh, in the mediations of justice already schematized and enacted by our intercorporeality, that the strong human bond required for the institutions of a just society is already being formed and tried.[7]

On "How We Are to and How We Are Not to Return to the Things Themselves"[1]

Stephen Watson

Within the schematics of classic Merleau-Ponty interpretation, Lefort's paper is as troublesome as it is enlightening. It will doubtless provoke the ire of those committed to defending the philosopher's text from the "structuralist" onslaughts that awaited it. Granted the precise affirmations of Lefort's earlier explications, the strong character of his deviation here may seem surprising, carrying with it the judgment of time that Merleau-Ponty thought to be so decisive. In fact Lefort's paper bears this judgment on its sleeve. In it we can find the infamous play of the signifier Merleau-Ponty introduced to contemporary French theorists come home to haunt him, as now even Lefort himself invokes a discourse that the speaking subject can neither control nor rely upon. Moreover, if transcendental presentation seems to be disrupted from without, it is also undercut from within. Lefort's affirmation of the Lacanian challenge to transcendental narcissism, far from providing the matrix of an originary return to self, instead silently disrobes all vestige of the Cartesian stronghold, whether understood as its constitutive foundation or its final *telos*, the *letzte Subjekt*, as Husserl called it.

Between them, between the challenges of a discourse that could not be contained and a desire that could not be named, appeals to an *Ursprungsklärung* of the flesh must renounce both the homogeneity and the assurances of classic transcendentalism, being delivered over instead to their other, to what Lefort calls "segregation, fission, and alterity." Moreover, the effects of these challenges impact far beyond the theoretical domains of epistemology and ontology, as Lefort's paper intimates in closing. The laterality upon which all phenomenology depended for its explications of the horizons of consciousness becomes, in the moment of its most extreme return to origins—precisely, that is, in its most radical explication of the very flesh of the *Ineinandersein* of self and world—the final recognition of being, to speak Hegelian, in *absoluten Anderssein:* dispersed, as Lefort puts it, both from "beneath and above this domain."

Those strongly committed to Merleau-Ponty remain entitled to conduct, as have those before them (e.g., Dufrenne, Ricoeur) the appropriate transcendental defense against these threats—*either* by appealing to the pure forms of sensibility—that is, the lived, the existential primacy of perception and the immediacy of the lived body—*or* by reinvoking the pure forms of grammar. To do so, however, threatens to divide the philosopher's text once more into the protocols of the *en soi* and the *pour soi*, which it so strongly resisted. Even so, there may be much in Merleau-Ponty's ambiguous work that tends to support, if not sustain, such defenses.

I am inclined to think that these strategies fail. The transcendental return to the silence of the perceived turns dogmatic in ways Husserl never fully grasped—as is evident in his claim to have phenomenologically *solved* Hume's denials concerning the appearances by appealing to a new superscience based upon "intuition," still plagued methodologically by the vagaries of "description" and epistemologically by those of verification.[2] Moreover, if Merleau-Ponty condemned the Husserlian strategy, it was one that he himself realized he had followed—or followed too much—in the *Phenomenology of Perception*. At best, as he realized, it provided a narrative of how thought is "not impossible"; at worst it simply begged the question, relying upon an access—and an excess— it could not guarantee.[3] The appeal to a science of pure forms, on the other hand, could occur only by forgetting the anticipatory status of the evidence that might bolster such arguments; forgetting that a Benveniste or a Chomsky operate not by transcendental but empirical necessities, necessities that are, to invoke the transcendentalist's lexicon, "putative." There is then a certain *Hexenkreis* to all transcendental defenses—either from "above" or "below." Lefort's invocation of the proper name and the transgression of desire are the signs of their failure, albeit by poisoning the well perhaps every bit as much as transcendental accounts appealed to what could never be adequated.

All attempts at theoretical reduction, transcendental or otherwise, as Merleau-Ponty knew, would be at best provisional.[4] We remain "at sea" within the perceived world, thrown into a dialectic between the sensible and the intelligible, which remains unresolvable—hence the problem of *l'intremonde* and its *Wechsel* between symbol and the symbolized, sign and the signified. From the early 1950s in which the problem of this *intremonde* emerges vis-à-vis structuralist considerations, Merleau-Ponty had already begun to undo the bonds of the flesh even before he had named it.[5] It involved, after all, a *chiasme* that was insurpassable—and unresolvable. Lefort's focusing upon the concept of dehiscence in the working notes to *The Visible and the Invisible* only further truncates it. But in fact as Merleau-Ponty put it quite straightforwardly—and despite his natural proclivities to follow the Husserlian subreption to the contrary—"appearance is not being but the phenomenon."[6]

Moreover, despite Lefort's apt concerns that Merleau-Ponty remained conspicuously silent about the risks (or the "cleavage") of the totalitarian state and democracy, it is true too that his endorsement of parliamentarianism in *The Adventures of the Dialectic* already occurs precisely out of the recognition that only here is there a break with the dialectical illusions of consensus, that only in preserving opposition do political institutions preserve the difference that preserves truth.[7] Notwithstanding the *glissements* of phenomenological *protention,* the ontological difference—that is, the *distention* of the phantasm—here too remains insurmountable.

All interpretation—"phenomenological" or otherise—arises always and only within a certain risk, depending upon what from the outset escapes the warrant of strict assertibility. And it is perhaps less the case that Merleau-Ponty did not recognize it, than that we need to recognize it again, truncating all the while the oversights that accompanied his own theoretical expositions. It is in this sense that we must concur with Lefort: Merleau-Ponty cannot be simply defended against his charges. We can say now with "structuralist" hindsight that, strictly taken, he was too quick to subsume the play of the signifier beneath the teleology of consciousness, too quick to construe the problem of the alterity of desire before the smile of the mother (too quick then to understand "Being" as flesh), and then too quick to think that the withdrawal of the phantasm could be identified as the latent horizon of consciousness, symbolic equivalent in the exchange between the sensible and the intelligible. Here we should simply affirm the developments Lefort calls up and deny Merleau-Ponty's advocates.

For the same reason, however, we must bar the "Levinasian" move that seems to hover in Lefort's appeals to the "third" as "the representative of otherness," stabilizing the dialectics at stake. If Levinas will doubtless assist us against the Cartesian stronghold within phenomenology—precisely in reopening the ethical dimension—that move will not overcome, let alone *solve*, the justificatory demands that motivated the latter. The primacy of practical reason will not, that is, solve the requisites of *theoria*, the obligations and demands of the other person will not fulfill the "demands" of *strenge Wissenschaft*, nor, finally, will the grounds or reasons underlying ethical commitments approach their modalities. As Derrida realized early on, Levinas's ethical transformations of phenomenology require themselves consideration on the confrontation between *theoria* and *praxis*, if you will "a systematic confrontation between Husserl and Kant on the one hand and Husserl and Fichte on the other."[8] Merleau-Ponty speaks in this regard from an abyss that Levinas bridges less than (perhaps quite legitimately on the latter's terms, i.e., those of the ethical and the rights of justice) he simply overlooks. This is not to say that *we* can do so without a risk that, despite its force, the Levinasian text is prone to dissolve (and Lefort to subsume in appealing still to representation, making the "third" "the representative of otherness").

To invoke again the rights of phenomenology at this point, that is, the rights of theory, is by no means, however, to accede to its demands, ones before which it failed as strongly and as radically as any form of Cartesianism. Nonetheless, if in the wake of the structuralist purge the lingering foundationalism that transcendental descriptions invoked remained unquestionably naive—perhaps they can be reread in its wake as the site of a certain remainder. Here we can recall with Merleau-Ponty that the chiasm of the visible and the invisible was both the "labyrinth" of first philosophy and the "ruins" of all objective thought. Doubtless it is precisely this that Lefort's text forces us to confront anew, both by truncating and trading still upon the risk of the "phenomena," the problem, that is, of the withdrawal, and perhaps, to use Merleau-Ponty's term, the "transcendence" of the phantasm. If in the failure of transcendentalism it becomes incumbent to grasp the fact that truth and certainty cannot be identified, what remains "true" too is that neither have they simply been rendered incommensurable. And if he was prone to oversight in confronting the event of their intertwining, it should be said too that no one recognized both the risk and the implications of this confrontation more than Merleau-Ponty.

PART 2

MERLEAU-PONTY AND LEVINAS ON ALTERITY

6

Two Texts
on Merleau-Ponty
by Emmanuel Levinas

Michael B. Smith

The two texts presented here for the first time in English, "Intersubjectivity" and "Sensibility," originally appeared, respectively, as "De l'intersubjectivité, notes sur Merleau-Ponty" in *Paradigmes de théologie philosophique* (Fribourg: Editions Universitaires, 1983) and as "De la sensibilité," the second and major portion of an article entitled "In Memoriam Alphonse de Waelhens," in the September 1984 issue of *Tijdschrift voor filosofie*. They were both reprinted in the collection of essays *Hors Sujet* (Montpellier: Fata Morgana, 1987).

Before discussing the content of these texts, several extrinsic factors make them of special interest. First, they were written quite recently, and hence the perspective they take up already encompasses their author's major theses. Second, the texts are quite parallel, offering the reader a stereoscopic sample of Levinas's manner of approaching a central philosophical problem—namely, that of our initial relation to other subjectivities, or the origin of intersubjectivity. Third, they are deeply intertextual: they take up the problem of alterity through a text of Merleau-Ponty's, "The Philosopher and His Shadow" (in *Signs*), which is itself a critical examination of Husserl's treatment of the perception of others.

The texts begin by retracing Merleau-Ponty's interpretation of the Husserlian reduction: though unsuccessful in what it purports to do, its significant spin-off is to expose the inner, inalienable elements of the constituted world within the very fabric of the constituting consciousness, a curious "anachronism." These elements turn out to be, in Merleau-Ponty's scheme of things, the basis of our knowing of ourselves (as one hand touches the other) and of our apprehension of other persons as well. But immediately after describing in admiring terms the way in which Merleau-Ponty explains the perception of other persons through a version of the Husserlian *Einfühlung* (I lend myself to others—i.e., I know them as variants of myself), Levinas introduces his own, radically different understanding of our relation to the other. The transition is abrupt, because he does not spend much ink in showing the shortcomings of the Husserl/Merleau-Ponty view. He merely indicates that Merleau-Ponty considers this relationship as one of knowledge, even though of a prepredicative or nonthematic variety. Both Husserl's "appresentation" and Merleau-Ponty's unorthodox mode of knowing account for a positive relationship in terms that denote lack, insufficiency, negativity.

Levinas's "note" concludes with a telegraphic series of key philosophical terms he has elaborated in his earlier works (dis-interestedness, non-in-difference, responsibility, love, etc.), to describe the realm of what appears to be a context-less and original meaning, the look of the other, or the face. These assertions can be little more than appeals to works in which the metaphysics of "otherwise than being" is elaborated, but they do remind us vividly of an underlying difference in the overall philosophies of Levinas and Merleau-Ponty: the latter's was always one of continuity (the relationship between body and mind), whereas Levinas posits an absolute break, which if bridged at all can only be crossed in one direction (from other to self/same), and only from the realm of being's other, which is not a mere negation of being, to being.

For the translator, aside from the very condensed, allusive style of these texts, there is a specific problem: the frequency of sentence fragments. Although French is generally more accepting of the so-called incomplete sentence, which is particularly to be expected in what the author refers to as a "note," the absence of the copula is so frequent as to justify the following remark of Alphonso Lingis, masterful translator of Levinas's major theses. He has said that Levinas's suppression of the copula "reflects the understanding of the work of language the book [*Otherwise Than Being, or Beyond Essence*] puts forth."[1] I have retained as much of this essential (or perhaps I should say "antiessential") stylistic feature as I thought English could reasonably tolerate.

Intersubjectivity:

Notes on Merleau-Ponty

Emmanuel Levinas

Husserl's transcendental reduction: phenomenology's methodical return upstream, starting out from the world as it appears in itself to natural or naive consciousness, toward an "absolute consciousness," the return to the "I think," assured of its noetic being, where "in parentheses," in the form of a noematic correlate, the things of the world would come to constitute themselves—this is, according to Merleau-Ponty, an operation as necessary to the isolation of areas of irreducibility as to the interpretation of the appearance of "things-nothing-but-things" (*blosse Sachen*) in their "constitution by the *cogito*."[2] According to his account, the irreducibility of these areas does not come from their exhibiting some radical strangeness, unconvertible into *givens* and eluding the reach and the grip (the *Auffassen* and the *Fassen*) of the knowledge that makes possible the idealist besiegement of being by thought. These areas are irreducible because, although located within the relative of the known world (i.e., within the order accessible in principle to the phenomenological reduction), they belong to the noetic context, to the stuff, to the flesh itself, of the *I think* and to its absolute. That belonging of the *I think* "to flesh" is not meant to be a metaphor: the perception of things in their objectivity implies, noetically and independently of any psychophysiologistic concern (for causality or conditioning), a movement of the senses and even of the legs and the entire body: everything that is called life of the body as body proper, as flesh embodying thought; flesh that allows itself to be associated by the subject with his or her body *objectively* perceived, such as it allows itself to be examined medically and investigated by the psychosomatic psychologist, and is thus a part of the mechanism of nature. Flesh, as objective body, is therefore constituted for consciousness possessed of "powers" already tributary to this body. Consciousness is in a situation of having already called upon what it is only supposed to constitute. This is a curious anachronism!

This anachronism is precisely incarnation, in which the belonging of spirit to flesh, which, as body, it constitutes, is not reducible to the noetic-noematic correlation, to the purely theoretical. Is this the disqualification of the transcendental reduction, thus charged with an inevitable methodological non sequitur, a kind of transcendental illusion? Is this the pure failure of the wisdom of the return to the self? Merleau-Ponty thinks that, for Husserl himself, the transcendental reduction is an inevitable philosophical itinerary leading toward a sphere of intelligibility that is not, of course, that of the objectification called for by positive science, but even more primordial than transcendental subjectivity. The original incarnation of thought, which cannot be expressed in terms of objectification (and which Husserl may have been suggesting in *Ideen I* by the term apperception), is, in Merleau-Ponty's view, prior to the taking up of any theoretical or practical position. An *Urdoxa*: a synthesis prior to all syntheses, "older" than the syntheses derived from an intellectual activity of the postulated *I think*, and making a synthesis of the *res extensa* and the *res cogitans*.

Flesh. Flesh, which is called the body proper, and which does indeed also show itself as body among bodies, but which in that case is no longer approached according to its concreteness, nor in its own sphere. It offers itself to biology, which treats it as a thematizable object—as *Körper* rather than as *Leiblichkeit*. This is not, surely, a way of going toward a false meaning, but certainly toward an already abstract meaning. Body proper, life. It [life] is *here*—that is, in a point in space—but being in that place, the point of departure for a feeling, a "point of view." Localization of this feeling that Descartes nevertheless included, in his "Second Metaphysical Meditation," among the acts encompassed by the *cogito* and not as *res extensa*. The body proper existing as habitation of a world, and the milieu and surroundings of which are not immediately "pure things," nor things invested with "value attributes" referring to axiological intentions, already noetic-noematic structures. The purely theoretical knowledge in which these things appear in this way, and from which the noetic-noematic model of intentionality is undoubtedly borrowed, is a possibility of this life, but one that is already derived from it. "There is undeniably something between transcendent Nature, naturalism's being in itself, and the immanence of mind, its acts, and its noema," Merleau-Ponty writes in *Signs* (166). An in-betweenness more originary than either!

Thus, according to Merleau-Ponty, who with extreme perspicacity returns to the exegesis of numerous texts from *Ideen II* (which the founder of phenomenology, however, never made up his mind to print and which appeared posthumously, thanks to the Husserl Archives of Louvain), Husserl's descriptions were no longer in the style of the transcendental philosophy proclaimed in 1913 in *Ideen I*. It is impossible to express sufficient admiration for the subtle beauty of Merleau-Ponty's analyses of that original incarnation of spirit in which Nature reveals its meaning in the essentially signifying (i.e., expressive, i.e., cultural) movements of the human body, going from gesture to language, to art, to poetry and science: in which Nature reveals its meaning (or soul?) in Culture. Doubtless his own itinerary allowed the French philosopher to say the unsaid [*le non-dit*], or at least the unpublished, of Husserl's thought, a thought the "possibilities" of which require throughout an attentive ear, despite the appearance of immobility or repetition of the major theses.

It is in sensibility, according to Merleau-Ponty, that the carnal (or the mental) manifests its ambiguity or ambivalence of the extension or interiority, in which the *felt* [*senti*], which is out there, is ipso facto a *feeling* [*sentir*]. The sensible content is itself inseparable from that incarnation, of which it is, according to Merleau-Ponty, the "reflection" or the "counterpart." "A universe with its 'subject' and 'object', the articulation of one upon the other" (S., 167). It is the articulation of the subject upon the object in a region where one no longer finds the intentional structure of the noetic-noematic, an articulation that Merleau-Ponty approaches by highlighting what is called the double touching [*double toucher*] of one hand that touches the other, and that, during this touching, is touched by the other hand. The overall phenomenon is structured as if the touch were a reflection on touching, and as if, according to a speculative expression of the philosopher, "space itself knows itself through my body" (S., 167). Here the human is but a moment or an articulation of an event of intelligibility, the heart of which is no longer enveloped or situated within the human being. We must note that antihumanist or nonhumanist tendency to refer the human to an ontology of anonymous being, a tendency characteristic of an entire era, which, while reflecting on anthropology, is mistrustful of the human. The propounded doctrine would seem all the more defensible for appearing indifferent to the drama of persons. Also, one might wonder whether, to a certain degree, Merleau-Ponty is not rehabilitating here, while deepening it, the sensualist conception of sensation, which was both feeling [*sentir*] and felt [*senti*], without empiricism having had to be startled at this psychism, which it construed without the dynamism of horizons, and without intentionality. The latter did not even emerge beyond the "sensible quality," not even in cases where the object detached itself in a way from carnal experience, distancing itself, and thus distinguishing itself from feeling [*sentir*].

For Merleau-Ponty, the passage of sensible qualities tied to carnal subjectivity toward the condition of objective qualities of the real is henceforth sought in intersubjective agreement on the sensible content. That presupposes the constitution of intersubjectivity. Merleau-Ponty accentuates everything in *Ideen II* that makes the relation with others depend upon that carnal structure of sensibility. The way the two hands touch one another remains the prototype, so to speak, of that relation.

"My right hand," Merleau-Ponty writes, "was present at the advent of active touching in my left hand: it is not otherwise that the body of the other comes to life before me when I shake another man's hand, or when I just look at him" (S., 168). The discovery of the felt [*senti*] as feeling [*sentant*] extends to the other's body without having given rise to any reasoning by analogy. The other person and I "are like the elements of one single intercorporeality" (S., 168): the co-presence of two hands, due to their belonging to the same body, is extended to the other person. The "esthesiological" community is seen as founding intersubjectivity and serving as a basis for the intropathy of intellectual communication, which is not directly given, and is produced by reconstruction. This is not taken as an indication of any deficiency in our perception of the other, but as the positive characteristic of that perception. "I lend myself to others, I create them out of my own thoughts. This is no failure to perceive others, it is the perception of others" (S., 159).

Still, one must wonder whether this way of affirming a positivity in a phenomenon that, at first sight and from a certain point of view, appears as privation does not require the indication of a new dimension that would accredit that positivity. Is not the insufficiency of "ap-presentation" compared to representation in the relation to the other the consequence of a finitude? Is it [that insufficiency] not the premise of a new relation between myself and the other, which is not limited to a deficient knowledge of the other? Is it truly nothing but knowledge? The latter remains in Merleau-Ponty, despite the originality of the pre-theoretical structure that he brings to light, precisely as pretheoretical, already in relation to the theoretical and already the shadow, as it were, of that to which it is related. Even if it stands out in contrast to the no-etic-noematic structure of idealizations, that structure is for Merleau-Ponty, already or still, knowledge, even if it is of an other modality. "Even when our knowledge of things is concerned," he says, "we know much more about them in the natural attitude than the theoretical attitude can tell us—and above all we know it in a different way" (S., 163).

Intersubjectivity, being constituted in sensibility described on the basis of the "reflected touching" of the hands touching one another, is structured according to the community between "touching" and "being touched," "the common act of feeling and being felt." A community that is affirmed in its agreement around being: around things and the world. In the phenomenological theory of intersubjectivity, it is always the *knowledge* of the alter ego that breaks egological isolation. Even the values that the alter ego takes on and that one attributes to it stand upon a prior knowledge. The idea that a sensibility may reach the other person *otherwise* than by the "gnosis" of touching, seeing, even if the seeing and contact are those of flesh with flesh, seems foreign to the analyses of the phenomenologists. The psychism is consciousness [*conscience*], and in the word "consciousness" the radical *science* [*science*] remains essential and primordial. Thus the order of consciousness is not broken by sociality any differently from the way it is by knowledge, which, joining the *known* [*su*] immediately coincides with what may have been foreign to it.

Whence a question. In the handshake that phenomenology attempts to understand on the basis of mutual knowledge [*connaissance*] (even if it is the double touching), does not the essential, extending beyond knowledge [*le connaître*], reside in confidence, devotion, and peace; and with an element of the gift from me to the other, and a certain indifference as to compensations in reciprocity and thus with ethical gratuity, which the handshake inaugurates and signifies, without being a simple code transmitting information about it? No more so than the caress that says love is merely the message or symbol of it, but rather, prior to that language, is itself already that love. One may especially wonder, then, whether such a "relation," the ethical relation, is not imposed across a *radical separation* between the two hands, which precisely do not belong to the same body, nor to a hypothetical or only metaphorical intercorporeality. It is that radical separation, and the entire ethical order of sociality, that seems to us to be *signified* in the nakedness of the face illuminating the human visage, but also in the expressivity of the person's whole sensible being, even in the hand one shakes.

On the basis of the face, in which the other is approached according to his or her ethical responsibility, sociality as the human possibility of approaching the other, the absolutely other, is signified—that is, commanded.[3] It is a possibility that does not borrow its excellence from the dignity of the One, the sociality of which may already seem compromised in multiplicity, but a possibility that is rather like a completely new modality that certifies, in and by the human, its own specific *goodness*. In its excellence, which is probably that of love, it is no longer simply the laws of being and of being's unity that rule. The spirituality of the social signifies precisely an "otherwise than being."

Does the distinction, which is still current in everyday parlance, between matter and spirit, have any less naive meaning today? The numerous variations on the theme of the Aristotelian distinction between matter and form, potency and act, or the variations on the theme of Cartesian dualism: Are these not called into question (beyond the simplifications we owe to progress in the natural sciences and certain models in the human sciences, beyond the speculation of transcendental idealism) thanks to the realism of socio-political doctrines or the contestation of subjectivity by modern philosophical anthopology, in which, with the principle of meaningfulness [*le sens*] "more original [*originel*] than the subject," the rift between *res extensa* and *res cogitans* disappears? We have asked ourselves, in this note, whether the distinction should continue to be sought in some intrinsic structure of matter and spirit [*esprit*] taken as constitutive essences of the world and as bound by the unity of the world. Perhaps the spiritual does not show, does not reveal, its specificity except at the moment of interruption of being's normal course: in the strangeness of humans to one another, but of humans capable of society in which the bond is no longer the integration of parts of a whole.

Perhaps the spiritual bond resides in the non-in-difference of persons toward one another, which is also called love, but which does not dissipate the difference of strangeness and is possible only on the basis of a word [*parole*] or an order coming, via the human face, from most high outside the world.

Sensibility

Emmanuel Levinas

In "The Philosopher and His Shadow,"[4] Merleau-Ponty, referring to texts in Husserl's *Ideen II*, suggests that the *transcendental reduction*, phenomenology's inaugural operation, may not have been, for its originator, solely a method that makes possible the perception of the reality of the world as it is constituted in a noetic-noematic correlation, with no remainder. The *reduction* may also have been supposed to circumscribe, or bring to light, the *irreducible*. This [irreducible] can be avoided only in the "constitution" of the things of the world called "pure things" or "things nothing but things" (*blosse Sachen*), given exclusively to vision and hearing as pure representations; and, without doubt, before the objects of the world are marked by "value" attributes, before appearing as "utensils" or cultural objects (which would imply a reference to the "incarnation" of consciousness) and before being related to other persons.

The irreducible in question here is therefore not (as opposed to the idea of the so-called realist philosophers) caused by the permanence, in the "world to be reduced," of some radical *difference* eluding relation: resisting the intentionality of consciousness, the grasp of *conceptualization*, the *taking up* that it involves; a difference refractory to *being given*, positing itself as an absolute and, in its alterity, so to speak, as "too strong" for thought and thus as if dooming to failure any transcendental idealism.[5] What is at stake is something entirely different! The irreducible that has been singled out here does not come from a noninteriorizable outside, an absolute transcendence. In the constituting consciousness itself, in its psychic content of the "I think" and its "intention," there is a paradoxical ambiguity: the texture of the *constituting* is stitched together with *threads* that also come from the realm of the *constituted*, without that origin having to correspond to any "intentional aim." These *threads* belong to the psychic cloth and, if one may say so, to the very *flesh* of the mind. The point is, this is not simply a metaphor: for example, the mental "gait" of thought is also, in the nonfigurative sense of the term, a walking and a movement of the human body; of a body that moves on legs to walk around the thing to be known, that leans over and straightens up to multiply and clarify the views of the real to be captured. Always unilateral views, views to be mutually confirmed, contested, or completed; movements of hands and fingers that explore, of a head that changes points of view, and of hearing; movements of contraction and decontraction of the eye muscles. These muscular acts and these perceptive acts are "mixed," tied to the exploratory activity of a skin that touches. They are lived in the form of "sensation," in which, as in the doctrine of empiricist sensualism, the *feeling* coincides, without any intentionality, with the *felt*.

These sensations are, surely, included, according to Descartes, in the broad notion of the *cogito* (as is the case with all feeling), and yet, already localizable, and through kinesthetic feeling, signifying movement. They are already thoughts then, that are, so to speak, extended and from the start superimposable onto regions of the body of the feeling and thinking subject. They are superimposable upon the objective movements of his or her organs and muscles, in which the flesh also appears as something quasiexterior, constituted, in its various parts, for the look, and, in all its surfaces, for touch, just as much as is a simple stone, in a noetic-noematic process of consciousness, such as Husserl describes it for the "things nothing but things" placed, using his expression, *facing* the "pure I." There is an ambiguity of the *mental* and the *extended*, which is characteristic of "physical" pain and pleasure, which is always localizable, and characteristic also of coenesthesia, in the general sensibility of corporeal *presence*, which is precisely the sensation of the spatial *here*.

What we have here is thought lived as extension and not just, as in the transcendental model, as *idea* of extension: extendedness belonging to the "flesh of thought, to thought having flesh": it [this conception of thought] is not the intentional correlate of extension, no matter how closely interfused we might imagine it to be with extension. Thus there is, in the transcendental reduction of sensibility, the manifestation of a vicious circle, or of an anachronism—of a constitution presupposing, or already giving itself, the constituted. In that insistence in *Ideen II* on what Husserl calls *conditioning* of the conscious by "one's own body," there appears to be a return to the phenomenological sources of the psycho-physiological doctrine in psychology. It [that doctrine] is justified on the basis of the reduction. It is a return that does not yet imply any naturalist prejudice, even though that return may, in the natural attitude, be expressed in terms of causality and favor a confusion between conditioning and causality. In the "natural attitude" prior to the reduction, that return announces and founds the psychophysiological method, once the phenomenological evidence of "conditioning" is taken up and prolonged by empirical information on the attachment of the psychic to the peripheral and central nervous systems.

This conditioning of the mental in "one's own body" that makes up what is called sensibility, this "incarnation" of thought that is phenomenologically described in *Ideen II*, which contrasts with the noetic-noematic structures—might it not be, in the Husserlian system, the effect of a certain prior *apperception* discussed in *Ideen I* (103) that could be understood as an original transcendental synthesis accomplished by the *I think*—like a putting together, in a noetic-noematic representation, of this *I think* itself and of extension via this already constructed *I think*?

But Merleau-Ponty has already accustomed us to the fact that the "body proper" or living flesh is a modality of original being, irreducible to the simple synthesis of pure nature (*res extensa*) and the double touching [*double toucher*] of one hand that touches the other, and that, during this touching, is touched by the other hand. The overall phenomenon is structured as if the touch were a reflection on touching, and as "noema" (S., 166). It is something whose ontology is inscribed within sensibility and in which the relationship of thought to extension is, at its most irreducible, the *inhabiting* of a world, an *incolere*, the inaugural event of culture. In sensibility, the relationship between *I* and the *other* of the world is not to be thought of as the assimilation of the world by the constituting act, but as *expression* of an inner in an outer, life as culture: the truth of knowledge would be, in this scheme of things, neither more nor less than a particular mode of culture.

Culture is not conceived of as coming along subsequently to add on axiological attributes (which would then be seen as secondary, founded on something else) to the preestablished, founding representation of the thing. The essentially cultural can be traced back to embodied thought expressing itself, to the very life of flesh manifesting its soul—the original signifying of the significant [*sensé*] or of the intelligible. It is a modality of meaning that is older than that of the dualist metaphysics of

Cartesianism or of the subject-object correlation that develops into transcendental philosophy. The subject-object correlation is a derivative
concept, and one that presupposes, in particular, the intersubjective
agreement that cultural forms require in order to be able to signify being
and world, and that truth requires in order to signify [within being and
world] objectivity. This agreement is established, according to Merleau-
Ponty, on the basis of flesh itself, on the basis of embodied spirituality,
on the basis of the sensible, which, in other persons, reappears as "a
flesh of one's flesh," like a right hand that, touching a left hand (its
"felt"), touches it ipso facto as a "feeling" hand, feeling the hand that
touched it.

It is in this phenomenon, according to this analysis, that *intropathy*
resides, and also the *Einfühlung* spoken of in German psychology, and
which Husserl's phenomenology takes as its point of reference. By virtue
of the fact that my right hand touching my left hand is touching a
"feeler" who experiences "kinesthetic and tactile sensation" similar to
those residing in my right hand, I immediately lend [*prêter*] to the hand
of the other person [*autrui*] that I shake—I lend to the felt hand—the
tactile and kinesthetic sensations of an actively feeling being. I lend them
to the other's hand in this contact itself just as I experienced them in my
left hand touched by my right. And I did this without any reasoning by
analogy whatsoever! I go from my hand to the other's hand as if both
hands belonged to the same body. This loan as esthesiological transfer
plays a fundamental role: it forms the basis of reconstructions for me of
the thought of other people, using my thought as point of departure.
And Merleau-Ponty writes (S., 159): "I lend myself to others, I create
them out of my own thoughts. This is no failure to perceive others; it is
the perception of others."

It is not our intent to cast doubts, in Merleau-Ponty's remarkable
analysis, upon the opening up of a path toward the recognition of other
people in the "I lend myself to others." But can the social unity toward
which it claims to proceed be thought solely on the basis of an
intercorporeity understood as the solidarity of an organism in its *esthetic*
unity? Is the meaning of intersubjectivity at the level of sociality attained
while being conceived by analogy with the image of the joining of a person's hands, "the right knowing what the left is doing"? Is the handshake
a "taking cognizance of" ["*prise de connaissance*"] and as it were a coinciding of two thought-worlds in the mutual knowledge of one by the
other? Is it not in the *difference*—the proximity of one's neighbor? In
difference that, as proximity, can be reduced neither to an attenuated
difference, nor to a partially abortive coincidence or assimilation, but a
difference that (and this adds new meaning to peace) is tendered not by

the psychism of intentionality and thematization, nor by a communication of information, but by non-in-difference, by responsibility-for-others; by *sentiment,* which originally is not "intentional pointing toward values," but rather peace breaking apperception-consciousness? Is it not then an *"attuning oneself"* to the other—that is, a giving of oneself to him or her? To be sure, not all sentiment is love, but all sentiment presupposes or inverts love. The handshake is not simply the notification of agreement, but prior to that notification the extraordinary event itself of peace, just as the caress, awakening in the touch, is already affection and not information about sentiment.

Moreover, how can a knowledge in which the perceived is neither grasped nor found in the object, but only lent to it, mean anything but the failure of perception's very intentions, even if this knowledge were to be only a "knowing differently" [*savoir autrement*], to use Merleau-Ponty's own term (S., 163)?

It is true that the Husserlian texts on *intropathy* that appear in *Ideen II* present the meaning of this *"knowledge"* in a manner that is particularly impressive by its phenomenological precision. These analyses, many years earlier than those presented in part 5 of Husserl's *Cartesian Meditations,* seem to us paradoxically richer than the latter. We are thinking particularly of the entire paragraph 56 of this dense but extremely rich book, and more precisely of those inimitable pages (*Ideen* II, 236–47) devoted to the comprehension of objects "invested with spirit," contrasted with our knowledge of all other meaningful objects; we are thinking of the admirable effort to sift out, from the phenomenological analysis of appresentation, sociality and society in their height and in the way in which they go beyond the perception of objects invested simply with "signification." Yet at no point in that very beautiful analysis is there a questioning of the (ultimately or originally) cognitive structure of lived experience, in order to rethink the cognitive access to the objectivity of the other on the basis of his or her proximity as neighbor, rather than founding the latter on the former. Sentiment remains till the end thought of on the basis of the knowledge of values.

At this point it would be appropriate, in our opinion, to ask the following question: Is it not the case that intropathy—beyond (or on the hither side of) acquired or even immediate knowledge concerning the existence of a thought external to my own, and uncovering the fact that there is out there "someone to speak to"—is itself already, and fully, a social relation? As expressed by Husserl in the personal form of a reflexive verb, *Ich fühle mich ein,* does it not already resonate like a feeling of sympathy, already like a friendship and almost like a kind of fraternal compassion—that is, like a taking upon oneself of the "undergoing" of the other person? Its excellence in intersubjectivity is to be assessed, then, not by the degree of adequation of the perceived with the real, but by the generosity of the "I lend myself to the other," by the ethical value of the gift, of the consent of the loan from myself to the other, loftier than the investment of being in pure knowledge. "To lend oneself to others" is not of the order of esthesic constitution. It is a "first move" granted to the other! To lend oneself: that is the very metaphor of sociality that insinuates itself in *contact*, which is ambiguous from the start. Sociality stemming from the signifying power of feeling [*sentiment*], already dulled in the purely qualitative and neutral sensation of touch and always about to reintroduce itself back into that sensation. Intersubjectivity is not the modality of a *sensation* that, in the example of the hands touching one another (in the "double touching" [*"double toucher"*] as it used to be called in psychology) would be the end point of pure knowledge. This is the case even if, in the ambiguity of insinuation,[6] which is a modality of the enigmatic or of the "vacillating" [*clignotant*] and not simply of the equivocal, there always remains the possibility of an un-saying [*dé-dire*], which still does not justify the pure and simple reduction.[7]

Surely there is in Husserl's analyses in *Ideen II*, on which many of Merleau-Ponty's analyses are based, a priority given to the tactile, the kinesthetic, localizable pain and pleasure, in comparison with other modes of the sensible, and in the reflections on touch and physical affectivity, an insistence on what sensation, as a way of knowing, means, at once in terms of movement and extension. Hence perhaps a certain priority given to the ambiguity of the sensible as [a form of] consciousness in which the mental element of the apprehension of things and the spatial element of the corporeal gestures of taking, in that same apprehension, go together. This is the original and originary [*originale et originelle*] condition of the body proper, the status of *Leiblichkeit*, solipsistic subjectivity and, in other people, the object "invested with spirit." But henceforth [there is a] priority of the flesh affirming itself in human spirituality and to the detriment of another ambiguity or ambivalence, that of the enigma of sensation-sentiment, which is played out in the passivity of the *senses affected* [*sens affectés*] by the sensorial, between the pure undergoing or suffering and eventual pain, and the *known* [*su*] of knowledge that remains behind as its residue or trace. It is a pure undergoing, eventual pain—solitude and abandonment like the concretization of suffering. It is solitude and abandonment, but thus, in the "privation" that is the desire for the other, [it is] this desire itself. It is an affectivity that carries within itself affection and love—secret structure or concretization of feeling. Should we say a waiting for God in this anticipatory feeling of the absolutely other? Not at first or immediately a call for help, but a pathway leading to the other, leading to the human. In the touch itself, the possibility of a helping hand. Or possibility of the caress, the kiss, the erotic.

The other, who is unique to the affection and who, by virtue of that uniqueness, is no longer a simple individual among individuals, grouped within some sort of common generic category, the unique other who precisely is other in relation to all and any generality, is bound to me socially. That person cannot be represented and given to knowledge in his or her uniqueness, because there is no science but of generality. But the nonrepresentable—is it not precisely the inside, which, *appresented* [*apprésenté*], is approachable? Indeed, appresentation is not only the last resort of a deficient representation, as certain of Husserl's texts would seem to lead us to believe. It is, in proximity, all the novelty of the social; proximity to the other, who, eluding possession, falls to my responsibility—that is, signifies in all the ethical excellence of obligation toward others, in fear for him or her, and love.

There is a misunderstanding or forgetfulness, also, in Husserl and Merleau-Ponty, of the enigma of sensation-feeling even more mysterious in the visual. The latter, being *uncovering* [*dévoilement*] par excellence, fully theoretical opening upon *being*, a fastening upon it in synthesis, seizes and conceptualizes more being than hands could carry off. But behold how in this universal investiture there lurks the dispossession which is dis-interestedness beneath the concretization of responsibility, of non-in-difference, of love. There is responsibility for the unique that shatters totality; responsibility before the unique that rebels against every category, a signifier beyond any concept, disengaged, for a moment, from all graspable form in the *nakedness* of its exposure to death, pure appresentation or expression in its supreme precariousness and in the imperative that calls out to me. Here is vision turning back, re-turning into nonvision, into the insinuation of a face, into vision's denial at the heart of vision, into that of which vision, already espousing a plastic form, is but forgetfulness and re-presentation.

One-Way Traffic:
The Ontology
of Decolonization
and its Ethics

Robert Bernasconi

L evinas refers to Merleau-Ponty explicitly in a number of places. In *Totality and Infinity* Levinas acknowledges his debt to Merleau-Ponty for having established the idea of the underlying solidarity between speech and thought in place of the myth of a disincarnate thought, a thought prior to speech (T.I., 205–6; *T.I.*, 180). Two discussions of the reading that Merleau-Ponty gives of Husserl in the essay "The Philosopher and His Shadow" have been translated for the present volume.[1]

Most penetrating perhaps, and certainly most difficult, is the encounter between the two thinkers that arises from Levinas's use of Merleau-Ponty as an interlocutor in the essay "Meaning and Sense" ("La Signification et le Sens"), to be found in his book *Humanisme de l'autre homme*. This essay will serve as my primary text. Levinas began to write it in 1961, the year of Merleau-Ponty's death. It was also the year of the publication of *Totality and Infinity* (French original), and so "Meaning and Sense" represents one of Levinas's first attempts to reformulate—and rethink—the insights developed there. Where *Totality and Infinity* relied largely on a language of alterity whose main recourse was negation in its various forms (denial, contradiction, etc.), "Meaning and Sense," particularly in its last pages, already points toward the still largely uninvestigated language of *Otherwise than being*, a language that one might provisionally characterize by its power to disturb.

In "Meaning and Sense," as indeed elsewhere, Levinas associates Merleau-Ponty with the phrase "fundamental historicity." Although I have not yet succeeded in finding the phrase in any of Merleau-Ponty's published works, there is hardly a book or an essay by him that does not seem to promise it. Similar phrases abound. To take "Eye and Mind" for example, Merleau-Ponty proposes there that scientific thinking return to "the soil of the sensible," both as it belongs to my own body and to the associated bodies of the "others" alongside me. By rediscovering its "primordial historicity," science will, according to Merleau-Ponty, once more become philosophy by learning to ground itself upon things themselves (Pr.P., 161; Œ., 13). "Primordial historicity" is not to be understood as an obstacle to truth, but a reason for a new conception of truth. "Since we are all hemmed in by history, it is up to us to understand that whatever truth we may have is to be gotten not in spite of but through our historical inherence" (S., 137; *S.*, 109).

The idea of fundamental historicity is associated in Merleau-Ponty with the idea that language conditions thought. Nevertheless, Levinas appears to want to take the difficult route of siding with Merleau-Ponty on the solidarity of thought and language, while challenging the latter's idea of fundamental historicity. As early as 1964, Derrida spelled out the difficulty: "For Levinas, the origin of meaning is nonhistory, is 'beyond history.' One would then have to ask whether it is any longer possible to identify thought and language as Levinas seeks to do."[2] Derrida passed this judgment largely on the basis of *Totality and Infinity*. Although he drew on "Meaning and Sense" for its account of the trace, it appeared too late for him to make extensive use of it. I shall suggest that "Meaning and Sense" not only shows why Levinas is at such pains to divorce Merleau-Ponty's two claims, but also indicates how he proposes to do so. That would explain why Merleau-Ponty plays such a prominent part in the essay.

Levinas explicitly acknowledges that the analyses to be found in the opening sections of "Meaning and Sense" are guided by Merleau-Ponty (C.P. 95; *H.H.*, 46). The difficulty one has in assessing the extent of Levinas's engagement with Merleau-Ponty arises from the fact that Levinas reworks his sources, very much as Merleau-Ponty reworks his. This is particularly true of "Meaning and Sense," where Levinas follows Merleau-Ponty's practice of taking up in his own voice the thought that he will eventually discard. Much of the time one is uncertain who is speaking. The first task, therefore, is to explore the structure of the essay, reconstruct and assess its argument, and investigate its sources. The complexity and range of Levinas's essay defies commentary in the conventional sense. More than usual his commentators cannot be sure who is speaking—he or they. I am well aware that my efforts here are no more than a provisional and somewhat tentative step toward a reading of the essay. Only some of the essay's themes, particularly that of transcultural ethical judgments, are taken up. I have already explored elsewhere[3] Levinas's discussion of the trace, which serves as the culmination of the essay.

"Meaning and Sense" begins by contrasting, in somewhat broad strokes, two rival claims on the relation of meaning and receptivity. The first, which is associated with the intellectualist tendency of Western philosophy from Plato to positivism, attempts to make good what is lacking in perception. The deficiency or finitude of perception is established by contrast (explicit or implicit) with the idea of a God for whom reality and intelligibility coincide. If the designation of this position as "intellectualism" seems unusual, this is because Levinas is using the term in a very broad sense to include "rationalist or empiricist, idealist or realist" variations (C.P., 76; *H.H.*, 20). The alternative view presents perception as an excellence and conceives it as bodily, not simply by virtue of human finitude, but essentially. As incarnate, cultural action "does not express a preexisting thought, but Being" to which it already belongs (C.P., 81; *H.H*, 27–28). This is Merleau-Ponty's standpoint and Levinas draws on a number of his works in order to reconstruct his position. Borrowing from the *Phenomenology of Perception*, Levinas rehearses both Merleau-Ponty's thesis that pure sensation corresponds to nothing in our experience (Ph.P., 3; *P.P.*, 9) and his discussion of horizon as that which guarantees the identity of the object (Ph.P., 68; *P.P.*, 82). Drawing on *Signs*, Levinas adds the lesson Merleau-Ponty learned from Saussure, that "it is the lateral relation of one sign to another which makes each of them significant" (S., 42; *S.*,53). This gives rise to the notion of a lateral universality that replaces the universality of Platonic Ideas. Levinas also highlights the way the assembling of the totality of being is assigned by Merleau-Ponty to the production of cultural objects (S., 181; *S.*, 228).

Levinas finds that the alternative philosophies just outlined have very different implications when it comes to the political question of colonization. The introduction of this political question might seem somewhat sudden, but it appears less so if one thinks of "Meaning and Sense" as a response to Merleau-Ponty's 1960 collection of essays, *Signs*. In that volume Merleau-Ponty placed philosophical essays alongside articles and interviews on current topics, mostly of political interest. A long preface sought to unite these interests by exploring the difficulties facing a philosopher who engages in political discussion. It began, "How different—how downright incongruous—the philosophical essays and the ad hoc, primarily political observations which make up this volume seem!" (S., 3; S., 7). If Levinas had felt that incongruity on first opening the book, there is certainly no hint of it in "Meaning and Sense." For Levinas, the politics of decolonization fits as perfectly with Merleau-Ponty's philosophy of language as colonization conforms with Platonism.

In the case of Platonism, which corresponds to what Levinas had earlier called intellectualism, the world of meanings prior to language and culture functions as a privileged culture dominating historical cultures and rendering them intelligible. That is to say, "there exists a culture that would consist in depreciating the purely historical cultures and in, as it were, colonizing the world beginning with the land in which this revolutionary culture arose—this philosophy which goes beyond cultures" (C.P., 84; H.H., 31). By contrast, the anti-Platonism of Merleau-Ponty subordinates the intellect to expression. The diversity of cultural expression, which had been relativized by Platonism's belief in an intelligible world of meaning situated prior to language, is now to be celebrated. Cultural differences are to be recognized as an inexhaustibly rich resource and not presented as a problem indicative of a deficiency or lack (C.P., 83; H.H., 30). Whereas Platonism's belief in a privileged culture that had already colonized the world by way of the timeless order of Platonic Ideas opened the way to a disregard for historical cultures (C.P., 84; H.H., 31), the thought of "fundamental historicity" is introduced by Merleau-Ponty to break Western thought's nostalgia for a culture capable of encompassing all historical cultures. Just as the passage from one language to another does not need to pass through an algorithmic language and does not require the support of a universal grammar, the contact between cultures is not mediated by the world of Ideas (C.P., 100; H.H., 54). Levinas concludes that "the political work of decolonization is thus attached to an ontology—to a thought of being, interpreted in its multiple and multivocal cultural meaning" (C.P., 86; H.H., 33).

That Merleau-Ponty was indeed at one time opposed to colonization is confirmed by a 1947 essay on Indochina, which was written as a reply to the Catholic writer François Mauriac. "The Vietnamese themselves have above all seen the 'corruption' of it [colonization]. It is in a precise sense scandalous that a Christian should show himself so incapable of getting outside himself and his 'ideas' and should refuse to see himself even for an instant through the eyes of others" (S., 324; S., 404). Colonization on this view follows from failing to see oneself from the outside. It arises insofar as one is locked within oneself. It seems therefore that colonization is not simply a political issue that comes to a head only in the attempt to derive a politics from ontology. And because it amounts to understanding everything within one's own terms, reducing the other to the same and imposing that understanding on the other, colonization does not end with the political process of decolonization. In *Humanism and Terror* Merleau-Ponty gives some indication of how widespread he finds the phenomenon of colonization, even within the political arena, by drawing a picture of Western humanism as a humanism of comprehension where "a few mount guard around the treasure of Western culture," while the rest remain subservient—not just to the few, but "to a certain idea of man and its supporting institutions." He draws a contrast between the way Western humanism appears to itself and the way it appears to those on whom it imposes itself. But the latter are not confined to inhabitants of some distant land. On this analysis "colonial exploitation" can also take place within a particular society (H.T., 175–76; *H.T.*, 189–90).

Before examining how in the course of developing his own position Levinas negotiates the alternatives, Platonism and anti-Platonism, it might be helpful to consider the difficulties he finds in situating Husserl with regard to them. In "Meaning and Sense" Husserl's transcendental philosophy is, after some hesitation and with certain important reservations, referred to as intellectualism (C.P., 76; *H.H.*, 20). Levinas follows this characterization later in the essay when it comes to the question of Husserl's position on culture. The phenomenological reduction and the constitution of the cultural world in transcendental and intuitive consciousness is said to amount to a Platonism in the sense of "an affirmation of the human independently of culture and history" (C.P., 101; *H.H.*, 56). But the ambiguity of Husserl's position on this issue leads Levinas to present it differently elsewhere.[4] In a brief, largely autobiographical, essay called "Signature," the emphasis goes the other way. Referring to Husserl's claim that ideas do not separate themselves from their genesis in a fundamentally temporal consciousness, Levinas writes: "In spite of his intellectualism and his certitude with respect to the excellence of the West, Husserl has thus brought into question the Platonic privilege, until then uncontested, of a continent which believes itself possessed of the right to colonize the world."[5]

That the tension is in Husserl's position on colonization and not just in Levinas's presentation of it could be illustrated by drawing on Husserl's "Vienna Lecture" with its identification of Greece as the source of that common cultural spirit that draws all of humanity under its spell (C., 277; *K.*, 322–23). But what is important here is that

Levinas's own position exhibits a similar tension. In both "Signature" and "Meaning and Sense" Levinas espouses a return to Platonism, in something like the way Husserl insists on a return to rationalism. That Levinas does so is quite remarkable, given his usual tendency to insist dramatically on his break with the previous history of Western philosophy. Nevertheless, this is not the old Platonism, any more than Husserl's rationalism was "the old rationalism," misguided and confused "in its entanglement in 'naturalism' and 'objectivism' " (C., 299; K., 347). Levinas characterizes his own position as a "return to Platonism in a new way," "a return to Greek wisdom, even though mediated by the whole development of contemporary philosophy" (C.P., 101; H.H., 56). In other words, it is a Platonism mediated by anti-Platonism.

Levinas's Platonism is anyway not Husserl's. According to Levinas, it is ethics that transcends history and culture, or is "prior to" them, as he would say. More precisely, it is the ethics of the face of the Other (C.P., 101; H.H., 56). It is not possible on this occasion to rehearse the details of Levinas's path-breaking philosophy, which this simple phrase is supposed to evoke. It will be necessary later to question the possibility of maintaining the independence of ethics and history, but this is what Levinas constantly calls for. "Signature" outlines his position succinctly: "By showing that the first meaning (signification) arises in morality—in the quasi-abstract epiphany of the face, which is laid bare and stripped of every quality—absolute—absolving itself of cultures, one draws out a limit to the comprehension of the Real by history and rediscovers Platonism" (R.P., 188; D.L., 379). The terms of the title of the essay "Meaning and Sense" are used to develop the same point.

The distinction between *meaning* and *sense* is a familiar one within phenomenology, but there is some reason for thinking that Levinas is drawing specifically on Merleau-Ponty's use of it insofar as both thinkers take advantage of the ambiguity of the French word *sens* as both sense and direction. This is Merleau-Ponty in the chapter on temporality in the *Phenomenology of Perception*: "We have no way of knowing what a picture or a thing is other than by looking at them, and their meaning (*signification*) is revealed only if we look at them from a certain point of view, from a certain distance and in a certain direction (*sens*), in short, only if we place at the service of the spectacle, our collusion with the world" (Ph.P., 429; P.P., 411; see T.I., 98; T.I., 71). In Merleau-Ponty the distinction corresponds to the two kinds or levels of intentionality, variously described as operative and thetic, founding and founded, or prepredicative and predicative. In adopting this distinction, Levinas nevertheless transforms it. Whereas Merleau-Ponty can talk of a "sense of history" (Ph.P., 448–49; P.P., 512), he would not refer, as Levinas does, to a "sense prior to history" (C.P., 102; *H.H.*, 57). Levinas uses the word *signification* when it is a question of cultural diversity. *Sens* is given an ethical weight. This is most pronounced in his use of the phrase *sens unique*, familiar from its use as a traffic direction: *rue à sens unique*, one-way street. Sense, in Levinas's understanding, is both unique and in a single direction. The asymmetrical, irreversible relation in favor of the Other is a kind of one-way traffic.

On this issue of transcultural understanding, Husserl, Levinas, and Merleau-Ponty share a recognition of the privilege held by the language of philosophy as it originated in Greece, the privilege of the *logos*. Levinas has often made this point, insisting, as he puts it in recent essays, that Greek wisdom must be distinguished from the Greek language, and that Judaism must be translated into Greek, the "language of the university," which presumably means in this context any of the Western languages.[6] The malleability of these languages plays for Levinas the role that Merleau-Ponty gives to transparency: "There is something irreplaceable in Western thought. . . . A culture is judged by its degree of transparency, by the consciousness it has of itself and others. In this respect, the West (in the broad sense of the term) is still the system of reference. It is the West which has invented the theoretical and practical means of becoming self-conscious and has opened up the way of truth" (S., 138; *S.*, 174).

Merleau-Ponty believes that it is precisely because he retains the standpoint of the West that he is so ready to learn from other cultures, at least more ready than if he had withdrawn into some kind of neutrality. In "Everywhere and Nowhere," answering the question of what the West can learn from Oriental philosophy, he suggests that Indian and Chinese philosophy might help us to rediscover the relationship to being that gave birth to philosophy, a relationship from which we have excluded ourselves "in becoming 'Westerners' " (S., 139; *S.*, 175–78). Merleau-Ponty is doing more than acknowledging the possibility that Western philosophy might be instructed by other cultures. It is as if he were suggesting that other cultures can play the role for Western philosophy that, according to "Eye and Mind," art plays in informing science. That is to say, they would return it to the soil of the sensible, or to what he also calls—and he uses the phrase in a way that suggests that he quite probably is borrowing it from Levinas (or Blanchot)—the "there is" (*il y a*).

In one place, Merleau-Ponty sets himself the task of understanding why what one culture produces has meaning for another, "even if it is not its original meaning." This is the question of "why we take the trouble to transform fetishes into art," the question of "*a* history or *a* universe of painting" (S., 68; *S.*, 84). Elsewhere he confirms that, if the lateral relationships between cultures awake echoes of one culture in the other, then it is necessary to restore the idea of a single history as the precondition of human communication. "What makes this connection of meaning between each aspect of a culture and all the rest, as between all the episodes of history, is the permanent, harmonious thought of this plurality of beings who recognize one another as *'semblables,'* even when some seek to enslave others, and who are so commonly situated that adversaries are often in a kind of complicity" (Pr.P., 10; *R.M.M.*, 408).

Thus Merleau-Ponty found that in order to compare distinct and separate cultures, it was necessary to place them under a common denominator. Like Husserl, he found himself struggling to distance himself from the kind of dogmatic rationalism that he associated with Hegel's *Weltgeist*. The task of maintaining the separation of "primordial historicity" from Hegelian historicity is not straightforward. When in an interview on Madagascar given in 1958 Merleau-Ponty resisted the idea of French withdrawal from Africa, it was on the grounds that France could continue to do good there and that it was better for France to be "a country which does something in history than . . . a country which submits to it." History is the guiding value. If Western civilization is superior it is not in respect of moral value, but what Merleau-Ponty calls "historical value" (S., 336; *S.*, 417–18). This is a consequence of the idea of "fundamental historicity" and helps explain why in *Otherwise than being* Levinas distances himself from it no less than four times (O.B., 45, 70, 160, 167; *A.Q.*, 57, 89, 204, 215).

But in "Meaning and Sense" this is not the main objection. There the issue against Merleau-Ponty is that by insisting that there is no level of meaning that escapes cultural determinacy, Merleau-Ponty deprives himself of the basis that would allow him to pass judgment on other cultures (C.P., 100; *H.H.*, 54). It is clear that we do issue such judgments, Merleau-Ponty included. His comments on torture in the interview "On Madagascar" are an example. I have already said enough about that interview to suggest that it marks a break from the strong opposition to colonization exhibited in the essay on Indochina. But the reality is rather more complex. In "On Indochina" Merleau-Ponty was clear that his approach was not rooted in abstract morality or arguments of principle but in concrete observation (S., 323; *S.*, 402). The same kind of reasoning operates in "On Madagascar." He does not attempt to deduce a policy from "a moral attitude." To illustrate what he means by a "moral attitude" he takes the case of someone who thinks that "in principle white men had no business in the rest of the world" and "that their only duty and their only role at present is to get out," irrespective of the difficulties that would leave the countries in (S., 329; *S.*, 409). Merleau-Ponty's approach to colonization is therefore not moralistic. It is guided by a recognition of political realities—and "history." Nevertheless, this does not mean that there is no place for morality, only that "it should not legislate without considering the case" (S., 323; S., 402). That leaves in place the question of the basis of the ethics that nevertheless still underlies the judgments. Because Merleau-Ponty never completed the promised metaphysics that he said would also deliver "the principle of an ethics" (Pr.P., 11; R.M.M., 409), Levinas's argument, which seems to say that Merleau-Ponty could *never* have written the ethics he needed to justify his judgments, has to be taken seriously.

And yet does Levinas's concern really lie in the judgments one culture passes on another? Levinas may say that "the norms of morality are not embarked in history and culture" (C.P., 100; H.H., 56), but he surely does not mean that such "norms" can be justified beyond history and culture. Levinas's work is concerned with the possibility of ethics rather than with the generation of a specific ethics. That is why the phrase "norms of morality" is so rare in his work. By the same token, the fact that Levinas writes of the "abstractness of the face" does not mean that he proposes a morality somehow distilled from the various instances of morality exhibited by different cultures (C.P., 100; H.H., 57). The face is abstract or absolute in the sense that it disturbs the concrete world. It does not, he says, settle into the horizons of the world. Moral judgments, which are concerned with the realm of history and culture, must negotiate the world and take their place there. But they are possible, according to Levinas, only because ethics is prior to history and independent of culture. The claim is that there is no room within Merleau-Ponty's ontology for the ethics (in his special sense) that underlies moral judgments, politics or, as Levinas himself would say, "justice." The judgments whose justification is lacking from Merleau-Ponty are not *ethical* in Levinas's sense. They are issued "on the basis of ethics," as his more precise formulation has it (C.P., 101; H.H., 56).

The ethical one-way traffic that Levinas celebrates in "Meaning and Sense" (C.P., 90–92; H.H., 40–42) does not express itself in a series of critical pronouncements. The orientation of ethics in Levinas is not the condemnation of others, but the moment of self-questioning. "To discover the orientation and the one-way sense (*l'orientation et le sens unique*) in the moral relationship is precisely to posit the ego as already put into question by the Other it desires, and, consequently, as criticized in the very straightforwardness of its movement" (C.P., 98; H.H., 53). It is only by a circuitous route that one can come to question the Other and never simply on one's own behalf.[7] In "Meaning and Sense" the neologism *illeity* maps the route that always passes through the Other (C.P.,

107; *H.H.*, 63). And yet would it not be a distortion of Levinas's thinking to suppose that the face-to-face relation with the Other can be transposed to the encounter between cultures? Levinas's claim is that the encounter with the Other puts me in question. But even if the encounter between cultures leads me to doubt the norms of my own culture *on the basis of* the practices of an alien culture, does that make the encounter ethical? For all the rhetoric of strangerhood, is not the Other always other than culture? Can the Other qua Other have a cultural identity?

On the other hand, would it not be highly paradoxical to find Levinas committed to a radical separation of culture and ethical alterity? However much the Other must maintain its "priority" over culture in order to secure its alterity, must not its immanence within culture also be secured? Is it not essential that Levinas redetermine the notion of culture in terms of his philosophy and not simply remain content with the concept he inherits?

In his contribution to the Seventeenth World Congress of Philosophy held in Montreal in 1983, Levinas began that task. Appropriately the title of the session, which Levinas also took as the title of his own paper, was "Philosophical Determination of the Idea of Culture." In this essay Levinas rehearsed, more systematically but perhaps less profoundly, many of the issues introduced in "Meaning and Sense." Once again the attempt is made to negotiate a way between a view of culture as mastery where knowledge assimilates alterity "to the unity of the One," and a conception of culture where the world is inhabited through poetry and art. Whereas the universalizing character of the first approach is in this essay associated with science rather than Platonism, it is once again opposed to a position identified as Merleau-Ponty's.

What is striking—and, it has to be said, within the context of this 1983 essay somewhat artificial—is the introduction of a third concept of culture, "ethical culture" (*D.P.I.C.*, 81). This notion of culture is associated with love, although not in the sense given it by literary culture, including the Bible. Love in the appropriate sense is "commanded by the face of the other man, who is not given within experience and does not come from the world" (*D.P.I.C.*, 82). Whatever reservations one might have about Levinas's presentation of "a culture which precedes the political" (*D.P.I.C.*, 80), it is important simply for its recognition that ethics as understood by Levinas does not leave the Platonic and the anti-Platonic, the scientific and the poetic, conceptions of culture in possession of the field. But what does ethical culture amount to?

If Levinas is proposing the idea of an "ethical culture" as a solution to the relation between ethics and culture, it seems to work only on the level of the magical. On the other hand, if it is offered as a term that invites us to think the inevitable tension between ethics and culture insofar as each calls for the other, then it imposes itself as a task for thinking. Indeed Levinas prefaces his introduction of the term "ethical culture" with a recognition of "the incessant possibility of the monstrous which is attested to by the fact . . . of Auschwitz, the symbol, model or reflection of our century in its horror across all continents." The reduction not of sense (*sens*) but of the meant (*sensé*) to the absurd is "perhaps also the philosophical determination of culture" (*D.P.I.C.*, 74).

The question that Levinas asks at the end of "Meaning and Sense" is whether the beyond being can be thought except insofar as it is reduced to culture (C.P., 102; *H.H.*, 57). The response to this question takes the form of a discussion of the trace. That Levinas during the course of this discussion finds himself led to introduce a reference to the Book of Exodus, which refers the trace to the Judeo-Christian tradition, does not decide the issue (C.P., 107; *H.H.*, 63). Levinas cannot here use the ploy employed with reference to love in the "Philosophical Determination of the Idea of Culture" of inviting us simply to put aside certain cultural connotations. He cannot, because one always needs such references, even if only to deny them. But the question is not whether culture is irreducible for thought, but whether ethics can always be reduced to culture.

The question runs parallel to one that Merleau-Ponty put to himself in *The Visible and the Invisible*: "How can one return from this perception fashioned by culture to the 'brute' or 'wild' perception?" (V.I., 212; *V.I.*, 265). Indeed Levinas in "Meaning and Sense" quotes what is ultimately the same question in another form, the form used by Merleau-Ponty when he asked at the Royaumont conference of 1957: "Where does this resistance of the unreflected to reflection come from?" (C.P., 98; *H.H.*, 51). In the essay that interested Levinas so much, "The Philosopher and His Shadow," Merleau-Ponty gave reflection as Husserl's answer. One cannot look for an access to the unreflected beyond that provided by reflection itself. Meanwhile in "Meaning and Sense" Levinas speculates that *sense* might provide an answer (C.P., 98; *H.H.*, 51). If one understands the distinction between the saying (*le dire*) and the said (*le dit*) as a revised version of that between sense and meaning, then one can perhaps understand what he had in mind.[8] Saying, the one-way address to the Other, is beyond history, just as the said that accompanies it is within history. They are so divorced that even the term "distinction" is misleading for appearing to correlate them. And yet they belong together insofar as every saying has a said and vice versa. Ethics and culture are similarly divorced and yet conjoined in so-called ethical culture.

However, none of this gets to the heart of Levinas's encounter with Merleau-Ponty in "Meaning and Sense." In addition to the question of judging civilizations and the problem of access to the unreflected, Levinas points to the ethical direction at the heart of Merleau-Ponty's ontology of decolonization, the saying in his said. Recognition of the equivalence of cultures is itself the effect of an "orientation" (C.P., 88; H.H., 37), which means in this context that it has an ethical source as the "soil" from which it arises, even if Merleau-Ponty is as ignorant of it as so-called wild perception is ignorant of itself (V.I., 213; V.I., 266–67). But is it not an imposition on Levinas's part to claim this? Does it not indeed amount to an interpretive violence, whether it be the violence of an attempt to colonize Merleau-Ponty's work so that Levinas can exploit it for his own benefit, or the violence of decolonization as the attempt to liberate truth from the cultural presuppositions of its expression (C.P., 101; H.H., 55)? Perhaps, but that is in accord with the tension that this reading of Levinas has unearthed, a tension all the more acute because Merleau-Ponty is constantly reminding Levinas of the historicity he often dismisses too quickly. Just as Levinas's ethical interpretation is itself violent, Merleau-Ponty's ethical stance of decolonization is a cultural and historical product. Is not this the gist of these lines from "Meaning and Sense" where Levinas quickly moves from recognizing the generosity of a thought that acknowledges "the abstract man in man" to recognizing the cultural specificity of this very generosity:

> It [Platonism] is overcome in the name of the generosity of Western thought itself, which, catching sight of the *abstract* man in men, proclaimed the absolute value of the person, and then encompassed in the respect it bears in the cultures in which these persons stand or in which they express themselves. Platonism is overcome with the very means which the universal thought issued from Plato supplied. It is overcome by this so much disparaged Western civilization, which was able to understand the particular cultures, which never understood themselves. [C.P., 101; H.H., 55]

Is not Levinas clearly attributing to the "West" a certain superiority?[9] The superiority would seem to lie in its capacity to understand. Indeed, Levinas seems to be suggesting that it would lie in its ability to understand other cultures better than they understood themselves. Could the "end of eurocentrism" be "the ultimate wisdom of Europe" (D.P.I.C., 74)? The "generosity" of Western thought, which at first sight seems to be an illustration of the one-way direction of ethics in favor of the Other, is quickly turned into a judgment on the relative intellectual powers of different cultures. It would seem, then, that once again the distinction between the ethical and the cultural is under pressure. Insofar as it remains in place, it gives rise to the conclusion that the ethics of asymmetry in favor of the Other is, when transferred to the cultural level, readily converted into an inequality in favor of the culture which produced that ethics of asymmetry. Levinas often expresses his enthusiasm for Western culture on precisely this point.[10] Indeed when Levinas does exercise his capacity to judge transculturally, this is the usual conclusion, which is not to say that he is ever forgetful of the barbarous acts that have been committed from a sense of moral superiority.

Merleau-Ponty is not far divorced from Levinas here. In 1947 in *Humanism and Terror*, he adopted what he later described as a "wait and see attitude to Marxism" (*une attitude d'attentisme marxiste*) (A.D., 228; A.D., 306–7). Under the force of events, he came to revise this position and eight years later put his earlier stance under scrutiny in the Epilogue to *Adventures of the Dialectic*. In *Adventures of the Dialectic* he singled out the Korean war in an effort to explain how he came to revise his position (A.D., 230; A.D., 310), but somewhat earlier (in 1950) he had already acknowledged that the extent of "the camps" had thrown "the meaning of the Russian system wholly open to question again" (S., 264; S., 332). The experience of disillusionment, which is so important in Merleau-Ponty's philosophy as the source of knowledge of oneself (Ph.P., 379; P.P., 434), here shows him that it is necessary to question a philosophy of history that divorces itself from self-criticism (A.D., 231; A.D., 311). Implicitly, Merleau-Ponty acknowledges the superiority of a thinking that accuses itself. Such thinking is ethical, in Levinas's sense.

Merleau-Ponty's revision of the political stance adopted in *Humanism and Terror* seems to leave in place the distinction that he made there between a "humanism of comprehension" and a "humanism in extension." As already mentioned, the former is a humanism that "subordinates empirical humanity to a certain idea of man and its supporting institutions." By contrast, a humanism in extension acknowledges in everyone "a power more precious than his productive capacity, not in virtue of being an organism endowed with such and such a talent, but as a being capable of self-determination and of situating himself in the world" (H.T., 176; H.T., 190). It is the latter, not the former, that corresponds with Levinas's phrase "the *abstract* man in men." It is the humanism in extension, which, of the two, most closely corresponds with Levinas's *Humanisme de l'autre homme* [Humanism of the other], the title Levinas gives to the collection in which he included "Meaning and Sense." Is it too much to suggest that "Meaning and Sense," far from being the place where, as at first sight appears, Levinas most acutely divorces ethics from culture and history, is one of the essays in which Levinas most profoundly understands the need to complicate further the relation between them? Would that not be confirmed by the trajectory that twenty years later leads from "Meaning and Sense" to "Philosophical Determination of the Idea of Culture"? In that case "Meaning and Sense" would not be a critique of Merleau-Ponty, but a superlative instance of one thinker learning from another across all the differences and misunderstandings that serve to separate them. To read Merleau-Ponty and Levinas in conjunction is to deepen our appreciation of both of them.

8

Listening
at the Abyss

Patrick Burke

A philosophical meditation does not end. At most, it is interrupted and, even then, only seriously by death. But the great philosophers of the past remain, nonetheless, our contemporaries. Their thoughts continue to structure the tensions we find in our questions about the world, our lives, and our history—questions that inversely make visible the rich and unresolved tensions in their works that they could see only partially and by virtue of which distinct traditions of meditation were born.

Merleau-Ponty's sudden death places before us another unfinished meditation, and it asks that we resume it. Not only is it a protracted and continuous rumination on the issues that concern philosophers most—perception, expression, history, thought, the world—but it has the distinct characteristic of suddenly turning in upon itself in its last years and inquiring into its own first and famous efforts to take up these perennial themes. Acutely aware of how his own thinking sought to disclose and resolve the tensions secretly polarizing Husserl's philosophy, Merleau-Ponty now concentrates, in *The Visible and the Invisible*, on how those same tensions insidiously entered his own thought in *Phenomenology of Perception*. Moreover, just as he labored to reveal the *impensé* of Husserl—that is, the circumscribed but "unthought of" dimension creatively animating Husserl's whole philosophical itinerary—so now Merleau-Ponty seeks to draw up the submerged *impensé* of his own thought. As part of his effort, Merleau-Ponty undertakes a radical reconsideration of the nature and method of ontology as fundamental philosophy. He subjects to criticism the dominant tendencies in the Western philosophical tradition to define the methodological basis of ontology in terms of reflection, dialectic, and intuition, and undertakes a final strenuous effort to free his own thinking from the prejudices implied in them.

But can one free oneself from old prejudices, old shadows and odors, without discovering them anew? Is there really a way out of the labyrinth? An exit? An escape? Is there on the other side a pure light in which to see, a pure air to breathe? Is this not to dream again the dream of presuppositionlessness? To suffer again the fall into one of the multiple variations of the fallacy of self-reference? In this paper I propose to discuss the frightfully rigorous, almost brutal, manner in which the later Merleau-Ponty took ownership of these questions in order to set ontological thinking on a new course. This will entail, first of all, a brief description of his new program for ontology, followed by a summary analysis of his proposal that reflection become hyperreflection, dialectic become hyperdialectic, and intuition become "auscultation in depth." This analysis will then be my entry into a discussion of the interrogative as the proper mode of our relationship with Being, and thus as the core of philosophical methodology. I will then examine the implications of this method for Merleau-Ponty's revisioning of ontology in terms of the "there is" (il y a) of abyssal or wild Being. In an effort to understand the relation between the "there is" and radical interrogation, I will briefly contrast Merleau-Ponty's use of "there is" with Levinas's description of il y a. Finally, I will risk showing how the "there is" can be understood as the most originary form of wonder, and how wonder is the abyssal dimension of Being and the heart of the methodology through which Being announces itself and by which Being is approached. This methodology I shall call "listening at the abyss."

I

In one of the "working notes" dated February 1959 and appended to the posthumously published work, *The Visible and the Invisible*, Merleau-Ponty writes that ontology involves a "return to Σιγή the Abyss."[1] This is an obvious reference to Claudel's *Art Poétique* on which Merleau-Ponty commented in an article devoted to Claudel and published in *Signs*. There he says:

> If this world is a poem, it is not because we see the meaning of
> it at first, but on the strength of its chance occurrences and

paradoxes. . . . Although Claudel, as we know, never stopped adoring the principle at work in all this mess, he once called it Silence, Abyss; and he never took back this ambiguous word: "Time is the means offered to everything whatsoever to be in order to be no longer. It is the *Invitation à mourir*, to every sentence to decompose in the explanatory, total harmony, to consummate the word of adoration in the ear of Sigé the Abyss."[2]

For Merleau-Ponty, ontology was to be a philosophical but also, to a certain extent, a poetic science of Being, an expression of the paradox of language as a mediation of Being, of the entrance that is a withdrawal, of the revealing that is a concealing, of the dialectic of time that binds together all the contrasting words that failed throughout the history of philosophy to name Being, which transfigures them by its interrogative force into an invocation to Silence. Ontology is the interrogative word of adoration in the ear of Sigé the Abyss. Because the word is essentially interrogative, the adoration that is the poised wonder of the philosopher is neither madness nor quietism. It is an appeal for a response, an active "listening" for what is *there* in the abyssal depths of Being; it is the "perceptual faith questioning itself about itself."[3] The perceptual faith is a prepossession of Being, it is what gives our questions their relevance and their anchorage. It is the confidence that there is an answer *there* at the same time that it prompts the question "What is there?" and even "What is the *there is?*"[4]

In my judgment, two notions of presence secretly polarized the *Phenomenology of Perception*. The first, the relation of presence-to, signified by *être-au-monde*, dominated the analysis of that famous work; the second, *Urpraesenz* understood as a preobjective and presubjective structure, factored as the *impensé* of these analyses, that toward which they were reaching, but which they could not bring fully to light. It is this second presence that is abyssal and that the later Merleau-Ponty identifies with fundamental thought, with the primitive "there is" (*il y a*). About fundamental thought, Merleau-Ponty argues:

[It is] fundamental because it is not borne by anything, but not fundamental as if with it one reached a foundation upon which one ought to base oneself and stay. As a matter of principle, fundamental thought is bottomless. It is, if you wish, an abyss.[5]

The abyss that is fundamental thought is to be found in the *écart*, the gap, the separation, the differentiation between the touching and the touched, the seeing and the seen, mind and world, self and others; it is the fissure that language tries to bridge and that the philosophical methods of reflection, dialectic, and intuition have historically attempted to close through their respective theories of meaning, only to ignore thereby how this "un-tamable" at once secretly nourishes and undermines the habits of thought and experience that they sought to establish. In order to be faithful to the more profound notion of presence, the later Merleau-Ponty summons ontology to a new approach, that of listening at the abyss.

In the early chapters of *The Visible and the Invisible* Merleau-Ponty shows how the methods of reflection, intuition, and dialectic are incommensurate with his new ontology. He argues that their use has engendered false paths or pointless detours for the philosophical life. Yet Merleau-Ponty does not claim that we can completely dispense with these methods in fashioning a fresh approach to the ontological question. If philosophy is not to be doomed to repeat their failures continually, it must radicalize these methods and, in so doing, abandon the foundations they purportedly uncover. By this he means that reflection must be transformed into hyperreflection, dialectic into hyperdialectic, and intuition into "auscultation in depth," and the foundation consequently disclosed by them is not some Archimedian point, but an abyss. How are these transformations to be accomplished in the case of each? Merleau-Ponty proposes the following.

Transcendental reflection, whether written in the ink of Descartes or Kant, seeks to reveal the conditions for the possibility of experience and of the world. The conditions for possibility are simply expressions of the essential traits of experience, not its foundation. Reflection is basically an eidetic activity and should not presume, as it does, to generate a progressive synthesis that would express the ontogenesis of the world. Nor should it ever claim, as it does, to dispense with perception in its grasp of Being. If this is so, reflection must question the fundamental presupposition of the transparency of its own operation. It must question its own adequacy in the face of experience from which it arises; it must ask whether its own operations are really amenable to experience, whether they can really disclose our envelopment within Being, or whether they simply reduce it to themselves. It ultimately must ask how it is able to do what it does and what the meaning of its own operations is vis-à-vis perception and the corporeal life of the body.

Once reflection becomes radically self-critical, it provides, according to Merleau-Ponty, an indispensable tool for ontology. Merleau-Ponty calls this self-critical reflection "hyperreflection":[6]

> [It would] take itself and the changes it introduces into the
> spectacle into account. . . . It must plunge into the world in-

stead of surveying it, it must descend toward it such as it is instead of working its way back up toward a prior possibility of thinking it—which would impose upon the world in advance the conditions for our control over it. It must question the world, it must enter into the forest of references that our interrogation arouses in it, and it must make it say, finally, what in its silence *it means to say.*[7]

The hyperreflection is essentially interrogative and the Being it seeks to disclose cannot be found independently of an interrogation of the perceptual beings of our experience. This Being is not something already known except perhaps in a most confused and unthematic way as a prepossession of the perceptual faith. Consequently, ontology as a disclosure of Being is also subject to the radical movement of interrogation and discovers therein its own abyssal character:

> We know neither what exactly is this order and this concordance of the world to which we thus entrust ourselves, nor therefore what the enterprise will result in, nor even if it is really possible.[8]

The interrogation that would elicit the voice of Being cannot therefore approach perceptual beings simply in terms of the conditions of their possibility, their essential characteristics. The hyperreflection makes use of eidetic reflection, but only in order to show the extent to which the lived experience of the world both converges with and diverges from the fixed eidetic invariants, the extent to which the world transcends the relation between thought and its object, the extent to which the separation of abyss between the touching and the touched comes to the reflective subject from the world.

Regarding *intuition*, Merleau-Ponty proposes, contrary to Husserl, that philosophy dispense with the "myths of inductivity and the *Wesenschau*"[9] predicated on the classic distinction between essence and existence, and that it try to grasp the Being of essence and the essence of Being as they are lived and as they motivate the existing world from its abyssal depths. Merleau-Ponty admits that ontology cannot dispense with intuition as a methodological tool, but he claims that it requires a different kind of intuition than that of the pure gaze of a worldless subject that flattens the world: rather one that is an opening out of the self from and upon the abyssal depths of the world, and which expresses the turning in of the world upon itself. Merleau-Ponty describes this intuition as an "auscultation or palpation in depth"[10] of the Being that surrounds us and makes its path through us.

Contrary to Bergson, Merleau-Ponty argues that this intuition is not a return to the immediate; it is not the effective fusion or perfect coincidence with Being in its original integrity. On the contrary, intuition is infected beyond remedy by a distance, an abyss, a divergence such as that found in the touching/touched, which is the condition for the "proximity" of Being, of the touching with the touched, and which must of necessity enter into its very definition and the definition of truth. So, rather than as coincidence and fusion, Merleau-Ponty defines intuition as proximity through distance. By implication, ontology cannot be defined by a method of return to an immediate that is unencumbered by depth. If it is a return to an immediate, it will be, first of all, an immediate that is always in relief and, therefore, always mediated by a horizon that is the only unmediated, the only true immediate with which, however, intuition cannot fuse, for it is forever "further on," abyssal by its very nature.

Regarding the *dialectical method*, Merleau-Ponty distinguishes between the bad dialectic and the good dialectic. The bad dialectic assumes that the dialectical process traverses only Being and not thought itself, in spite of the stated equivalence of thought and being in Hegel's writing. It fails to notice that its definition of the dialectic is likewise subjected to the movement of dialectic, that the dialectic traverses thought about the dialectic, so that any particular thesis about the form and content of the dialectic can be surpassed. That is why Merleau-Ponty says that it would be better not even to name the dialectic if we want to maintain its spirit, for it is "essentially and by definition unstable."[11]

Merleau-Ponty has, of course, just named it, just constructed a thesis about it, and by implication he must grant that his description can suffer reversals. Merleau-Ponty is willing to grant this in the spirit of dialectic, which resists positive designation. That is why he proposes a "hyperdialectic" as the definition of the good dialectic—that is, one that "criticizes itself and surpasses itself as a separate statement."[12] The good dialectic knows only what it is not and does not know what it is. It is, thus, a dialectic without a final synthesis. According to Merleau-Ponty, philosophy itself must become the good dialectic, which means that philosophy must cease being a philosophy and join an ambiguous movement of self-manifestation, of self-mediation that is at the heart of Being itself:

[Within] the Being that lies before the cleavage operated by reflection, about it, on its horizon, not outside of us and not in us, but there where the two movements cross, "there is" something.[13]

This is the prepredicative Being of primordial presence, which submits to formulation precisely to the extent that formulation is itself submitted to the process of reversibility, which it discloses within it. Thus, the hyperdialectic is that labyrinthian thought of labyrinthian Being, of the Being that cannot be positively intuited or reflected through a positive judgment, but which thought must follow into the night without knowing the route in advance or whether it is indeed traversable, and along which and in terms of which thought discovers its own inherent logic of reversibility beneath reflection and intuition and the imperative of noncontradiction. The good dialectic is the dialectic that remains thus situated.

II

For Merleau-Ponty, the method of ontology will be the hyperdialectic characterized by hyperreflection and intuition as auscultation-in-depth, which seek to awaken Being from its silence, to articulate Being through its own voice, through its own native and operative speech. This voice is to be listened for within the abyss of noncoincidence between the touching and the touched, the seeing and the seen, which institutes these reversible domains and is, paradoxically, the secret of their bond. The key to this method is radical interrogation. A brief analysis of the meaning of this interrogation will more fully disclose the meaning of the question motivating Merleau-Ponty's ontology and allow us, therefore, to indicate more precisely the nonfoundational character of this ontology.

In *The Visible and the Invisible* Merleau-Ponty argues that the ontological question about the meaning of Being is not *an sit*. That question is artificial, for in the end it presupposes the very existence that it questions and that still needs to be elucidated. Likewise it is not the *quid sit* insofar as the meaning of Being would be that of a pure essence, beneath or above a manifold of limited beings. According to Merleau-Ponty, the question about the meaning of Being, about *what it is* for the world to exist, comes down to the question "What do I know?"[14] This at first seems surprising. It sounds as though Merleau-Ponty is asking for an illuminating inventory of the things that we know implicitly and take as self-evident. But right from the start Merleau-Ponty cautions us that the ontological question is not a question of mere cognition:

> Being and the world are not for the philosopher unknowns
> such as are to be determined through their relation with
> known terms, where both known and unknown terms belong in

advance to the same order of *variables* which an active thought seeks to approximate as closely as possible.[15]

The ontological question in the form of "What do I know?" is, according to Merleau-Ponty, a question to the second power. It reveals that same inverse movement of self-mediation that is the principle of dialectic: "What do I know?" aims not only at things, but also at knowing and thus aims at itself as a question. In thus becoming radical:

> [The question] intimates that the interrogative is not a mode derived by inversion or reversal of the indicative and the positive, is neither an affirmation nor a negation veiled or expected, but an original manner of aiming at something, as it were a *question-knowing*, which by principle no statement or "answer" can go beyond and which, perhaps, therefore, is the proper mode of our relationship with Being as though it were the mute and reticent interlocutor of our questions.[16]

Thus the ontological question itself, when its power is released, becomes coextensive with the methodology by which Being can be approached. The question of the method is resolved by the method of the question. The question about the meaning of Being in the form of "What do I know?" is radical in its intent to presuppose nothing about Being, about knowing, about questioning, and about answering. Yet it is a kind of knowing. It knows itself as a question at the same time that it questions the meaning of knowing; it knows that Being traverses it, that it belongs to Being by simply being a question at the very moment it questions the meaning of Being and the being of the question. But because it is thus constantly in this state of self-mediation, of paradox, this question-knowing provides a reflective and intuitive access to Being, which philosophers of intuition and reflection quickly sought to close up by trying to prove that the answer was already contained in the question; for them the "meaning" of Being was prior to the question, for it was contained a priori in the mind, so that through reflection or eidetic variation the mind could come to a pure intuition of what is already immanent in the question of Being. For these philosophers, the judgment, the positive or indicative statement, is our proper relation to Being, and the interrogative is in no way the fundamental of an original access to Being. For Merleau-Ponty, there is no positive statement that does not have an interrogative halo. He points out:

> Husserl himself never obtained one sole *Wesenschau* that he did

> not subsequently take up again and rework, not to disown it,
> but in order to make it say what at first it had not quite said.[17]

Making Being say what it has not quite said is precisely the function of the philosophical interrogation, and thus the distinctive act of the philosopher is to maintain through reflection and intuition the paradoxical interrogative openness. This does not mean that the ontological question has no answer. On the contrary, it means that we do not know a priori what answers are forthcoming. It means that if answers come, it will be only as a result of our having recognized the interrogative space, the abyss, within which alone Being can freely and continually manifest itself.

Reflection dislodges the mind from its empirical nesting place, but only to catch glimpses of a light shining through empirical beings, to harken to a voice deep within them. Thus, from this reflection born as a question, intuition is engendered. But intuition has only empirical beings in front of it and not Being as a positive datum. Mediated by empirical beings, guided by hyperdialectic and hyperreflection, intuition is an interrogative listening to what is not empirical, for what is there in their abyssal depths.

By describing the methodology of his new ontology in this manner, Merleau-Ponty is not committing himself to some irrationalist thesis about the groundlessness of Being. He is not saying that beneath Being there is chaos or nothingness. Through the interrogative listening, Merleau-Ponty discerns that the question of the ground is simply not applicable to Being because, as a question, it begs itself, presupposing as it does from the outset that Being can be "derived" from something, whether that something be the Absolute Subject (*Ens Realissimum*), or a fully positive nature in itself, or the primordial chaos, or whatever. On the contrary, Being is the generative openness within each of these insofar as they can function as ground, and is the condition for thinking them as such and for the very asking of the question. Abyssal Being envelops the conditioned/condition schema and thus cannot be subject to it. Questioning foundations is part of the interrogative listening, which, in turn, calls itself into question insofar as it is hyperreflective and hyperdialectical. Both the uncritical search for foundations and the uncritical denial of foundations presume a more stable and more structured notion of Being, and in that way beg their own questions. In this respect, Merleau-Ponty leaves behind the *Fundierung* model operative in the *Phenomenology of Perception;* it involved a less rigorous and less critical use of the methods of reflection, dialectic, and intuition. In *The Visible and the Invisible* he challenges this model decisively when he argues:

The progress of the inquiry toward the center is not the movement from the conditioned to the condition, from the founded
unto the *Grund:* the so-called *Grund* is *Abgrund*. But the abyss
one thus discovers is not such by lack of ground, it is the upsurge of a *Hoheit* which supports from above . . . that is, of a
negativity that comes to the world.[18]

Significant in this quotation is the mention of the abyss as the
upsurge of a negativity that comes to the world. In another passage, he
describes this negativity as *"separation (écart)* which, in first approxima-
tion, forms meaning . . . is a *natural* negativity, a first institution, always
already there."[19] This separation is active, it is the dehiscence of Being,
the eternal splitting open of Being into the touching and the touched,
the seeing and the seen, the site of their differentiation as well as their
union and intimacy. The *Hoheit* (or height) that supports from above is
the "there is" (*il y a*), which, in its most advanced form, is philosophical
wonder poised on the whole history of philosophy and culture, and joining the movement of transcendence that animates them from within.
The groundlessness of Being, if we must speak of it, is the groundlessness of the ground that continues to surrender to the radical interrogation that it nonetheless sustains.

III

For Merleau-Ponty, the question about the meaning of Being is equivalent to "What do I know?" But it is my contention that all the nuances in
"What do I know?" are more fully expressed in "What is the *there is*?" of
the sensible world, of nature.[20] For Merleau-Ponty, this question expresses the enigma that nature "presents itself as already there before us
and yet as new before our gaze."[21] It is the enigma of a presence with a
temporal depth that exceeds that of the positional "there is" of reflective consciousness, and which points to a nonpositional "there is," which
is one with what "is there," which is the originary openness of what is
there before it is "there" for reflective consciousness, before mind and
world have been set apart by reflection: it is the abyssal presence of "that
primordial being which is not yet the subject-being nor the object-being
and which in every respect baffles reflection."[22]

By describing the "there is" in this manner, it would seem that
Merleau-Ponty is advocating a notion of presence prior to individual
things and persons. As a presence of that which has yet no structure, form,
or direction, it would appear that he is proposing a notion of Being as an

indeterminate and undifferentiated state prior to the organizing and stabilizing functions of thought and language to which Heidegger says *Dasein* is called in the self-comprehension of Being. It would appear that he is interpreting *il y a* in the manner of Levinas. For both:

1. *Il y a*, the third-person pronoun in the impersonal form of the verb, refers to brute Being, to being in general.[23]
2. Brute Being is (a) impersonal, (b) indeterminate, (c) anonymous, (d) inextinguishable, (e) inevitable, and (f) infinite. It is glimpsed as an absolutely inevitable presence that engulfs the mind, a field and force of inexhaustible depth and power.[24]
3. *Il y a* transcends the distinction between subject and object, interior and exterior.
4. It is not through thought that we seize it.
5. *Il y a* is not yet the givenness of the objective world.

The difference between the two thinkers on this topic is, however, quite significant.

For Levinas, the indetermination of brute Being is almost as absolute as that of the *en-soi* of Sartre, with the exception that, for Levinas, brute Being is not something static as it is for Sartre; rather, it is a field of force, of movement, conceived in a Heraclitean manner as a kind of eternal flow. Unlike Heraclitus's notion, this movement is chaotic and does not exhibit an underlying synthetic principle, a *logos*.

For Merleau-Ponty, the indeterminacy of brute Being is only relative, it is the indeterminacy of what is prior to the *blosse Sachen*. Like Heraclitus, Merleau-Ponty argues that brute Being is not chaotic, but is under the spell of the *logos*, of a synthetic principle within it, encompassing it, and even coterminous with it. For Merleau-Ponty, the *il y a* transcends the exterior-interior distinction, but this does not mean that it is the absence of exterior and interior, of mind and world. Rather, the savage presence to which it refers is the *Urstiftung* of both. It is the *logos* that internalizes itself as mind by expressing itself as world. Both mind and world are the reverse sides of the eternal dehiscence of Being, a movement that is not, therefore, a completely indeterminate chaotic flow.

In addition to these differences, for Merleau-Ponty, the experience of *il y a* as the experience of abyssal presence in the elusive and perpetual intertwining of the seeing and the visible is not, as it is for Levinas, the experience of night, the *exclusion absolue de la lumière*.[25] It is the experience of light dappled with shadow, of the "secret blackness of milk," of a depth of Being into which the mind is drawn and within which the mind cannot find its own bottom. It is the experience of the abyssal Being that includes the being of the mind and is, thus, contrary to

Levinas, not the absence of subjectivity, although certainly it is not yet its determinate presence. The experience of brute presence and the brute presence itself are both described by the word *il y a*. This points to another and most significant difference between Merleau-Ponty and Levinas. For Levinas, the *il y a* is brute Being, and the experience of *il y a* does not blend into and become reversible with brute Being, as Merleau-Ponty will argue. Rather, it is one of horror or repulsion at the eternity of Being, the horror of not being able to die. It is Hamlet's realization that "to be or not to be" is not a genuine dichotomy, for it collapses under the weight of eternal Being expressed in "perchance to dream." *L'horreur exécute la condamnation à la réalité perpetuelle, le "sans issue" de l'existence.*[26] Horror, for Levinas, is thus not to be confused with Heidegger's notion of *Angst* poised on the thought of nothingness.

IV

For Merleau-Ponty, the experience that we call *il y a* is neither horror nor *Angst*, but is wonder or astonishment at presence. There is an important sense in which this wonder is narcissistic, and this is what must be elucidated. To do so will deepen what I meant when I said that the "there is" is one with what "is there," and will reveal how the "there is" is the openness of Being upon itself, an openness that is abyssal and eternal.

Let me begin by first discussing wonder as an act and attitude of the perceiving subject and from there take up the question of its relation to Being more fully. Consider the following passage:

> The effective, present, ultimate and primary being, the thing it-
> self, are in principle apprehended in transparency through
> their perspectives, offer themselves therefore only to someone
> who wishes not to have them but to see them, not to hold them
> as with forceps . . . but to let them be and to witness their con-
> tinued being—to someone who therefore limits himself to giv-
> ing them the hollow, the free space they ask for in return, the
> resonance they require, who follows their own movement, who
> is therefore not a nothingness the full being would come to
> stop up, but a question consonant with the porous being which
> it questions and from which it obtains not an *answer*, but a con-
> firmation of its astonishment. It is necessary to comprehend
> perception as this interrogative thought which lets the per-
> ceived world be rather than posit it.[27]

In *Phenomenology of Perception* Merleau-Ponty argued that, unless the "putting out of play" or "bracketing" of the familiar world takes place as a lived experience that evokes a feeling of *wonder* at the strangeness and mystery of the world, the phenomenological reduction would amount to a mere academic exercise of suspending the judgments of the natural attitude. Wonder, therefore, was presented as the source and motive of the phenomenological reduction,[28] which should actively return categorical reflection to its origins in the vast regions of the prereflective and, hence, present reflection with its limit and its task. But in the above passage we see that Merleau-Ponty goes further. Wonder is the motivating power of perception itself. It is the originary question that the look addresses to the world, but, unlike the questions of cognition, does so without expectation or demand, with only a "wish" that this open world remain open to its savage witness. Wonder must be understood, then, as the most primitive openness upon Being, and openness must be grasped in the interrogative mode. Wonder as the originary mode and force of all interrogation is "an ontological organ"[29] because it allows us to grasp Being as it passes through our perceptual life and sustains it from within.

This primitive interrogation or wonder is the strangest of all experiences because it is openness upon the strange. It is strangeness itself. Merleau-Ponty resumes Claudel's analysis of the strange as it appears in banal questions such as "What time is it?," "Where am I?" As long as we feel "at home," as long as one consults a watch or a map for the "answer," these questions are not strange. But there are moments when the sense of home becomes infected by a kind of disease (which the philosopher knows only too well), when the clock and the map suddenly become conspicuous in themselves, stand out against a background in terms of which they appear to have been arbitrarily placed, when the questions find themselves animated by a deeper questioning: "but where are these reference events and these landmarks themselves? . . . Where is the World itself?"[30]

These are the questions of the sick or threatened individual beyond the frontiers of the familiar world who, wanting to "situate his levels and measure his standards"[31] in order to dissipate the strangeness, ends up increasing it. For there is no end to the process, there is no absolute dimension in terms of which everything else can be determined or measured; and so the imagination, in search of totality, finds itself flooded by something wild and unseen, by the simultaneity and eternity of everything, by an abyssal presence, both visible and invisible, out of which it (the imagination) arises but which it cannot frame. Certainly this is not the threat of nothingness referenced by Heidegger; it comes closer to Levinas's analysis of the *il y a* as the "silence of infinite spaces of which Pascal spoke."[32] This experience was defined by Kant as that of the sublime, as experiences rooted in the power of the aesthetic imagination to embrace the greatest magnitude or force and present one even greater. Here, in Merleau-Ponty's discussion of primitive interrogation or wonder, the process is reversed; the imagination does not "present" as much as it is "presented with" something always further beyond it, does not so much open as it is opened. We find ourselves borne up by a wave of Being that outstrips our power to think it or imagine it. The "there is," as the most rudimentary openness at the core of perception, is wonder, a condition of permanent tension that defines us and our relation to the world:

> We ourselves are one sole continued question, a perpetual en-
> terprise of taking our bearings on the constellations of the
> world, and of taking the bearings of the things on our dimen-
> sions . . . [an] appeal for totality to which no objective being
> answers.[33]

Wonder, then, is not so much one act or attitude among others of the subject as it is the instituting act or attitude that defines the subject, that motivates all his or her acts from the most rudimentary perception to the most abstract thinking.

According to Merleau-Ponty, besides being true of the perceiver, it is also the case that "the existing world exists in the interrogative mode."[34]

What does this mean? What can it mean? If the human exists in the interrogative mode through his or her wonder, does it mean that wonder not only is what binds the world to the subject, but also the proper mode of being of each and the central dimension of the Being they inhabit? Can we go so far as to say that Being wonders in us and is thus open upon itself? Is wonder, thus understood, no longer merely an act or attitude defining the subject? Does it precede the subject-object distinction? Is it somehow not only the halo of all perception, experience, and thought, not only their motivating power as well, but also their very condition within Being? Is it, perhaps, the halo of Being itself, the nimbus it secretes around its savage darkness, the sign of its presence, its openness, the foreshadowing of its future? We say that the human wonders. Perhaps this is too prosaic! Should we not say, rather, that the human is in wonder, that wonder has him or her, is his or her element, that in which he or she originally dwells—that all the acts and attitudes proper to the subject are cut out of the fabric of wonder, which is Being's relation to itself?

This interrogative ensemble stakes out something wild, fantastic, even perhaps ludicrous. In order to decide the meaning and value of what it opens us upon, or if it does so at all, let us look carefully into that strange statement: "The existing world exists in the interrogative mode."

We understand how the human exists in the interrogative mode: his or her very presence is a question, an active wondering. But the existing of the world, its presence, is not a self-questioning, and yet we want to say that its presence is an "openness" beyond the confines of positivity and plenitude, that it is a presence in depth, in promise. Presence is "openness," so Merleau-Ponty would teach us, and the originary openness is interrogative. In the case of the world, are we saying that its presence is interrogative *because* it supports my interrogative probing, and is not just a confirmation but also a function of my astonishment? Or is this to reinstate, within presence, the primacy of the subject-object distinction?

Presence in the most fundamental sense, as "originating," refers to a structure prior to the subject-object distinction. To speak of a presence in this sense is not to deny it, as does Levinas, the power that is realized in each of these terms. It is not as if the subject is to be understood in terms of something that in no way exhibits its power. It is only to say that that power cannot be thought by itself. It is only to say that the order of the subject and the order of the object emerge as distinct from a condition wherein they were distinguishable only in principle, being so thoroughly engulfed each by each that at this level it becomes preposterous to even speak of them as "two"—two terms, two orders. Rather we must speak of a single structure, a single life, whose prime characteristic is that of reversibility, recognized, or perhaps postulated, by the philosopher after having abstracted the completely interwoven features of this single structure.

It is through Merleau-Ponty's notion of reversibility, which he calls the "ultimate truth," that we can understand how the world exists in the interrogative mode. In the later thought of Merleau-Ponty, the notion of "reversibility" radicalizes the notion of "dialectic" as it was employed in *Phenomenology of Perception*. The intentional dialectic may suffice as a second-order description of the epistemic relation of subject to world, but at the ontological level, Merleau-Ponty argues that the subject and the world are *Ineinander*, in one another, each being the reverse side of the other. The intentional dialectic assumes an ontological difference between the being of the subject and the being of the world, which, through the notion of reversibility, Merleau-Ponty would leave aside. Ultimately subject and world are of the same Being and the reversibility that defines their intimacy (in a way the notion of dialectic never could) allows us to see that wonder is, in the last analysis, Being's openness upon itself; all the traces and first beginnings of which are laid out in the world, temporarily culminating in the human who is the reverse side of the world come into precarious possession of itself. Openness cannot be generated; all generation presupposes openness. The flesh, as the most fundamental category of Merleau-Ponty's new ontology, is alone capable of signifying this wonder in the world, this presence, this interrogative openness of Being. The reversibility between the touching and the touched, the seeing and the seen, which defines the flesh, reveals *both sides* of the "there is" of which I spoke above (the experience of brute presence and the brute presence itself) when I said that the "there is" is both the primary emergent being *and* the openness upon it, which is originary wonder.

Thus Merleau-Ponty would teach us that wonder is not only the most primitive mode of consciousness and the principle of the development of the higher modes of consciousness, but also that it is prior to consciousness, ordinarily defined as relation to an object, and that consciousness is one of its modes. We do not constitute our wonder, we find it in all our acts and attitudes, but beyond any identifiable act and attitude, we have a surplus of it, as though it were not as much our contact with Being as Being's upsurgence within us, around us. Distinct conscious life arises as a result of a "dehiscence" of Being, that bursting open, that primordial self-differentiation of Being, which is the perpetual advent of wonder within the brute presence of the world, which is its reverse side. Merleau-Ponty suggests the image of Being as a perpetual process of self-transcendence, of infolding and unfolding, each whirl and whorl of which is invisibly motivated by wonder at its own presence. In the mode of the "I think" consciousness wonders at the presence of things, but in the mode of "there is" Being, wondering in us, wonders at its own presence, wonders at its wondering. In this sense, wonder can be described as essentially narcissistic.

V

The spirit that animates Merleau-Ponty's writing from beginning to end is wonder that there is something to see and something to say. If philosophy is ever to advance beyond the monotonous repetition of its traditional "isms," its methodology must finally elicit and be elicited by, mirror and be mirrored by, transform and be transformed by, this wonder that is now no longer (and never was) the proper possession of the human, but of Being. But in stating this as a directive, does Merleau-Ponty's philosophy not betray its own critique of the methods of dialectic, intuition, and reflection, which in the end revert to the questions of the previous efforts of ontology? Is not Merleau-Ponty implicitly claiming that his philosophy is closer to promoting the truth of Being? And does this claim not subtly presume what Merleau-Ponty explicitly denies—that is, an intuition in principle commensurate to and fused with Being?

Merleau-Ponty is familiar with all traps of self-reference. He knows that if he speaks, his sentences, in whatever form they take, work against themselves, call themselves into question, especially the sentence that indicates the questionability of every sentence. Merleau-Ponty says that there is no exit from this predicament, this labyrinth: "The task of philosophy should be to describe this labyrinth, to elaborate a concept of being such that its contradictions, neither accepted nor 'transcended,' still have their place."[35]

In the last analysis, all the sentences of fundamental philosophy are no more and no less than words of adoration in the ear of Silence, the Abyss. For philosophy to be called back to primordial wonder is, in the end, to be called to silence, and yet it is a silence that can be found only in the abyss between the fugitive words that Being nonetheless provokes and even requires. Philosophy must speak, but this speaking serves only to intensify the wonder and the silence.

We leave Merleau-Ponty "posed on the visible, like a bird, clinging to the visible,"[36] as in a Japanese painting a blackbird perched over an abyss, listening. There is (il y a) a bridge across the abyss, it is signified by the letter "Y." To cross it requires a descent to that point where reversibility occurs, that pivot which is the eternal dehiscence, "il y a," so as to join that movement of wonder, of transcendence toward that which may not, in fact or in principle, be given in experience, a *Hoheit* beyond the visible, a sublime, a Silence.

9

Alterity
and the Paradox
of Being

Wayne J. Froman

n his essay "Violence and Metaphysics," Jacques Derrida, in comparing Husserl and Levinas on the question of alterity, observes that for Husserl, things, along with others, display characteristics of alterity:

> Bodies, transcendent and natural things, are others in general for my consciousness. They are outside, and their transcendence is the sign of an already irreducible alterity. Levinas does not think so: Husserl does, and thinks that "other" already means something when things are in question.[1]

For Merleau-Ponty, things do display characteristics of alterity. In *Phenomenology of Perception*, Merleau-Ponty discloses how perception opens beyond the explicit content of perception to the perceiver's original bodily habitation of the world, where things figure as terms of bodily intentionality. Things, however, are not exhaustively accessible to perception. The simultaneous transcendence and accessibility of things makes for the "thingness of things." The simultaneous transcendence and accessibility of the world makes for the "worldness of the world." World-as-perceived and phenomenal body are two poles of the perceptual field. The act intrinsic to perception plays a role in the structuration of that field. I live my body, and through my body, I live the world.

With regard to other persons, *Phenomenology of Perception* establishes that theoretical solipsism is always based on being-in-the-world
with the Other and consequently is a self-contradictory position. In addition to being-in-the-world, the Other is being-for-itself, just as I am both
in-the-world and being-for-itself. In order to clarify the myself-other
structure more fully, it will be necessary to understand how the human
being is *simultaneously* being in-the-world and being-for-itself. The issue,
which comes up repeatedly as Merleau-Ponty's effort to disclose the
original content of perception proceeds in *Phenomenology of Perception*, is
addressed in the third and concluding part of the book, "Being-For-
Itself and Being-In-the-World," but not resolved there.

In *Phenomenology of Perception*, the clarification of the relation between the explicit content of perception of a thing, and the dynamics
among the contributing senses that result in the equilibrated perception
of the thing, proceeds considerably further than the clarification of the
"depth-dynamics" involved in the experience of an Other. This, I think,
is not an indication that at this point Merleau-Ponty has overlooked difficulties peculiar to the phenomenological clarification of my awareness of
the Other as a conscious perceiver. Quite the contrary. I think that this is
an indication of Merleau-Ponty's philosophical sensitivity to those difficulties. And I am not saying that at this point he was avoiding difficulties
rather than addressing them. I will explain myself further presently. As
far as *Phenomenology of Perception* is concerned, both the thing and the
Other are transcendent to me, but at the same time, my perception of
them is what makes me cognizant of this.

What does the later work, particularly *The Visible and the Invisible*,
have to say about the alterity of things and Others? First, a word about
the transition from *Phenomenology of Perception* to *The Visible and the Invisible*. In the final section of *Phenomenology of Perception*, "Being-For-
Itself and Being-In-The-World," Merleau-Ponty finds that neither the
cogito, nor temporality, nor freedom set the perceiver off as a subject
divorced from the world as perceived. These findings underscore the
problem that develops throughout *Phenomenology of Perception*, the difficulty of attempting to describe the dynamic that yields the perceptual
field, of which the world and the perceiver are two poles, from the point
of view of a perceiver perceiving the content that this process has already
yielded. It would appear that this point of view is itself generated by the
dynamic that Merleau-Ponty would disclose.

In *Phenomenology of Perception*, Merleau-Ponty, even while describing the dynamics of the perceptual field including the act intrinsic
to perception, dynamics that generate the explicit content of perception, does not employ the language of "constitution." Although I will

not make a case for it here, I think that this is because from *The Structure of Behavior* on, in exploring the relation between consciousness and nature in a sense broad enough to include given social structures (which is how he first defines his task), Merleau-Ponty's work is oriented by an interest in the possibility of what "transcendental creativity" suggests in Husserlian terms, or by the possibility of an originary transformation of the perceptual field that is indicated by Merleau-Ponty's project of "awakening experience anterior to all traditions." I think that Merleau-Ponty was cognizant of the limitations of the analysis of the passive and active syntheses of constitution in getting through to this possibility. Although I am not making the case, I will venture to say that the failure to recognize this orientation is the source of misunderstandings of Merleau-Ponty's work that regard it as of regional interest only.

Despite the comparatively infrequent usage of the language of "constitution," I think that the difficulty that develops throughout *Phenomenology of Perception*, and that is reinforced by part 3 of the book, the difficulty of attempting to describe the dynamic that yields the perceptual field from the point of view of a perceiver perceiving the content that this process has already yielded, bears comparison with the paradoxes of the dynamic of constitution identified by Husserl in *The Crisis of European Sciences and Transcendental Phenomenology*. Husserl sums up the trouble by observing that the *epochē* leads to a state of affairs where:

> The subjective part of the world swallows up, so to speak, the whole world and thus itself too. What an absurdity!

And then Husserl adds:

> Or is this a paradox which can be sensibly resolved, even a necessary one, arising necessarily out of the constant tension between the power of what is taken for granted in the natural objective attitude (the power of "common sense") and the opposed attitude of the "disinterested spectator"?[2]

Merleau-Ponty's way of addressing the difficulty is to proceed with a "phenomenology of phenomenology," which, as the essay "The Philosopher and His Shadow" makes clear, Merleau-Ponty found consistent with the direction of Husserl's thought. I agree with Jacques Taminiaux when he says in his essay "Phenomenology in Merleau-Ponty's Late Work" that "a close study of Merleau-Ponty's last writings shows that there is no question of refuting Husserl."[3]

Taminiaux does not specifically discuss the transition from *Phe-*

nomenology of Perception to *The Visible and the Invisible* in terms of contending with the difficulty that I suggest, despite the infrequent use of the language of constitution, is essentially the absurdity or the paradox of "subjectivity swallowing itself up," identified by Husserl. Taminiaux does compare that transition with the transition between *Being and Time* and Heidegger's later work. He writes: "*The Visible and the Invisible* is Merleau-Ponty's *Kehre.*"[4] If there is a likeness, and I think that there is, it is not a question of Merleau-Ponty's repeating the turn in Heidegger's thought. Rather, I think, a failure to understand the radical nature of Merleau-Ponty's concern with an originary transformation of perception, as indicated by his project of "awakening experience anterior to all traditions," is a failure to understand one means of preventing the question concerning the meaning of Being from leading to a metaphysical conception of Being, in Heidegger's sense of metaphysics, a misreading that Heidegger evidently found virtually unavoidable. If for Heidegger, the difficulty encountered when "subjectivity swallows itself up" would result from beginning with subjectivity as a metaphysical ground, for Merleau-Ponty, the recognition of the implications of the dynamic of *reversibility*, suggested by Husserl in *Ideen II*, and discovered by Merleau-Ponty in the art of painting, is what makes it possible for him to set out to work through the difficulty posed by *Phenomenology of Perception* and to proceed with the project of "awakening experience anterior to all traditions." This dynamic takes place neither inside nor outside a metaphysical subject. This recognition is what makes it possible for him to proceed with the task that he undertook in *Phenomenology of Perception*, a rediscovery of "the system 'Self-others-things' as it comes into being."[5]

What becomes of alterity? Let us consider the opening description of reversibility in *The Visible and the Invisible*, in the chapter "Reflection and Interrogation":

> For after all, sure as it is that I see my table, that my vision terminates in it, that it holds and stops my gaze with its insurmountable density, as sure even as it is that when, seated before my table, I think of the Pont de la Concorde, I am not then in my thoughts but am at the Pont de la Concorde, and finally sure as it is that at the horizon of all these visions or quasi-visions it is the world itself I inhabit, the natural world and the historical world, with all the human traces of which it is made—still as soon as I attend to it this conviction is just as strongly contested, by the very fact that this vision is *mine.*[6]
>
> Now that I have in perception the thing itself, and not a representation, I will only add that the thing is at the end of my gaze and, in general, at the end of my exploration. Without

assuming anything from what the science of the body of the other can teach me, I must acknowledge that the table before me sustains a singular relation with my eyes and my body: I see it only if it is within their radius of action; above it there is the dark mass of my forehead, beneath it the more indecisive contour of my cheeks—both of these visible at the limit and capable of hiding the table, as if my vision of the world itself were formed from a certain point of the world.[7]

The fact that this vision is *mine*—that is, that I find that my vision of the world itself is formed from a certain point of the world—marks my visibility, my place in the field of the Sensible. It also marks a recognition that other perceptions of the world can be formed at other particular points of the world:

Everything comes to pass as though my power to reach the world and my power to entrench myself in phantasms only came one with the other; even more: as though the access to the world were but the other face of a withdrawal and this retreat to the margin of the world a servitude and another expression of my natural power to enter into it. The world is what I perceive, but as soon as we examine and express its absolute proximity, it also becomes, inexplicably, irremediable distance. The "natural" man holds on to both ends of the chain, thinks *at the same time* that his perception enters into the things and that it is formed this side of his body.[8]

The enigma of reversibility, the dynamic whereby my sensing is as it is because I am of the Sensible, is that while the proximity of the world and its irremediable distance are at odds, while they prevent one another from being fully realized, there is no rent in perception, it is not torn in pieces, but rather as a "natural" person, my perception, in effect, makes the two go together. It is when we try to understand this that we find ourselves in a quandary. And this is the enigma that Merleau-Ponty sets out to interrogate in *The Visible and the Invisible*.

The interrogation is to proceed without imposing an external law and framework upon the opposing vectors in perception, without ceasing to be a way of deciphering the being with which we are in contact, the being in the process of manifesting itself, the situational being[9]—a loss of contact that Merleau-Ponty associates with the "bad dialectic" that "begins almost with the dialectic."[10] This interrogation is to be "hyperdialectical," an interrogation that is "capable of reaching truth because it envisages without restriction the plurality of relationships and *what has been called* ambiguity."[11]

The hyperdialectic is another name for the phenomenology of phenomenology, of which, Merleau-Ponty observes, Husserl had begun to speak in his late work, and which Merleau-Ponty finds necessary in order to work through the difficulty posed by *Phenomenology of Perception* and to rediscover the system "Self-others-things" as *it comes into being.* The description of reversibility finds that things are transcendent to the perceiver and that it is perception that makes the perceiver cognizant of this. The alterity of things is maintained in *The Visible and the Invisible.*

What about other people? After discussing reversibility in perception of things, Merleau-Ponty, in the chapter "Reflection and Interrogation," turns to the question of Others. He discusses it in terms of an added complexity in the enigma of perception of the world. "The other men who see 'as we do,' whom we see seeing and who see us seeing, present us with but an amplification of the same paradox."[12] "The intervention of the other does not resolve the internal paradox of my perception: it adds to it this other enigma: of the propagation of my own most secret life in another—another enigma, but yet the same one, since, from all the evidence, it is only through the world that I can leave myself."[13]

In *Phenomenology of Perception* the discussion of the "depth-dynamics" involved in the experience of an Other does not proceed as far as the discussion of the "depth-dynamics" involved in perceiving a thing. In the opening discussion of reversibility in *The Visible and the Invisible*, the alterity of Others is presented in terms of how that alterity amplifies the alterity of things. Again, I do not think that Merleau-Ponty's postponement of a direct analysis of the difficulties peculiar to the alterity of Others is an indication that he has overlooked the problems involved in a clarification of my awareness of the Other as a conscious perceiver. I think that it is an indication of his philosophical sensitivity to those difficulties. And it is not a question of avoiding them. The crux of the matter is identified by Derrida in "Violence and Metaphysics," in the course of his analysis of alterity in Levinas and Husserl. Derrida writes:

> Levinas *in fact* speaks of the infinitely other, but by refusing to acknowledge an intentional modification of the ego—which would be a violent and totalitarian act for him—he deprives himself of the very foundation and possibility of his own language. . . . To return, as to the only possible point of departure, to the intentional phenomenon in which the other appears as other, and lends itself to language, *to every possible*

language, is perhaps to give oneself over to violence, or to make oneself its accomplice at least, and to *acquiesce*—in the critical sense—to the violence of the fact; but in question, then, is an irreducible zone of factuality, an original, transcendental violence, previous to every ethical choice, even supposed by ethical nonviolence.[14]

The violence in question is the very identification of an Other as such insofar as this is accomplished by way of a negation of that which is intrinsic to the other person and resistant to subsumption as a particular modification of an "ego in general." Merleau-Ponty was acutely alert to this "transcendental violence." I have made a case elsewhere that the problematic of language is a generating axis of Merleau-Ponty's work.[15] That generating axis is oriented by an awareness of the imminent possibility of acquiescence to this "transcendental violence." This is not to say that a silent identification of the Other as such deflects Merleau-Ponty's philosophical itinerary. Such a silent identification is not immune to this "transcendental violence." The question is whether there may be a basis for addressing the issue without acquiescing to this "transcendental violence."

Merleau-Ponty's alertness to this "transcendental violence" surfaces in *The Visible and the Invisible*. In *Phenomenology of Perception* the return to the phenomenal body as a constant in the original content of perception is incomplete as long as sexual or affective intentionality and the appearance of speech as a different mode of gesture are left out of account, and the clarification of these relations with others is incomplete as long as the "phenomenology of phenomenology" called for by *Phenomenology of Perception* has not been undertaken. When it comes to the other pole of the perceptual field, the world as perceived, the clarification of the encounter with others does not proceed as far as the clarification of the "depth-perception" of things.

When Merleau-Ponty finds a way through to that "phenomenology of phenomenology" in the dynamic of reversibility, and he begins to examine the implications of that dynamic, he describes the alterity of Others as an amplification of the enigma posed by the alterity of things. As a "natural" person, I live a simultaneous lack of certitude, on the one hand, that the things as I perceive them are what my own perception tells me they are, a lack of certitude resulting not only from the transcendence of the things as such but as well from my perception of other perceivers who command their own perceived world, and on the other hand, a conviction that the "private worlds" open upon one sole common world. When I try to understand how I make the two go together, it appears as though the tension between them is irresolvable. The alterity of others persists as an apparent obstacle to the return to the originary dynamic of perception.

After the initial determination of the limitation of the philosophy of reflection to penetrate the enigma of "perceptual faith," Merleau-Ponty turns to the possibility that the phenomenological ontology of Jean-Paul Sartre in *Being and Nothingness*, if reconstructed from the point of view indicated at the end of that work—one that would take up Being and Nothingness within a broader sense of Being that contains them—could penetrate this enigma. In the course of that examination, Merleau-Ponty's alertness to the "transcendental violence," the deeper reason, I think, for his postponement of a direct engagement of the difficulty peculiar to the alterity of others in contrast to the alterity of things, is made explicit. Merleau-Ponty points out that the phenomenological ontology of *Being and Nothingness* appears at first to succeed where other philosophies fail in guaranteeing the alterity of the other and quitting solipsism, and then he observes:

> Yet we are not at the end of our troubles, and the labyrinth is still more difficult than we thought. For if we formulate what we have just said into theses—that is: the other can be for me, and hence can be only my being seen, the other is the unknown incumbent of that zone of the not-mine which I am indeed obliged to mark out with dotted lines in being, since I feel myself seen—this agnosticism in regard to the other's being for himself, which appeared to guarantee his alterity, suddenly appears as the worst of infringements upon it. For he who states it implies that it is applicable to all those who hear him. He does not speak only of himself, of his own perspective, and for himself; he speaks for all. He says: *the For Itself* (in general) is alone . . . , or: *the being for another* is the death of the For Itself, or things of this kind—without specifying whether this concerns the being for itself such as he lives it or the being for itself such as . . . the others experience it. This singular that he permits himself—the For Itself, the For the Other—indicates that he means to speak in the name of all, that in his description he implies the power to speak for all, whereas the description contests this power. Hence I only apparently . . . respect the radical originality of the for itself of another and his being for me.[16]

Is this "infringement," this "transcendental violence," a necessity established by the nature of the alterity of Others? Derrida specifies a feature of the alterity of Others (in contrast to the alterity of things)—a feature recognized, Derrida finds, by both Husserl and Levinas—that suggests that this is so:

> [The alterity of things] is incomparable to the alterity of Others, which is also irreducible, and adds to the dimension of incompleteness (the body of the Other in space, the history of our relations, etc.) a more profound dimension of nonoriginality—the radical impossibility of going around to see things from the other side.[17]

I think that this does not mean that I cannot see the things from the Other's vantage point alone, because I also cannot see "from the thing's vantage point." Rather, getting around the other side here refers to a possibility that Merleau-Ponty found at the limits of phenomenology, accessible to "phenomenology of phenomenology," and that he made explicit in "The Philosopher and His Shadow":

> Originally a project to gain intellectual possession of the world, constitution becomes increasingly, as Husserl's thought matures, the means of unveiling a back side of things that we have not constituted.[18]

Given the way that the alterity of others amplifies the enigma of "perceptual faith," the inability "to see things from the other side" where the alterity of Others is concerned would apparently leave two options: either the "transcendental violence" of a philosophical effort that addresses the question of the Other in order to penetrate the enigma of "perceptual faith," or an acceptance of the impossibility of the "phenomenology of phenomenology" that is to return to the originary dynamic of perception. Access to *l'être sauvage* would be barred by the Other. The return to the originary dynamic of perception, begun in *Phenomenology of Perception*, would necessarily fall short. I think that Merleau-Ponty understood this from early on and that this is why his approach toward originary philosophical utterance that would "awaken experience anterior to all traditions" was oriented by the problematic of the alterity of the other.

Derrida finds that the radicality of Levinas's work pertaining to the nature of alterity lies in the way in which it opens a question concerning the basis or the origin of philosophical interrogation of the zone of "transcendental violence." I think that this question opens up in Merleau-Ponty's work as well, and I think that there are indications that

Merleau-Ponty could have made this question explicit and responded in a manner that would transform "the problem of the Other" in a manner projected in a Working Note for *The Visible and the Invisible*:

> What is interesting is not an expedient to solve the "problem of the other"—It is a transformation of the problem. . . .
>
> Whence the essential problem = not to make common in the sense of creation *ex nihilo* of a common situation, of a common event plus engagement by reason of the past, but in the sense of uttering—language—[19]

Consider the following passage from the chapter "The Intertwining—The Chiasm":

> My voice is bound to the mass of my own life as is the voice of no one else. But if I am close enough to the other who speaks to hear his breath and feel his effervescence and his fatigue, I almost witness, in him as in myself, the awesome birth of vociferation. As there is a reflexivity of the touch, of sight, and of the touch-vision system, there is a reflexivity of the movements of phonation and of hearing; they have their sonorous inscription, the vociferations have in me their motor echo. This new reversibility and the emergence of the flesh as expression are the point of insertion of speaking and thinking in the world of silence.[20]

This "motor echo" can exceed the circuit of myself and my speech and "resound" in my interlocutor where in turn it can result in a "motor echo" that enters the circuit of my interlocutor and his speech, and can exceed that circuit and "resound" in me. The overlap of the fields of phonation and hearing awakens this echo in a manner analogous to that in which the overlap of the fields of vision and locomotion awaken an "echo" in the body, one that can exceed the circuit of a painter's touch-vision system, and as a painting, awaken further "echoes" in those who view the painting. Merleau-Ponty describes a painting in these terms:

> "Nature is on the inside," says Cézanne. Quality, light, color, depth, which are there before us, are there only because they awaken an echo in our body and because the body welcomes them.
>
> Things have an internal equivalent in me; they arouse in me a carnal formula of their presence. Why shouldn't these in their turn give rise to some visible shape in which anyone else

would recognize those motifs which support his own inspection of the world?[21]

When Merleau-Ponty says that the "body interposed is not itself a thing, an interstitial matter, a connective tissue, but a *sensible for itself*, which means not that absurdity: color that sees itself, surface that touches itself—but this paradox [?]: a set of colors and surfaces inhabited by a touch, a vision,"[22] we can add by a sonority as well. "Motor echoes" awakened by movements of phonation and hearing "resound" through the reliefs or hollows in "the flesh," the layered being that both I and my interlocutor are. This paradox of the Sensible Sentient is what can find its resemblance elsewhere, in the things that assemble incompossible sensibilia, and in other Sensible Sentients. The dynamic of "motor echoes" makes it possible that just as at times I can see another's seeing, or touch another's touching, at times I can hear another's hearing. It also makes possible what Merleau-Ponty describes in a preliminary landscape of *l'être sauvage* at the end of "The Philosopher and His Shadow," when comparing how we first become aware of others in that domain with how we face people in anger or love: "faces, gestures, spoken words to which our own respond without thoughts intervening, to the point that we sometimes turn [others'] words back upon them even before they have reached us, as surely as, more surely than, if we had understood."[23] The paradox of the Sensible Sentient that can find its resemblance elsewhere is a paradox of Being, Merleau-Ponty emphasizes, and not a paradox of man. It is not a paradox of reflection that would be disarmed, in effect, once we could recognize that it goes no further than reflection.[24]

The dynamic of "motor echoes" of phonation and hearing is anterior to the zone of "transcendental violence." This is the case because the more profound dimension of the alterity of others, in contrast to the alterity of things as identified by Derrida in Levinas's work and in Husserl's—"the radical impossibility of going around to see things from the other side"—is not decisive. Sonority is essentially a "sounding" that is not arrested by an impossibility of seeing another side. Unlike Visibility, Sonority is *not* essentially an "unveiling" and is *not* defined by Visibility's proclivity toward dissimulating and forgetting, or negating, what is not made manifest by Visibility. Merleau-Ponty observed that the reversibility of phonation and hearing is "incomparably more agile" than the reversibility of seeing and "capable of weaving relations between bodies that this time will not only enlarge, but will pass definitively beyond the circle of the visible."[25] The "motor echo" that can reach me beyond the circuit of my interlocutor and his speech can provide a foundation and possibility for language in which the alterity of others can be maintained without acquiescence to "transcendental violence" by virtue of a declaration concerning what is first declared impossible to perceive. That is how Merleau-Ponty describes Sartre's declaration concerning the I-Other structure:

> There is, to be sure, no question of a reciprocal relationship between me and the other, since I am alone to be myself, since I am for myself the sole original of humanity, and the philosophy of vision is right in emphasizing the inevitable dissymmetry of the I-Other relation. But, in spite of all appearances, it is the philosophy of vision that installs itself dogmatically in all the situations at the same time, by declaring them impenetrable, by thinking each of them as the absolute negation of the others.[26]

While the zone of "transcendental violence" could be an irreducible zone of factuality were "the radical impossibility of going around to see things from the other side" to define the I-Other relation through and through, the reversibility of phonation and hearing indicates a basis or an origin of philosophical interrogation of the zone of "transcendental violence" because that reversibility is capable of exceeding the "circle of the visible." Consequently, it indicates that the options of (1) addressing the question of alterity of others while acquiescing, in one way or another, to "transcendental violence," in order to return to the originary dynamic of perception, and (2) concluding that a return to this dynamic is ultimately impossible, are not exhaustive.

Nor is it necessary, in order to renounce violence without renouncing the possibility of awakening experience anterior to all traditions, to practice writing as an infinite multiplication of signs. That would mean the deferral of an effort to come to terms with the integral being, which Merleau-Ponty finds, is not "before me, but at the intersection of my views and at the intersection of my views with those of others, at the intersection of my acts and at the intersection of my acts with those of others,"[27] and let us specify, this includes the intersection of both words that are written and words that are spoken. Derrida, while suggesting the possibility of inverting what Levinas says about the distinctions between speech and writing, observes that to practice the infinite multiplication of signs and thus "[to practice] writing as *deferral* and as an *economy of death* [means] forgetting—at very least—the other, the infinitely other as death."[28] The "at very least" is why Derrida proceeds to say that "the limit between violence and nonviolence is perhaps not between speech and writing but within each of them."[29]

To deny the inextricable involvement, the intersections, including those of writing and speech, that "[make] the sensible world and the historical world be always intermundane spaces . . . under the pretext that [this involvement] can be broken up by the accidents of my body, by death, or simply by my freedom,"[30] or to treat this "order of involvement" as a transcendental, intemporal order, would, Merleau-Ponty observes, be opposing errors. And he writes:

> The principle of principles here is that one cannot judge the powers of life by those of death, nor define without arbitrariness life as the sum of forces that resist death, as if it were the necessary and sufficient definition of Being to be the suppression of non-being.[31]

This "principle of principles" was at work in what Merleau-Ponty had to say from the start. It is what made it possible for him to identify the dynamic of reversibility, which takes place neither inside nor outside a subject divorced from the world as perceived, as a way to work through the difficulty posed by *Phenomenology of Perception.* It is what makes it possible for us to identify indications that he could have made explicit the question concerning the basis for philosophical interrogation of "transcendental violence" and awakened experience anterior to all traditions without acquiescing to that violence. It is, I think, of the essence of phenomenology and of the "phenomenology of phenomenology" or hyperdialectic that Merleau-Ponty initiated after *Phenomenology of Perception.* Despite the irremediable incompleteness of his work, it is a principle of principles that he got at more decisively than had others whose words remain at stake in his own writings.

PART 3

OTHER EXPLORATIONS OF ALTERITY IN MERLEAU-PONTY: PHILOSOPHY OF NATURE, DERRIDA, AND HEGEL

10

Merleau-Ponty and Deep Ecology

Monika Langer

I

It is no secret that we are facing unprecedented "environmental problems" whose potential consequences could resemble those of a nuclear holocaust.[1] It is less well known that a number of ecophilosophers have argued that current measures designed to rectify the situation actually serve to camouflage it and facilitate its continuance. As they have noted, the dilemma lies much deeper than present approaches suggest. At issue are not only our relations with "the other"—more specifically, with the nonhuman other—but also the entire ontology that underpins our dominant Western conception of alterity.[2] An appropriate response to "the environmental crisis" thus requires no less than a rejection of our present, predominantly Cartesian ontology, and the development of a radically different ontology. This would mean a profound transformation in our conception of alterity and, in keeping with that, a fundamental alteration in our relations with the nonhuman other.

In this chapter, I shall show that Merleau-Ponty's philosophy has much to offer in this endeavor. As we shall see, Merleau-Ponty in fact outlines the main features of the requisite new ontology, based on his thorough critique of our Cartesian mode of comprehension. In Merleau-Ponty's new type of comprehension, the nonhuman other is no longer inert, alien, meaningless, and even threatening for a sovereign, self-transparent ego. For Merleau-Ponty, self and nonself, human and nonhuman, intertwine in a mutual enfolding, such that comprehension itself becomes a relation of "embrace" with the other. Ontology and alterity, thus understood, put us well on the way to resolving "the environmental crisis."

This potential contribution from Merleau-Ponty's philosophy is by no means readily apparent, however, as his works offer no sustained treatment of themes that have become the hallmark of "environmentalism" as it is popularly understood—themes such as the protection of the "environment," the conservation of natural "resources," the development of "appropriate" technologies, the recognition of animal rights, and the inherent value of wilderness. It is hardly surprising, therefore, that in general the literature devoted to "environmental" concerns has drawn relatively little on Merleau-Ponty's thought. Instead, where a phenomenological approach has been adopted the focus has almost invariably centered on Heidegger's reflections on technology, "care," and "letting be."[3] To ascertain the relevance of Merleau-Ponty's writings, it is necessary to indicate the principal concepts and concerns expressed in the literature generally characterized as "environmental."

"Environmentalism" designates a contemporary social-political movement that seeks to ameliorate or eliminate environmental problems. Inherently fluid and diverse, this global movement encompasses two main forms, which were first distinguished as "shallow and deep ecology" by the Norwegian philosopher Arne Naess in a 1972 lecture subsequently summarized in *Inquiry* 16 under the title "The Shallow and the Deep Long-Range Ecology Movement."[4] Given its negative connotations, the label "shallow ecology" has since then often been replaced by "reform environmentalism" or "reform ecology."[5] In any case, this approach is essentially anthropocentric—that is, it confines all intrinsic value to humans, typically regarding them as the apex of evolution (usually because it considers them the sole possessors of self-awareness and rationality). Consequently, it aims to protect and preserve the environment—including nature—primarily for human benefit. Adherents of reform environmentalism believe that the solutions to "environmental problems" lie in relatively minor procedural and legal modifications, technological innovations and "fixes," and the like. Their proposals thus do not necessitate any radical transformation in perspective or values; nevertheless, many a reform environmentalist has developed into a deep ecologist. The latter's approach is *eco*centric rather than *anthropo*centric, a shift expressed, for example, in the principle of biocentric egalitarianism, which stipulates that intrinsic value is equally distributed throughout the biosphere. Nature's value is no longer tied to human interests; rather, deep ecologists perceive nature as intrinsically valuable and humans as "an integral, creative, value contributing expression of nature's ways."[6] Concern thus focuses on the planet Earth's life as a whole, and "environmental problems" are seen as symptomatic of humans' fundamentally flawed way of life. Since that lifestyle is bound up with a certain ontology, a radical ontological shift becomes imperative.[7] Merleau-Ponty's philosophy can, I suggest, make a very significant contribution to effecting such a shift.

In an article examining the relationship between deep ecology and Green politics, Bennett and Sylvan summarize the dominant attitudes that render humans' lifestyle—especially that of the West—so destructive: the view that only humans have intrinsic value and that nature is a resource (of ample supplies); domination over nature and pursuit of material economic growth; consumerism, competition, and emphasis on high technologies; centralization and a hierarchical power structure.[8] A number of contemporary authors have argued—very convincingly, it seems to me—that the crux of this lifestyle lies in a profoundly reductionist ontology. (Some, like Heidegger, prefer to speak of metaphysics here.) Whether they trace its source back to Plato (or even Socrates) or—as is more often the case—back to the sixteenth/seventeenth-century scientific and philosophic revolution, such writers generally stress that this reductionism effectively *uprooted* humans and rendered them homeless in a world perceived as radically *other*, essentially alien and meaningless—even hostile and threatening to what, by contrast, was defensively deemed of paramount importance—namely, the human "mind" or "soul." Everything "outside" this human "essence"—even the human body—thus seemed to require ruthless subjugation and control. Descartes's philosophy provides the classic expression of this deracination with its consequent juxtaposition of mutually exclusive, inherently irreconcilable abstractions: "subject" versus "object," "mind" versus "matter," "internal" versus "external," "activity" versus "passivity," "self" versus "other(s)," and so on. The Cartesian/scientific paradigm, which reduced the (so-called) physical world to essentially atomistic, inert, quantifiable matter in motion observed by a dispassionate, detached human mind, paved the way for the lifestyle whose ravages have prompted the emergence of environmentalism.[9]

So firmly entrenched now are the assumptions of the Cartesian/scientific worldview in the very fabric of modern daily life—at least in the West—that even those wholeheartedly committed to eliminating its dualism and reversing its devaluation of nature frequently perpetuate the dominant paradigm unwittingly themselves. If Erazim Kohák is right, this phenomenon is hardly surprising; he suggests in his *The Embers and the Stars: A Philosophical Inquiry into the Moral Sense of Nature* that we have embodied our scientific constructs in a world of artifacts where most of us spend much, or even all, our lives. Kohák notes:

> The contrast between an "austere" ontology said to be the Way
> of Truth and the rich ontology of lived experience, dismissed
> as the Way of Seeming, is as old as Parmenides. In our time,
> however, it has come to seem far more convincing because of a

second, experiential development. With the expansion of our technology, we have, in effect, translated our concepts into artifacts, radically restructuring not only our conception of nature but the texture of our ordinary experience as well. . . . On a primordial, intuitive level, we preform our conceptions of nature not in an intimate interaction with God's living nature but amidst a set of artifacts which conform to our construct of reality as matter, dead, meaningless, propelled by blind force. . . . Once we come to take it for "nature," then our impersonal nature-construct appears an accurate description.[10]

Kohák contends that the (Husserlian) phenomenological reduction must therefore involve *"not only a conceptual, but a practical bracketing"* of artifacts, which allows their forgotten, human meaning to become visible.[11] We will need to take up this notion of a truly radical bracketing in assessing Merleau-Ponty's contribution to deep ecology. For now it suffices to elucidate the dilemma detectable within environmentalism itself. As Lorne Neil Evernden notes in *The Natural Alien: Humankind and Environment*, the very use of the term "environment" and its derivatives is counterproductive; as is environmentalists' recourse to what we might call co-opted ecology, their problem-solving approach, and their appeal for an environmental ethics. Briefly, Evernden's point—well justified, it seems to me—is that all this encourages us to continue our current manner of viewing the world instead of questioning the basic assumptions reflected in our contemporary categories.[12]

The common meaning of "environment" is particularly illuminating in this regard. The term signifies something surrounding, surrounding objects, surroundings. It connotes a physical thing rather than a "network of relationships" and frequently invites images of so-called natural scenery. Evernden stresses:

> In a very real sense there can only *be* environment in a society that holds certain assumptions, and there can only be an environmental crisis in a society that believes in environment. . . . The environment exists because it was made visible by the act of making it separate. It exists because we have excised it from the context of our lives.[13]

Drawing on J. H. van den Berg's work, Evernden suggests that this excision involves a twofold transformation whereby nature becomes a discrete, external thing devoid of any human element, while humans become individuals. Leonardo's *Mona Lisa* perhaps best indicates this remarkable development: "The famous enigmatic smile reveals a realm of privacy which we can glimpse but never know or possess, and the true individual is born. But the individual is created by pulling significance inward, and nature retreats outward as the thing we know as landscape."[14] The overemphasis on vision, and the Renaissance painters' preoccupation with linear perspective, are integral to this intriguing metamorphosis, contends Evernden.[15] In discussing Merleau-Ponty's stress on perspective, vision, and painting, we shall want to reconsider Evernden's claims. Here the noteworthy point is that the very notion of *environment* results from, reflects, and reinforces a fundamental rupture with nature and an implicit denial of relationships, in favor of things. By accepting the term and utilizing its derivatives, environmentalists themselves obscure the fact that at issue is *not* the protection and reparation of *things*, but the restoration of reciprocity, of primordial *interrelationships*. Such a stance fails to establish that "environmentalism, in the deepest sense, is *not* about environment." It thereby conceals the disturbing truth that, as Evernden puts it so well: "we are not *in* an environmental crisis, but *are* the environmental crisis."[16]

This unfortunate obfuscation of their fundamental concern has been compounded by environmentalists' reliance on ecologists to secure credibility with the public and with government agencies.[17] Like environmentalists, ecologists are a diverse group; consequently, among both lay people and academics there is considerable confusion about the essence of a proper ecology. Strictly speaking, ecology is a biological science that traces the interconnections of living beings and natural processes, describes "the basic patterns of ecological functions" applying to all wholes, and identifies "ecological principles and laws."[18] The focus on structures, systems, processes, organisms, and wholes would seem to preclude reductionism; nevertheless, some forms of "scientific systems ecology" have sought to sever any connection with natural history and have, in effect, adopted the mechanistic assumptions of classical physics as well as the general concern with prediction, manipulation, and control. They have thus converged with the dominant Cartesian scientific paradigm and have become closely allied with resource management. According to Evernden, the latter essentially supports more efficient exploitation.[19] In light of this, the term *deep* ecology becomes very significant; for it is the very paradigm itself that deep ecologists are concerned to question.

Deep ecologists Bill Devall and George Sessions underline the centrality of such questioning in their book *Deep Ecology: Living as if Nature Mattered*: "Deep ecology is a process of ever-deeper questioning of ourselves, the assumptions of the dominant worldview in our culture, and the meaning and truth of our reality"; and: "The essence of deep ecology is to keep asking more searching questions about human life, society, and Nature as in the Western philosophical tradition of Socrates."[20] Although it is by no means evident that Socrates himself philosophized from what we would today call a deep ecological stance, his legendary wonder and persistent questioning do indeed constitute the core of deep ecology. Given that such wonder permeates Merleau-Ponty's writings and that the latter embody a profound questioning, we shall find ourselves at the very heart of the deep ecology movement in pondering their significance. We shall see, however, that Merleau-Ponty's potential contribution to this movement is by no means exhausted in affirming deep ecology's emphasis on interrogation.

Ecophilosophical inquiry is holistic and transdisciplinary in its stress on the inextricable intertwining of all forms of life. It attempts to transcend anthropocentrism, eliminate the fact/value split, achieve an appropriate relational understanding, and approximate "the ideal of living lightly with frugality and voluntary simplicity."[21] Many deep ecologists (or ecophilosophers) consequently focus on nature's intrinsic value or "the cultivation of a state of being that sustains the widest and deepest identification"—an identification that Naess calls "Self-realization."[22] In their open-ended "dialogue with nature," deep ecologists seek a "comprehensive vision" in which theoretical, experiential, and practical aspects are integrally connected.[23] Merleau-Ponty's philosophy has a great deal to offer for the development of such an integral vision, as I shall now proceed to show.

II

We have seen that deep ecology is highly critical of the prevailing Cartesian/scientific worldview, which dichotomizes reality, denies reciprocity, declares the nonhuman realm devoid of meaning, and renders humans rootless in a world reduced to quantifiable lumps of lifeless matter. We have seen that deep ecologists recognize the need for a radical ontological shift from the dominant paradigm to modes of perception, conception, and valuation that restore primordial interrelationships. Such a paradigm shift calls for an inquiry that is holistic and transdisciplinary, and directs itself to the prepersonal, personal, and transpersonal levels of experience. It involves an inherently ongoing "dialogue with nature," which seeks to recognize our participation in a dynamic network of relationships, to reestablish our roots in the natural world, and to realize a creative integration of theory, experience, and praxis. We have seen that interrogation and wonder are central to the endeavor, and that deep ecology is aptly characterized as "a process of ever-deeper questioning of ourselves, the assumptions of the dominant worldview of our culture, and the meaning and truth of our reality." It remains to consider what contribution Merleau-Ponty's philosophy can make to this inquiry.

In his marvelous essay "Eye and Mind," Merleau-Ponty notes that "science manipulates things and gives up living in them. . . . [Its] fundamental bias is to treat everything as though it were an object-in-general—as though it meant nothing to us and yet was predestined for our own use."[24] Having lost any "feeling for the opaqueness of the world," scientific thinking "has become a sort of absolute artificialism," which threatens to precipitate "a sleep, or a nightmare, from which there is no awakening."[25] For Merleau-Ponty, as for contemporary deep ecologists, it is not a question of abolishing science, but of understanding its meaning and scope, revealing its implicit ontology, and questioning its pretension to absoluteness. It is a matter, says Merleau-Ponty, of prompting scientific thinking to "return to the 'there is' which underlies it; to the site, the soil of the sensible and opened world such as it is in our life and for our body."[26] As he sees it, such a return requires the "'destruction' of the objectivist ontology of the Cartesians," and the renunciation of the method that, by "the destruction of beliefs, the symbolic murder of the others and of the world, the split between vision and the visible, between thought and being," leaves us with "mutilated fragments" of reality.[27]

Merleau-Ponty calls for a radical "philosophical interrogation," which, instead of attempting "to separate itself from all being," takes "as its theme the umbilical bond that binds it always to Being." Such an interrogation would recognize Being as self-affirming meaning, *that without which* there would be neither world nor language nor anything at all." This interrogation would eschew Cartesian abstraction in favor of "the total contact of someone who, living in the world and in Being, means to see his life fully, particularly his life of knowledge, and who, an inhabitant of the world, tries to think himself in the world, to think the world in himself . . . and to form finally the signification 'Being.' "[28] Merleau-Ponty points out that the abandoning of Cartesian ontology in no way implies undertaking some esoteric exercise. On the contrary, "all we must do is situate ourselves within the being we are dealing with, instead of looking at it from the outside—or, *what amounts to the same thing*, what we have to do is put it back into the fabric of our life."[29] Merleau-Ponty's entire philosophy constitutes a comprehensive effort to do exactly that.

We saw earlier that in calling for a new ontology, deep ecology emphasizes the need for a radical reassessment of perception. Merleau-Ponty embarks on such a reassessment with his study of behavior, a study that aims "to understand the relations of consciousness and nature."[30] Popular and scientific thinking have generally (in modern times) considered nature to be a multiplicity of mutually external things or events that exist in themselves (*en soi*). When it has not followed the popular view that consciousness and nature present two juxtaposed orders of reality, science has generally simply reduced the one to the other (as in behaviorism) without any radical questioning of underlying assumptions. Drawing on physics, physiology, biology, and especially psychology in his study, Merleau-Ponty shows that the findings of the various sciences themselves indicate the inadequacy of their ontological underpinning and call for a fundamentally different conception of nature, consciousness, and understanding itself. Since the notion of behavior is in itself neutral regarding the traditional distinctions between the "mental" and the "material," Merleau-Ponty employs it as his point of departure for reassessing the classical conceptions without prejudging the outcome.[31] Evidently, we cannot here retrace Merleau-Ponty's detailed examination of major scientific studies of behavior (focusing on behaviorism and Gestalt psychology); hence, the following comments must suffice.

In *The Structure of Behavior* Merleau-Ponty shows that it is untenable to regard an organism as a material mass of juxtaposed parts, to consider its behavior a mechanical reaction triggered by environmental stimuli, and to equate understanding behavior with the interpretation of data collected by a detached spectator (whose reality is explicitly or tacitly considered to be of a different order from that of the observed organism). Merleau-Ponty points out the irreparable flaws in the cleavage between the objective and the subjective, and in the concomitant notion of objectivity— which deprives observed behavior of any inherent intentionality or value. Moreover, physico-mathematical analyses fare no better in understanding behavior than do realistic analyses in mechanistic science.

On the basis of modern physiology and psychology, Merleau-Ponty argues that "value and signification" must be considered "intrinsic determinations of the organism," and that these are accessible only "to a new mode of 'comprehension,' " which does not proceed by isolating elements or inspecting an allegedly "inert tableau." Such understanding would preclude any return to vitalism or animism. It would not be an intellection directed to logical significations in a world deemed "complete." Nor would it define "matter," "life," and "mind" as different kinds of beings or different orders of reality, and seek to explain the "higher" by the "lower" or, resorting to anthropomorphism, the "lower" by the "higher." Instead, this new type of comprehension would consider the "physical," "vital," and mental "to be three dialectics" or "three planes of signification or three forms of unity." Further, it would recognize that it is itself not the comprehension of a pure consciousness, but that of a perceiver who, in perceiving the behavior of another perceiving organism, participates in and constitutes the perceived world. Whether seeking to understand a natural "thing," an organism, one's own behavior or that of other people, such comprehension would be attuned to the prelogical "meaning which springs forth," to the character and intrinsic law of a whole. Merleau-Ponty emphasizes that, as biology admits, behavior is meaningful and hinges on "the vital significance of situations." In virtue of having a structure, behavior escapes the traditional categories of "thing" and "consciousness" (or "idea"); it is neither the functioning of an automaton, nor the manifestation of a pure consciousness—whether in our own case or that of animals. Instead, behavior is "an embodied dialectic which radiates over a milieu immanent to it." Merleau-Ponty's description of the phenomenon of behavior as it is apprehended in perceptual experience testifies to the fact that "the animal, to an extent which varies according to the integration of its behavior, is certainly *another existence*"—and this does not require a return to any theory about "the soul of brutes." It does, however, mean acknowledging the intentionality in the animal's manner of relating to its milieu—in short, recognizing the animal's "being-in-the-world" and the world's "being-for-the-animal." Such a holistic comprehension of behavior carries in its wake a radical transformation of our traditional conceptions of the world in its entirety. As Merleau-Ponty notes, to the extent that "it harbors living beings," the world stops being a mass of material and "opens up."[32]

Merleau-Ponty's study of behavior shows that we must discard the assumption of an external observer and embrace the notion of knowledge as an apprehension of existences whose meaning reveals itself to us in perception.[33] It therefore becomes necessary to elucidate perception by focusing specifically on that act itself—which Merleau-Ponty does in his *Phenomenology of Perception*. The center of gravity thus moves from perceived nature to the human perceiver—a crucial investigation, given Evernden's claim that we ourselves *are* the environmental crisis. Picking up on themes emerging in the second half of *The Structure of Behavior*, Merleau-Ponty proceeds to show that perceptual consciousness is neither mechanistic nor disembodied. Consequently, we must discard our traditional empiricist and intellectualist conceptions of ourselves and recognize that we are incarnate subjectivities, who thus are inherently situated, perspectival participants in a shared world.

Far from being pure minds floating blissfully unaffected above a plenum of inert matter, we are ourselves—as Saint-Exupéry said—"but a network of relationships" and, as such, are inextricably intertwined with a world we inhabit.[34] In reestablishing the mind's "roots" in the body and the world[35] Merleau-Ponty describes how "objective thinking"—which dominates our (Western) culture, underlying as it does our common sense, our sciences, and our traditional philosophies—distorts our lived experience, alienating us from ourselves, our world, and other people. Eliminating that estrangement requires that we affirm the prereflective, prepersonal dialogue between the phenomenal body and preobjective world, instead of continuing to negate it. By drawing our attention to the existence of that primordial communication and describing its rich dialectic, Merleau-Ponty's interrogation of perception helps us to achieve the requisite affirmation.

Following his phenomenological investigation and description of perception, Merleau-Ponty not only explored (mainly in essays and lectures) the implications of abandoning objective thought with respect to language, history, politics, psychology, sociology, and philosophy, but also addressed himself explicitly to the concept of nature in a series of lectures (of which we unfortunately possess only "themes"). In the *Phenomenology of Perception* Merleau-Ponty's discussion of "the natural world" had centered on overturning the common conception that the world is a totality of ready-made things. Merleau-Ponty there described the genesis of objectivity, showing that "thinghood" is the product of that prepersonal dialogue whose foundation is the body-subject's power of anchoring itself in a preobjective world through the exercise of its sensory organs. Although thus inseparable from the perceiver to whose sensory powers they "speak," things emerged as irreducible to the human; their nonhuman, inexhaustible core precluded absorption.

In the sections of *Themes from the Lectures at the Collège de France 1952–1960* devoted to the concept of nature, Merleau-Ponty's focus is no longer the coming into being of objectivity for a human perceiver, but the being of nature as such. To espouse an objectivist concept of nature is to forget our own source and support, says Merleau-Ponty, noting that Descartes and even Marx himself seem to have presupposed such a concept. Instead of adopting the Cartesian view that still prevails, Merleau-Ponty contends that "we must recognize that primordial being which is not yet the subject-being nor the object-being. . . . From this primordial being to us, there is no deviation, nor any break."[36] Merleau-Ponty points out that starting from the conception of nature as a realm of "pure things," Husserl was prompted to explore the basis of that notion and eventually described "the earth . . . as the homeland and historicity of bodily subjects who are not yet disengaged observers, as the ground of truth."[37] Noting that contemporary sciences are themselves moving beyond dogmatic objectivity, Merleau-Ponty picks up their insights as well as the thread of Husserl's reflections, and devotes his own efforts to developing the new ontology implicit in the transformation of the concept of nature.[38]

In rejecting the mechanistic conception of nature, Merleau-Ponty simultaneously rules out any notion of nature as a spirit in things or a projection of humans. As he emphasizes:

> [Nature] is *that which makes there be*, simply, and at a single stroke such a coherent structure of being (*de l'être*), which we then laboriously express in speaking of a "space-time continuum." . . . Nature . . . stands at the horizon of our thought as a fact which there can be no question of deducing.[39]

This fundamental facticity of nature does not, however, imply an "all or nothing" ontological principle. Contrary to neo-Darwinist claims, organisms and animal societies manifest "invariance *through fluctuation*," so that qualitative differences emerge by rearrangements that resume and transfigure "already latent activities." Consequently, Merleau-Ponty insists that "one cannot conceive of the relations between species or between the species and man in terms of a hierarchy"; moreover, all zoology presupposes humans' "methodical *Einfühlung* into animal behavior," with animals participating in our perceptive life and we in animality.[40] The investigation of nature thus brings Merleau-Ponty back to the study of our perceptual experience; but he is now able to go beyond his previous phenomenological descriptions to ponder "brute being" ("*l'être brut*") as disclosed in our contact with the world. That contact is one of *Ineinander*, for the human body both perceives and inhabits nature. Merleau-Ponty stresses that it is untenable to postulate either a descent of consciousness into, or a production of consciousness by, a body considered an object. Rather, "all corporeality is already symbolism" and the human body is "a metamorphosis of life." Our perceptual experience belies the traditional conception of ourselves as a composite of two natures, and reveals instead that we comprise a double being (*un être double*), which is perceived and perceives itself. Thus understood, the body itself "embraces a philosophy of the flesh as the visibility of the invisible," and induces wonder in face of Being to which it itself belongs.[41]

Merleau-Ponty's last writings center on this intertwining of the visible and the invisible, as he endeavors to express "our living bond with nature" and draw our attention to that primordial "dehiscence," which, in opening us to the world, establishes a "kinship" and "participation" such that "it is impossible to say that nature ends here and that man or expression starts here."[42] Painting is a celebration par excellence of this enigma of "universal flesh," which precludes our considering nature as *surrounding* us (or, alternatively, as surrounded by us).[43] Already in *The Structure of Behavior* Merleau-Ponty had noted that art is especially suited to breaking perception out of "a narrow circle of human 'milieus' [to] become . . . perception of a 'universe.' "[44] In "Eye and Mind" he describes how painting can awaken us to our prereflective "embrace" with the world—that is, to the miraculous relation of *Ineinander*, which the Cartesian/scientific ontology denies and obscures. The vision of the painter—who is clearly neither a disembodied mind nor a mechanical eye—essentially interrogates the visible so as to render the meaning (itself invisible) that "radiates beyond" it, visible in a painting. To do so, the painter's vision neither posits nor tries to possess the visible; instead, it "lets the perceived world be."[45] This does not, however, imply indifference; for the painter's vision inhabits the visible and allows its latent meaning to come to expression in the painting. The painter is moreover a visible seer and, as such, inextricably belongs to the world that her/his vision is interrogating. Not only does he or she actually experience being "looked at by the things,"[46] but with the help of a mirror he or she can paint a self-portrait expressing the paradoxical reversibility of the self-sensing seer. (The inclusion of the mirror and canvas in the self-portrait can elaborate the reversibility of painter painting self in the act of painting self.) The painter's activity thus overturns the traditional categories and dichotomies—such as mind versus body, human versus world, self versus other(s), subject versus object, internal versus external, activity versus passivity.

In bringing to our attention the inextricable intertwining of the visible and the invisible, painting restores the depth of Being to a world rendered flat by " 'technicized' thinking."[47] By the same stroke, it dispels the persistent illusion of a disembodied spectator in showing how the seer is inherently part of the seen and coils back over it in an embrace that lets a new meaning emerge. Paradoxically, a profoundly "cultural" activity (painting) and its product—which is usually considered a "cultural object" par excellence—are thus particularly suited for restoring our rootedness in our own carnality and in that of the natural world as a whole. A painting—itself a visible—discloses its meaning only insofar as the viewer's vision is not a look that reduces it to blobs of color on a (flat) canvas. Just as the painter's vision must take up its abode in the visible, which invites expression, so the viewer's vision must let itself be drawn into the painting in such a way that that viewer *feels* the pleasant coolness of the breeze, the lushness of the grass, and the rippling of the stream depicted by the artist. Moreover, the elements that animate the painting—such as lighting and shadows—must draw the viewer's vision without becoming visible themselves. Only by going beyond the visible—a transcending sustained throughout by that very visible—to inhabit the painting, can the viewer comprehend the meaning the painter sought to convey. In thus responding to the painting's solicitation, the viewer accomplishes the relation of *Ineinander* by a dialectical movement akin to that of the painter—namely, a prepersonal installing of vision beyond itself in a visible, in such a way as to open a hollow for the emergence of meaning.

Merleau-Ponty's phenomenological investigations and descriptions suggest that painting (in the double sense of the term) has the potential to transform us experientially in a manner consonant with the new ontology that deep ecology demands. Further, philosophical reflection on painting can help us articulate and develop such a new ontology—as Merleau-Ponty's writings amply testify. They indicate that, as Marcuse was to claim much later in *The Aesthetic Dimension: Toward a Critique of Marxist Aesthetics*, art is especially effective for breaking through the one-dimensional reality maintained by operational (objective) thought. To put it in Marcuse's words: "Art breaks open a dimension inaccessible to other experience, a dimension in which human beings, nature, and things no longer stand under the law of the established reality principle."[48] Merleau-Ponty's reflections on painting suggest that Kohák's call for a "practical bracketing" neglects the liberating power of art. In drawing our attention to "the living world of nature" on the one hand and the "world of artifacts" (i.e., "tools"), which "have no intrinsic sense of their own" on the other, Kohák's "invitation to look and to see" is itself curiously *unseeing* with respect to art. Thus it misses the very vision that is perhaps best able to restore the living, intrinsically meaningful world. This is not, of course, to deny the need for a critique of our artifacts, but rather to suggest that painting might well help us to see the world—including nature, ourselves, and artifacts—afresh.[49]

Similarly, Merleau-Ponty's interrogation of painting can provide an important corrective complement to Evernden's presentation. It is undoubtedly the case that vision—including that of the painter—*can* congeal the world by assuming the modality of the Sartrean stare, and so can contribute to the illusion that there is a pure consciousness confronting meaningless matter. Nonetheless, the distance inherent in vision and the Renaissance painters' perspectival techniques do not by any means make such destructive objectification inevitable. On the contrary,

Merleau-Ponty stresses that distance is essential to depth; without these, we could not be open to the world and it could not be inherently meaningful. While acknowledging the possibility of "seeing without staring," Evernden misses the richness of the painter's seeing, and so fails to recognize that painting is itself superbly suited for dissolving the dichotomies expressed in the *Mona Lisa*. As Merleau-Ponty points out, painters have always known that vision enables us to be absent from ourselves and "present at the fission of Being from the inside"; they have always known that we are fundamentally open to the world and, through vision, "are everywhere all at once."[50] Thus, by being true to their own experience of vision, painters can help us undo the withdrawal of meaning from the world into an allegedly privatized Mona Lisa-like "self."

In conclusion, let us summarize the potential contribution of Merleau-Ponty's philosophy to deep ecology. From the consideration of his writings presented here, we can see that Merleau-Ponty's philosophy effectively anticipates deep ecology's basic concerns and responds to them in a way that can contribute very significantly to current ecophilosophical inquiries. Emphasizing the centrality of an ongoing *holistic interrogation* (one of "total contact," as he stipulates in *The Visible and the Invisible*), Merleau-Ponty undertakes a very sustained critique of the Cartesian/scientific paradigm that lies at the source of our current ecological crises. Drawing on the insights and shortcomings of a whole range of other disciplines, Merleau-Ponty shows that traditional notions of "consciousness" and "nature" must be rejected; that organisms' behavior manifests *intrinsic value and meaning*; that the *structure* of behavior is simply inaccessible to traditional understanding and requires a *new type of comprehension*—one that we today would call "ecocentric." Merleau-Ponty stresses that such a new comprehension radically alters our traditional perceptions of ourselves and of the world as such. He therefore pursues the critique of "objective thinking" by interrogating the various facets of perceptual life and showing how traditional distortions of perception manifest the need for a fundamental shift of ontology. Consequently, Merleau-Ponty follows his comprehensive critiques of the dominant paradigm with studies that seek to develop a new ontology. To this end, he elaborates and profoundly deepens insights that emerged in the course of his earlier critical interrogations. Thus, he now goes beyond the phenomenological descriptions of the prepersonal body-subject and preobjective perceived world, to engage in a more radical inquiry into the being and meaning of "universal flesh." Earlier he had described inherently meaningful behavioral forms, and had called for a new sort of comprehension to which those forms would be accessible.

Now Merleau-Ponty embarks on a description of the being of nature; the manner in which meaning is to be understood as the invisible counterpart of the visible; the way in which visible and invisible intertwine in vision; the fundamental *Ineinander* of ourselves and world, which requires that comprehension itself become a relation of "embrace"; and the paradoxical reversibility of self-sensing flesh that escapes all our categories, dissolves our dichotomies, and installs us beyond ourselves so that we are in kinship and participation with the whole world—and, through it, with Being.

This description of our prereflective intertwining with the world, and of the emergence of meaning in that dynamic network, significantly deepens the current ecophilosophical notions of intrinsic value (or inherent significance) and Self-realization. Merleau-Ponty's description enables us to see more clearly why it is not a matter of choosing between these notions, for they signify the same phenomenon. There can be no question of locating value in some*thing* lying "over there"; rather, it becomes evident that it is a question of recognizing that—as Merleau-Ponty's interrogation of painting shows—we are both "here" and "there." In short, we and the world truly form one dynamic, meaningful whole—as we recognize in Self-realization. The latter, as described by Merleau-Ponty's "new mode of comprehension," emerges more clearly as incorporating the theoretical, experiential, and practical aspects of our existence in a "total contact" of "embrace" with the world.

Finally, Merleau-Ponty's new ontology enables us to see more clearly why there can be no question of any dichotomy between "nature" and "culture," nor any conception of "environment" in the traditional sense. The deepened comprehension that Merleau-Ponty's philosophy articulates thus puts us on the path to resolving that "environmental crisis" that we *are* as long as we cling to our old ontology. Much, of course, remains to be done along the way. A working note of March 1961 indicates that Merleau-Ponty himself was planning to undertake a comprehensive description of Nature as "the man-animality *intertwining*," and to explore far more fully how truth and subjectivity are to be understood from the perspective of the new ontology he was developing.[51] It is up to today's ecophilosophers to continue that exploration.

11

Merleau-Ponty
and Derrida:
Writing on Writing

Hugh J. Silverman

What is writing on writing? Who writes on writing? What writing writes about writing? Is writing an act or an effect? In phenomenology, writing is an act. In semiology, writing is an effect. In interrogation, writing is placed in question in an act of inquiry. In deconstruction, writing is the inscription of a differential space.

For Merleau-Ponty, interrogation asks about writing. It announces that writing is not itself an entity, or a product, or a result. For Merleau-Ponty, writing is style. For Derrida, writing is difference. For Derrida, writing is neither speaking nor the graphic effect of speech.

Style in Merleau-Ponty is expression. Writing for Derrida is the inscription of signature. Expression for Merleau-Ponty results in signification. Signature for Derrida results in traces. The elaboration of the place of difference is the marking off of a textuality—scriptive textuality—in which writing is neither act nor effect but in which writing operates at the conjuncture of style and inscription, expression and signature, signification and trace. The task here is to elucidate this place where writing makes a difference.

Style/Writing

What is in a style? The question echoes the Shakespearean: What is in a name? The answer is not inconsequential. Merleau-Ponty writes:

> Style is what makes all signification possible. Before signs or emblems become for everyone, even the artist, the simple index of already given significations, there must be that fruitful moment when signs have *given form* to experience or when an operant and latent meaning finds the emblems which should liberate it, making it manageable for the artist and accessible to others. If we really want to understand the origin of signification—and unless we do, we shall not understand any other creation or any other culture, for we shall fall back upon the supposition of an intelligible world in which everything is signified in advance—we must give up every signification that is already institutionalized and return to the starting point of a nonsignifying world. This is always what faces the creator, at least with respect to what he is about to say.[1]

"Style is what makes all signification possible." Style is at "the origin of signification." Style is not just *a* style; it is that which conditions all signification. Style—whether in painting or writing—is not "a certain number of ideas or tics that [the painter or writer] can inventory but a manner of formulation that is just as recognizable for others and just as little visible to (the painter or writer) as one's own silhouette or one's everyday gestures" (P.W., 58). While literary or art historians attempt to offer a list of the elements that constitute a writer's or painter's style—Proust is ponderous, penetrating, thoughtful, subjective; Monet is light, airy, glimmering, pastellike—these are not what *constitute* style itself. They are rather an itemization of some features of an artistic result, pieces of an endless list that is necessarily reformulated and reformulatable in what Foucault would describe as new discursive frameworks.[2] These descriptive units, collectable, presentable, and impressive as they may be, still do not account for style. They are at best indicators of a style at work in a particular esthetic object or set of objects. They hardly constitute style per se. Rather style per se makes each of these particular significations possible. Style for Merleau-Ponty partakes of a "nonsignifying world," a condition that anticipates signification but itself is not differentiated into specific determinations. Style is not an emanation of the writer or artist, nor is it an effect of the written or painted product. Style is located at that place where signs "give form to" the world of experience, where signification becomes possible.

For style to be the very possibility of signification, it must be presignificatory. This does not mean that it is preobjective nor even presubjective. And yet in a sense, style is neither objective nor subjective. Earlier in Merleau-Ponty's writings, the interweaving of subjective and objective would have been called "ambiguity."[3] In *The Visible and the Invisible* it takes shape as the chiasmatic intertwining of visible and invisible.[4] Style inserts itself in the ambiguous domain, in the place of the intertwining, where differentiation has not yet resolved itself into the objective or the subjective, where specifications are not yet relevant, and where a distinct position cannot be found, asserted, or offered. Style is the in-forming, the giving form to what is not yet formed, not yet specified, not yet shaped. The writer's style is not a determinate form, yet it is the forming of the formation of writing. The writer writes. In writing, style is enacted. The enactment of style is not the production of an object nor the invocation of a concept. The enactment of style is the bringing into being of a whole orientation toward the world, toward culture, toward persons, and toward one's own experience of the world, culture, and other people.

Style is the stylizing of language. Language is shaped, articulated, brought into being by way of style. Style is the rendering specifiable of what is as yet unspecified in language. Style is not the set of specifications themselves, but rather that through which determination and specification are brought about. The style of a writer is the style of the writer's language. An analysis of—or even an algorithm for—a writer's language will not render a full account of the writer's style. The style of writing is for Merleau-Ponty *an indirect language*, a language that is neither produced nor accessed directly. Although Merleau-Ponty often characterizes style with respect to painting, style in writing plays a similar role. The style of writing "claims to retrieve things as they are" (P.W., 101). This is not the direct language of everyday speech and conventional discourse. The style of writing seeks to retrieve everything in its narrative grasp. Writers writing can only conceive of themselves "in an established language" (painters by contrast are able to refashion language) (P.W., 100). Painting is not the sole proprietor of indirect language. Indirect language also operates in writers writing. Writers writing, however, must enact style by reincorporating it into a language that is already there, already imbued with a past, already recognizable despite the transformations introduced by the new writing. Style shapes new writing, it does not create a new object.

Robbe-Grillet's novelty does not lie in a refashioning of language as in Mondrian's painting, rather his novels speak language as a retrieval of language such that it speaks differently. Writing in Robbe-Grillet is a reincorporation of language such that the descriptive repetitions, geometrical constructions, and perceptual *"constatations"* are still language, still French or English translation. However *what* it says casts the body of language such that its past is reintegrated in a new way. The past of the writer's language is "not just a dominated past but also an understood past" (P.W., 101), a past that is not only controlled in a new way but is also recognizable by those who might not yet know it. Writing, then, is shaped out of its past, returned to its past, and augmented by its past for the present of its readership. Style makes it possible for language to speak in a particular way. Style makes the past speak in a recognizable shape—even after the writer is gone.

For another language, a language that is critical, philosophical, and universal, Merleau-Ponty states, it is "essential to pursue self-possession, to master through criticism the secret of its own inventions of style, to talk about speech instead of only using it. In a word, the spirit of language is or pretends to be spirit for itself, to have nothing that does not come from itself" (P.W., 101). Critical language, critical writing seeks to explore how style introduces novelty, how style serves as the precondition for the reincorporation of language, and elaborates how style forms its own preconditions. To elucidate how style could be the style of a writer writing, a literary movement affirming itself in a variety of writings, or a period forming itself as a kind of *Zeitgeist* are some of the tasks of a critical language. But a critical language also has a revolutionary task, one of interrogating writing, understanding style and styles, getting the indirect language of writing to speak for itself.

Merleau-Ponty's account of style is itself located in the context of the early 1950s when it was most fully formulated. His understanding is often set off against Malraux's views, most notably in *La création artistique*. Merleau-Ponty's account of style is thereby itself located in a time in which a certain style of thinking was operative. Developing out of a phenomenological tradition, his thought moved beyond it and was limited by it. His own style picked up the relevant pieces of that tradition and reincorporated them into a philosophical writing that was distinctively his own. Yet he was limited by the style of his time, his language—as he says—was recognizable albeit difficult. It forged ahead while at the same time reintegrating its phenomenological past.

By contrast, Derrida's style—equally difficult, effectively perplexing to some, becoming eminently familiar to others—operates a new language, a new writing. This new writing, inscribing itself in the late 1960s (and in the couple of decades thereafter), cannot claim to speak as Merleau-Ponty's own philosophical language does. Yet it cannot dissociate itself entirely from Merleau-Ponty's writing. The Derridean mode of writing is not simply a style—though in one of the more restricted senses of style, it certainly has identifiable characteristics. But style for Merleau-Ponty, as should now be evident, is not a specifiable set of features. Indirect language is the precondition for writing itself. With Derrida, however, writing itself occupies a place analogous to that of style in Merleau-Ponty. Indeed, "analogous" is too weak: there is a distinct place of juxta-positional contact between the Merleau-Pontean account of style and the Derridean formulation of writing.

One would expect that style and writing are not the same. As is evident in Merleau-Ponty, style is the precondition for writing. Yet in Derrida, writing is not simply the product nor the correlate of speech. Derridean writing, or *écriture*, is not the opposite of speech, just as style for Merleau-Ponty is not the opposite of language. For Merleau-Ponty style is an indirect language that conditions writing itself. For Derrida writing is the inscription of difference between speech and writing, between word and concept, between the sensible and the intelligible. Just as style for Merleau-Ponty is chiasmatic (operating the intertwining of the visible and the invisible, the spoken and the unspoken, the specifiable and the unspecified indirect language of writing), similarly *l'écriture* for Derrida is inscribed in a place of difference, marking off the inside and the outside of written language, setting the margins of text and context, delimiting what is one's own and what is not one's own.

For Derrida writing (*l'écriture*) is difference (or more specifically *différance*). *Différance* is neither a word nor a concept, neither phoné nor graphè, neither the signifier nor the signified. *Différance* is spacing (*espacement*) and spacing is the opening up of a space where difference is inscribed, where the indecidability of *différance* as neither deferral nor differing, neither the temporal putting off nor the spatial distanciation can establish itself as having priority, as resolving itself on one side of the opposition or the other. *Différance* is hardly identical with Merleau-Ponty's "ambiguity" in the early writings and "chiasm" at the end of his career, yet the indecidability of *différance* certainly marks a similar if not corresponding place in the Merleau-Pontean enterprise. *Différance* is also the *pharmakon*: neither a poison nor a remedy, neither what kills nor what cures—it is a medicine that could turn either way: too much could kill, just the right amount could cure. Writing is a *pharmakon*. Too much can make us forget, lose the capacity to remember; too little and we cannot remember all there is to remember. Writing, following Rousseau, is a "dangerous supplement." Derrida suggests that writing is like masturbation, which, as Rousseau confesses, can add on to sexual relations with the other, or replace them even to the extent that the other has no place. Yet writing for Derrida has no determinate effect: its determination is to be indecidable just as style for Merleau-Ponty remains chiasmatic.

What of style for Derrida? In "Qual Quelle," Derrida writes:

> But, if there is a timbre and a style, will it be concluded that
> here the source *presents itself?*
>   *Point.* And this is why *I* loses itself here, or in any event ex-
> poses itself in the operation of mastery. The timbre of my
> voice, the style of my writing are that which for (a) me never
> will have been present. I neither hear nor recognize the timbre
> of my voice. If my style marks itself, it is only on a surface
> which remains invisible and illegible for me.[5]

Speaking of Valéry, Derrida writes, "*if there is* one literary event, it
is inscribed by style" (*Margins,* 296). This one literary event—*Ereignis* in
Heidegger (an appropriation, happening, enownment, advent)—is the
inscription of a style: a marking of what is one's own, a proclamation of
ownness. Style inscribes ownness—not as *I* but as appropriation. Style
for Derrida marks an event: not a momentary event but the persistence
of event in writing. Style is not the prose of the world but the inscription
of ownness in writing. And writing, as we have remarked, is differential
and itself "spacing."

Style is also the stylus, the writing instrument, the tool for the
marking of words, lines, margins. The stylus, the pen, the pointed thing
writes, inscribes, delineates. As Derrida elaborates in *Spurs,* the style of
Nietzsche, his styles are manifold.[6] Yet each involves the use of the writing tool, the male instrument. Truth, by contrast, is associated with
woman. Woman is the disclosure that *aletheia* portends. Woman is the
veil and unveiling of truth, the *Unverborgenheit* that Heidegger offers as
an account of truth. The truth in writing, the truth of writing, is not in
the style. Its truth is in the writing, but the writing takes place—as a
literary event—as style.

The inscription of the difference at the juncture of Merleau-
Pontean style and Derridean writing is their inverse: namely, Merleau-
Pontean writing and Derridean style. While style, for Merleau-Ponty, is a
way of being-in the-world, writing, for Derrida, is the differential space
in which readings must necessarily take place. The *scriptive* textuality that
results from this juxtaposition becomes even more evident in the intersection of Merleau-Pontean expression and Derridean signature.

Expression/Signature

Merleau-Ponty writes: "expression always goes beyond what it transforms" (P.W., 69). And Derrida asks: "Does the absolute singularity of

an event of the signature ever occur?" (*Margins*, 328). For Merleau-Ponty, expression enters into his basic understanding of language and its activities. As early as *Phenomenology of Perception*, speech (*la parole*) is characterized in terms of expression and gesture. The gestural, the embodied orientation toward not only objects but also articulation, is linked to anthropological studies—particularly those of Leroi-Gouran—which show the direct correlation between types of gesture and speech itself.

With Merleau-Ponty, as with a long tradition, speech is not writing, speaking is not written language. Yet writing or written language carries with it what he calls *speaking speech* and *spoken speech*. "Speaking speech" (*parole parlante*) is the direct articulation of sense through words and gesture and general bodily comportment. "Spoken speech" (*parole parlée*) is the produced cultural artifact that enters into the literary and many esthetic forms such as painting, writing, sculpture, and the like. But "spoken speech" need not be exclusively high culture. Grocery lists, course descriptions, and legal documents are also "spoken speech." However, even for Merleau-Ponty, the distinction between spoken speech and speaking speech is not so simple. "Spoken speech" is already imbued with "speaking speech." An orientation toward expression—as result—is already implied by "speaking speech." "Speaking speech" wants to say—something. What it wants to say is not only speech itself but also meaning. And it wants to say it in "spoken speech." The wanting-to-say in spoken speech by speaking speech is expression. Gesture is one form of expression—one way in which our embodied being-in-the-world takes shape in the speaking of and into spoken speech. The interlacing of speaking speech and spoken speech is crucial here. Expression is that interlacing such that the writing of writing, for instance, is not just the production of new reincorporated cultural artifacts but also—and even more importantly—the speaking of speech.

In *Prose of the World*, writing (like painting and other forms of indirect language) is expression—the speaking of spoken speech. What is crucial here is that expression is an orientation toward the world through language. The expressive language of writing is not the same as that of painting, for instance. The eighteenth-century Lessing (in the *Laocöon*) affirmed that the distinction between the plastic arts and poetry indeed makes a difference. But even the Roman poet Horace had called attention to the difference and the relation. For Lessing, however, it was "expression" that marked the difference. Painting expresses differently than poetry, the plastic arts do not express feeling, emotion, and intensity in the same way as poetry or writing. Many nineteenth-century writers (including Peacock and Shelley) were preoccupied with the debate over the distinction between poetry and prose. And even a century later Sartre's *What is Literature?* prompts the divergent responses on the one hand in Barthes's *Writing Degree Zero* and on the other hand in Merleau-Ponty's *Prose of the World*. Here, however, expression is not just an effect or feature of writing, but rather an intricate link with style. Expression "always goes beyond what it transforms." Expression cannot be located simply in writing itself, rather expression takes writing beyond itself. It transforms writing and carries writing to an understanding that goes beyond it. Expression, then, for Merleau-Ponty is both an activity of writing and an effect that transforms it.

The correlation between Merleau-Pontean expression and Derridean signature is not obvious. One would expect that expression (as a phenomenological activity) operates in opposition to meaning or content. And indeed Derrida at times offers such an account of expression—as just one more of those binary oppositions that partake of the text of metaphysics and that are available for a deconstructive reading. Expression—one might suggest—is active, noetic, and experiential. Content is objective, noematic, and analyzable. Yet for Merleau-Ponty, expression is not just a correlate of content. Expression is a characteristic of a whole orientation of thought and being. Writing as expression is both productive and transformative. Derridean signature is an inscription of identity, an indecidable marking of ownness, an indication and expression of what is one's own in writing. Derridean signature marks difference in writing—the *différance* of writing. It marks the authorial inscription of writing. Signature is not just a sign or indicator, it is also the making of the particular signs of a particular text: this text (and not any other), this text with this context and not another, this text bounded and limited in these ways.

As Derrida remarks in "Signature Event Context,"[7] communication is a "signature event." Communication—writing—is not just an object that is passed around, read, and accepted or rejected. Communication is also an event, an event not of presence but of presentation. Communication, building upon both the hermeneutic and semiotic models, is both event and message. Communication is a paper delivered at a conference, a message transmitted, and a bringing in of what was previously not said. Communication is a "signature event" made into a text—or "texted" (a *signature événement qu'on texte*). But what is it "to text" a "signature event"? To text a "signature event" is to delimit an expression in such a way that it is authorially marked, to enter into the differential space of style and expression (as Merleau-Ponty would understand them) and to inscribe a particularity, to replace the singularity of the person who signed with the signature. The signature takes the place of the actual person. A comparison of signatures on a bank check will suffice to determine identity. The signature communicates.

To the question "does the absolute singularity of an event of the signature ever occur?" the answer cannot be other than equivocal. "Signature events" are supposed to be individual and singular. Counterfeits and mistaken identities do occur. But the "signature event" itself is an occurrence that marks what is unique. And when the signature is reproduced—as is Derrida's at the end of the last essay in *Margins of Philosophy*—is that signature the same as *the* signature event? To the extent that the graphic marks are reproduced with each copy of the book, the signature is reproduced—counterfeited of sorts. But there would be no legal case against the publishers. The signature has not been stolen—not a letter of it. The signature has been reproduced in a book published under Derrida's authorship. Hence Derrida's signature is authorized. But is each time it is reproduced an authorized version? Or is the authority of each reproduction a concession that Derrida makes—a concession that need not be licenced each time? Surely it must have been licenced at least once—by way of a contract signed by Jacques Derrida. But would the singularity of *that* signature event authorize all the others? In a sense, the answer must surely be yes. In another sense, the signature is not the signing, the making of a sign. The signing, the production of signification or at least the traces thereof, are reproducible without prejudice to the publisher—indeed as things seem to be going the publisher is doing quite well by it. But what is communicated in the signature event is a reading of communication, the expression—as Merleau-Ponty would call it—of a positionality as text, as writing.

The signature marks writing as correlative with a style that is one's own. The scriptural textuality of signature/expression inscribes an authorial place in which writing takes shape, in which writing not only takes on style, but in which and by which it *has* style. The style of writing is the signature event of expression. The writing of style is the differential marking of expression as "signature event."

Signification/Trace

The question of signification preoccupied Merleau-Ponty from the earliest stages of his philosophical career. How signification intersects with style and expression fills out his account of writing. Signification is not reducible either to "meaning" or "sense." The sense of expression or the sense of style is the orientation of writing—the direction of its articulation, the path it sets for itself. The meaning of expression or the meaning of style is the articulation of its identities. The meaning of expression and the meaning of style are its conceptual specificities. What characterizes their signification is marked out where meaning and sense meet one another, where the indirect language of style and expression articulate themselves with a determinate identity: Kafka's style, as expressed in *The Trial (Der Prozess)*, or Wordsworth's style expressed in his "Lines Composed Above Tintern Abbey." Its signification is the particular formulation of a sign system—Kafka's sign system, Wordsworth's sign system—each animated by a vitality and expression of meaning.

To the extent that Derridean traces mark off the differential spaces left open in a signifying system, writing takes style to its limits. To the extent that Derridean traces permeate writing, they iterate the very signatures that constitute a style. Traces are left by a style that seeks to impose itself, to make a mark, to achieve an identity, to affirm a set of conditions that set limits to a particular type of formulation. Style not only produces traces, it also uses them:

> Style would seem to advance in the manner of a *spur* of sorts (*éperon*) . . . style also uses its spur (*éperon*) as a means of protection against the terrifying, blinding, mortal threat [of that] which *presents* itself, which obstinately thrusts itself into view. And style thereby protects the presence, the content, the thing itself, meaning, truth—on the condition at least that it should not *already* (*déjà*) be that gaping chasm which has been deflowered in the unveiling of the difference. *Already* (*déjà*) such is the name for what has been effaced or subtracted beforehand, but which has nevertheless left behind a mark, a signature which is retracted in that very thing from which it is withdrawn.[8]

Style, then, advances, proceeds from wherever it is. It goes ahead, carrying on with its task, presenting itself as what needs to be presented. Style is not a position of its own. Rather style goes forth in order to establish a position. It establishes a position by forming a set of identities not as positivities but as marks of what is no longer, what has been erased from the surfaces, what is other than what has been thematized. In this sense, the traces are not even identities. Rather they are marks, signatures, inscriptions that account for neither the absence of that which forms the style nor the presence of some sort of meaning, truth, thing itself that is described, narrated, identified, clarified, articulated, or even expressed. The marks or signatures are neither the marking of a style nor the style that is marked in an inscription. In the unveiling of difference, one would expect there to be truth. This was the Heideggerian dream, but with Derrida the unveiling, the disclosure, the opening is not the appearance of truth itself but rather the mark of the truth that has been styled by "a stroke of the pen."

As already noted, the pen is a stylus, a writing instrument, ready to mark out whatever writing is prescribed. What it marks out is the truth of what is said; it marks out a disclosure, which reveals something other than itself. What is other than itself is that which is disclosed. Marking the disclosure, marking the difference, marking the marking does not amount to anything contentful, anything upon which to base anything else. The marking of the difference for Derrida is writing itself. Style marks the difference. The difference that is marked in writing. The stylus writes writing with style. Thus Derrida notes:

> The *éperon*, which is translated *sporo* in Frankish or High German, *spor* in Gaelic, is pronounced *spur* in English. In *Les mots anglais* Mallarmé relates it to the verb *to spurn*: that is to disdain, to rebuff, to reject scornfully. Although this may not be a particularly fascinating homonym, there is still a necessary historic and semantic operation from one language to the other evident in the fact that the English *spur*, the *éperon*, is the "same word" as the German *Spur:* or, in other words, trace, wake, indication, mark.[9]

All this etymological and translinguistic magic is pertinent to the extent that it indicates some sort of link between the *stylus*, a *style*, and a *trace*. The trace, which Heidegger sometimes identifies with the gods who have fled, leaving an abyss (*ein Abgrund*) in the place of some sure ground (*Grund*), is not that which is marked, nor is it the marking. It is neither the active agent nor the passive patient. The mark, along with the signature or the writing, remains differential. And the movement from "spur" to "trace" is itself a differential movement.

What, one might ask, does the trace have to do with Merleau-Pontean signification? The question is particularly acute when one remembers that signification—understood as meaning—is associated with truth in Derrida, and truth or meaning are surely other than the writing of difference that the trace identifies. Yet in Merleau-Ponty, the project of signification is not a result, nor is it an agent. Signification arises out of the expression of a style through the indirect language of the body, of painting, of architecture. Signification is not the effect of signifying, nor is it the signifier. Signification is that chiasmatic domain in which neither expressing nor expressed have any priority, where neither the visible nor the invisible take precedence. Signification is itself a fabric of perceptual and experiential relationality. Formed by indirect as well as direct language, signification is styled in writing and expressed in the enactment of an embodied being-in-the-world. Like the trace, signification is neither an agent nor a result, neither a producer nor a produced, neither an initiation nor an effect. Like the trace, signification is differential. Signification has no identity other than the stylizing activity that produces that which signifies. Signification is not what is written, nor is it the writer. The trace is neither the stylus nor the thing that is given style. The trace is neither that which is true nor the writing of what is true. The trace is the marking off of what is disclosed in the being true of any particular thing or content. The trace like signification has no positive identity. It is differential in the case of the trace and chiasmatic in the case of signification.

Writing, then, for Derrida is a dispersed network of traces. The traces are given style by the stylus that writes them. Writing is the tracing out and delimiting of its own network, its own text. Writing for Derrida marks out the domain of a textuality that sets itself off from Merleau-Pontean style. Merleau-Pontean style could achieve the "prose of the world." Yet it can do so only by its achievement of expression and enactment of signification. Merleau-Pontean style cannot be a private, individual activity. It must enter into the texture of the world—in that way and only in that way can it fulfill its political necessity—namely, to be style, expression, and signification in a social context where communication, understanding, and action are not only valued but also an indispensable feature of writing and its realization of itself as an indirect language. Correspondingly, Derridean writing, signature, and traces hardly occupy an isolated, independent, solitary space. Writing, signature, and trace operate in the formation of a fabric of meaning, truth, and reality that are constituted textually as institutions, social formations, and communicative constructions. Textually, they could have been otherwise. This looming presence of alterity marks the difference in which Derridean writing operates, where it sets limits to itself as identity, and outlines the frame that keeps it from becoming fully other. Hence Derridean writing marks its own limits, identifies its outside, its externality, and thereby makes itself difference. That writing is difference—even the difference that sets Derridean writing off from Merleau-Pontean style—is the mark of a scriptive textuality that will have been expressed if only as a dispersed complex of traces here in this essay—which I mark off at this juncture. . . .

12

Hegel and Merleau-Ponty: Radical Essentialism

Joseph C. Flay

I n his essay, "Hegel's Existentialism," Merleau-Ponty developed an insight of Jean Hyppolite's, which recognized Hegel's understanding of the openness of existence.[1] Hyppolite's thesis was, to be sure, an important contribution both to Hegel studies and to the historical-philosophical dialogue in twentieth-century philosophy, but it still fell short of a complete insight into Hegel's own radical position; for it depended on preserving a longtime distinction between, on the one hand, the young Hegel (Hegel through the time of the writing of the *Phenomenology of Spirit*[2]) and, on the other hand, the older or mature Hegel who, only a few years later with the writing of the *Science of Logic*,[3] the *Philosophy of Right*,[4] and the *Outline of the Encyclopedia of the Philosophical Sciences*,[5] was supposed to have been transformed into the rigid system-builder who collapsed existence and everything individual into a bloodless and closed universe of categorical thought. In addition to the influence of Hyppolite, Merleau-Ponty also retained much of Kojève's view of Hegel and of the latter's doctrine concerning the so-called end of history. Although he was somewhat critical of Kojève, to whom he had attentively listened together with others in the 1930s, so far as I know, Merleau-Ponty remained deeply influenced by Kojève, as well as by Hyppolite, to the end of his life.[6]

This essay is not intended to offer any radical reinterpretation of Merleau-Ponty's philosophy. The argument is simply that Merleau-Ponty missed something important in Hegel's system, which, had he seen it, would perhaps have allowed him to go much further in his own thought. In short, I shall maintain that at the heart of the "mature Hegel" there is a doctrine of essence that supports the view of being that Merleau-Ponty and Hyppolite saw in the *Phenomenology*. I shall call this doctrine "radical essentialism." I want to maintain that it is not Merleau-Ponty against Hegel, but Merleau-Ponty as *un copain de Hegel*.

In order to focus what I want to argue, I should like to cite several passages from *Adventures of the Dialectic*. The first two are comments on politics:

> Politics is never the encounter between conscience and individual happenings, nor is it ever the simple application of a philosophy of history. Politics is never able to see the whole directly. It is always aiming at the incomplete synthesis, a given cycle of time, or a group of problems. It is not pure morality, nor is it a chapter in a universal history which has already been written. Rather it is an action in the process of self-invention.
> [A.D., 4]

The second comment on politics is made in the course of a discussion of Weber, Lenin, and Trotsky: "In politics, truth is perhaps only [the] art of inventing what will later appear to have been required by time" (A.D., 28–29).

Third, there is the following remark about history: "History does not work according to a model; it is, in fact, the advent of meaning" (A.D., 17).

Finally, there is a rich view of dialectic:

> Dialectic is not the idea of a reciprocal action, nor that of the solidarity of opposites and of their sublation. Dialectic is not a development which starts itself again, nor the cross-growth of a quality that establishes as a new order a change which until then had been quantitative—these are consequences or aspects of the dialectic. . . . There is dialectic only in that type of being in which a junction of subjects occurs, being which is not only a spectacle that each subject presents to itself for its own benefit but which is rather their common residence, the place of their exchange and of their reciprocal interpretation. The dialectic does not, as Sartre claims, provide finality, that is to say, the presence of the whole in that which, by its nature, exists in

separate parts; rather it provides the global and primordial co-hesion of a field of experience wherein each element opens onto the others. . . . It is a thought which does not constitute the whole but which is situated in it. It has a past and a future which are not its own simple negation; it is incomplete so long as it does not pass into other perspectives and into the per-spectives of others. Nothing is more foreign to it than the Kantian conception of an ideality of the world which is the same in everyone, just as the number two or the triangle is the same in every mind, outside of meetings or exchanges: the nat-ural and human world is unique, not because it is parallelly constituted in everyone or because the "I think" is indiscern-ible in myself and in the other, but because we are imitatable and participatable through each other in this relationship with it. [A.D., 203–4]

One of the most important consequences of these four passages is that it follows from them that there are limits not only to philosophical thought, but to all thought where thought is reflectively brought to bear on projects for the future and on an understanding of the past and the present. If we for the moment allow the word "philosophy" to stand as representative for all such thought, there is a "space" or a "gap" be-tween philosophy and nonphilosophy, which cannot be bridged. That means that there is a radical contingency that belongs to reality because there is radical otherness.

But secondly, it follows that essence—the heart of what a thing or event is—(1) is always in the making and never complete, (2) appears as the necessity of what the thing or event is, but only *after the fact*, post hoc, (3) is a matter of the *advent of meaning*, and (4) is always situated. Looked at in this way, we have a true perversion of the traditional signification of essence. And yet what Merleau-Ponty has so ably articulated here makes sense and seems to speak to the concrete problem of the sense of things or their essence.

In the present paper I want to suggest that Merleau-Ponty's posi-tion can be clarified and pushed much further once we realize that there was present in the so-called mature Hegel a doctrine of essence and of freedom that furnished the fundamental explanation for this radical contingency and otherness, and this seemingly perverse sense of neces-sity and essence (as only post hoc), and which has still to this day not been systematically developed as a categorial critique within any other philo-sophical position. It will lay a foundation not only for Merleau-Ponty's own thought in a way that he and others did not understand at all, but will also, once understood, allow us to comprehend the rationality of a view of essence that holds it to be radically contingent. Furthermore, it will allow us to understand this in a way that does not reduce everything to only a moment of dialectic to be encompassed within an ultimate absolute necessity—that is, within an ultimate synchronous structure existing outside time, in eternity. In short, there is a radical otherness implied in the categorial critique that constitutes Hegel's *Science of Logic*.

I shall first state, rather bluntly and merely for the sake of making it clear, my position (and the position of others in Hegel studies today) concerning the radical misinterpretation of Hegel that has given us the Hegel who actually influenced the history of philosophy that came after him. Second, I shall briefly sketch Hegel's doctrine of essence and in particular those parts of the doctrine that deal with (a) the relationship between necessity and contingency and (b) the rejection of cause-effect and the defense of radical reciprocity. Finally, I shall suggest some precise ways in which "the mature Hegel," thus understood, becomes the ally and not the enemy of Merleau-Ponty, and the way in which the historical-philosophical dialogue can now proceed if this authentic Hegelian view of radical essence and the otherness implied by it is considered.

Right-Wing Hegel

I will not spend much time on the misinterpretation of Hegel, because to be thorough about the matter would take much more than a single essay. An outline of the origins of the "traditional" interpretation of Hegel is approximately the following. The perversion of Hegel that led to what I claim is a radical misunderstanding had essentially two sources: Hegel's successors and Hegel himself.[7] First, even before Hegel's death, the right- and left-wing interpretations of Hegel's philosophy emerged. The dispute was quickly settled, however; for both agreed that the right-wing interpretation of Hegel was the authentic Hegel. Left-wing Hegelianism, and most importantly Marx and his followers, capitulated to the right. The left proceeded in its various developments as a critique of Hegel. The ideological motivations of the right-wing—both politically and theologically—therefore won the day, and the Hegel who came to have an explicit historical influence on philosophy and on thought in general was the so-called conservative Hegel of the system.

The perversion can be characterized in general as a view that turned Hegel into a modern version of a conservative Platonism, with a traditional doctrine of the hegemony of essence over existence and appearance, of necessity over contingency, and of eternity over temporality and history. It took on an important twentieth-century form with the lectures of Kojève, but the message remained essentially the same. Consequently, in Kojève's lectures one will find almost nothing of any value or accuracy concerning Hegel's philosophy. There is great drama and romance in Kojève, and we have an excellent view of Kojève's own philosophy, but there is little Hegel there.[8]

But, secondly, the cause of the perversion was not only the ideology of conservative German theology and politics alone, but also the presence in Hegel's system of a radical ambiguity that seemed, to traditionalist eyes, totally out of place. That is to say, ambiguities arose in Hegel's system, and it was assumed that if one were to be able to get an "intelligible" view of Hegel—intelligible from the Platonist-Aristotelian view of in what intelligibility ought to consist (a view that still for the most part controls philosophy today)—one must eliminate all ambiguity and choose a "consistent" formulation of what Hegel said. Consequently, system won out over method; and whatever dialectic remained did so only to the point where political and religious closure was demanded in order to satisfy the traditional sense of systematic thought. So we might say that Hegel is in part responsible for the distortions that came to represent his philosophy; for he embraced an ambiguity that seemed to the conservative, traditionalist mind to generate paradoxes rather than a rational system.

The reason for this state of affairs was glimpsed by Hegel himself. From the beginning of his Jena years, Hegel envisioned himself as standing in two epochs simultaneously: in the grand and matured epoch of the past, which began with the pre-Socratics and led through the long tradition up to Hegel himself; and in the epoch of the future of which post-Kantian philosophy, and in particular Hegel himself, was only the beginning. He lived in the dawn of a new age according to him, a time in which the old tasks of philosophy had been resolved and the new tasks were only beginning to emerge. The ambiguity and paradox that was troublesome for "consistent interpretation" arose from the following situation: as the bearer of what he characterized as "the infancy" of the new age, Hegel could in fact not adequately sort out the new from the old. The new and the old lay in his system together, and the import of the new was no more understood by Hegel—by his own admission—than the new world of the infant is understood by the infant. So, Hegel himself was not beyond confusing his own position.[9]

But the ambiguity that was responsible for the perversion of Hegel's philosophy is precisely what is important for the discovery of the real Hegel; for if we are to learn as much as possible from Hegel's contribution to the historical-philosophical dialogue, we must preserve this ambiguity and recognize that what seems to be paradox, from the point of view of tradition, is in fact the heart of the truth. The core of this ambiguity lay in his doctrine of essence as contained in his "science of logic." In what follows, I want now to attempt to sketch Hegel's radically new view of essence and to understand it as we, who stand firmly in Hegel's "new epoch," can now understand it.[10] In the last section I shall return to this matter of Hegel's own misunderstanding of himself at times and his resort from time to time to the Platonic-Aristotelian conception of philosophy.

Hegel's Doctrine of Essence

Hegel's doctrine of essence involves a thorough critique of what the traditional categories putatively gave as the structure of what is lasting and universal in all things. Whatever Hegel's differences from the tradition, there is a certain agreement with what I am calling, in order to show its universality, the Platonic-Aristotelian position. This position was due to the Socratic Anxiety, an anxiety about the costs and risks of *not* establishing a stable, consistent, unchanging domain of meaning and sense for the cosmos.[11] What caused problems to traditionalists is that Hegel seemed simply to have violated the Socratic concern for stability and thus exacerbated the anxiety; for on the whole the traditional oppositions, which were constituted by sets of categories standing against each other and which were meant to be resolved as oppositions by opting for the side of constancy and stability in all cases, were rejected by Hegel as oppositions that were too rigid and involved, too sharp an opposition to be true to reality. Hegel argued that the oppositions between what in general was seen to belong to the ephemeral, on the one hand, and to the eternal, on the other hand, had to be critiqued because they were too abstract. In what follows I want briefly to sketch the development of some of these categories as they appear in his *Science of Logic*.

Hegel's doctrine of essence succeeds his doctrine of being. The doctrine of being contains a dialectical critique of those categories that purported to establish the nature of being—that is to say, which purported to establish the nature of the *happening* of whatever exists. There are two main sorts of categories, the one sort constituted by categories of quality, the other by categories of quantity. At the very beginning of his discussion of the nature of "Being," Hegel takes up the opposition championed by the "thinking of the understanding" and faithfully followed by most of the tradition since Parmenides—namely, that being is the ultimate and unchanging nature of what is, and that it excludes and has as its absolute opposite "nothing" or "nonbeing." But Hegel shows in a dialectic, following faithfully the spirit of Socratic questioning, that if one maintains that being as "pure, undifferentiated being" is held to be the absolute, it in fact becomes indistinguishable from what is to be excluded from it—namely, nonbeing. His critique then shows that, if the distinction between being and nonbeing is to be preserved—as is the intention of those who champion "pure being"—then being and nonbeing will have to be understood as elements of "becoming." In the "belonging-together" of "being" and "nonbeing" in "becoming" we have preserved their difference and at the same time have shown that, if "being" is the first and ultimate category embracing what-is, then being is becoming. The only true being is the being that embraces the differences inherent in becoming.[12] This sort of critique is what constitutes throughout Hegel's logic/metaphysics his positive doctrines.

The upshot of Hegel's dialectical critique, in which one by one all the categories held formerly to establish for us the happening of whatever is are shown to be now inadequate to do the job they pretended to do, is to consider the ancient and ubiquitous doctrine that there must be some ultimate measure that finally contains all other measures of things in their happening. From the ancient *moira* of Parmenides, which fixed all things from the beginning, to the regulative ideas of Kant, a fixed and ultimate measure, either real or ideal, had been held to be necessary for the intelligibility of what-is.

Hegel's critique shows us that the claim for an ultimate measure is unwarranted and that, instead, both each and every thing as well as the "whole" of things is simply a system of many different internal measures that operate simultaneously and spontaneously. Neither a quantitative determination of qualia nor a qualitative determination of quanta reveal the real nature of anything so long as some measure or other is taken as external and independent—that is, as itself not measured by something else that itself exists in the domain of being as becoming. The truth is, rather, that reality in its happening, in the upsurge of being, is a matter of thoroughgoing reciprocity and thus a matter of contingency and radical otherness: the nature of what comes to be is not predeterminable. It is true, Hegel argues, that everything has its measure; but it is also true that there is not a *prius* as a single measure for all things. Rather there is a self-measuring of reality. The limit of the happening of reality—that is, of being—is fixed neither by *moira* nor by a set of regulative ideals, but by reality itself as a multiplicity of realities that furnish the measure of each other and therefore ultimately of themselves. This entails a radical otherness to being, an otherness not absorbed by some measure that, in the last instance, yields an ultimate identity; rather, the measure of what-is leaves us to the contingencies of the constant and unending reconstitution of what-is.

The doctrine of essence, which follows this analysis of measure, is the attempt to determine in just what way being can be fixed if the measure of things is of this character. Traditionally there arose distinctions between the following sorts of pairs, the first member of which was held to fix or order the second: essence as what is essential, as opposed to the inessential or accidental; essence as the abiding reality, as opposed to mere show or the ephemerality of appearances; the fundamental law on the basis of which the positing of what-is occurs, and the dependent, posited being; identity, as opposed to difference; ground, as opposed to what is grounded; form, as opposed to matter and content; whole, as opposed to parts; force, as opposed to its mere expression; inner, as opposed to outer; the absolute, as opposed to its expression as attributes and modifications; necessity, as opposed to contingency; substance, as opposed to accident; and cause, as opposed to effect. In each of these, the first member of the pair speaks to the eternal, the stable, the lasting, and the self-identical, while the second addresses the temporal, the unstable, the ephemeral, and the differentiated. The task of the tradition was to make constant and universally intelligible the measure of all measures—that is, to articulate an overarching power that would give unity and eternal stability to what-is by making a hierarchy of each pair with the first member ordering the second. Inasmuch as the sheer being of things was open to contingency and otherness, the traditional task of essence was to tame being.

Hegel's critique shows that, like the attempt to grant stability to being itself, this attempt fails as well. His general argument, repeated mutatis mutandis for each of the pairs, is that the choice of anything to represent the "stable," and so forth, is purely arbitrary. For example, let us take the pair cause-effect. It is traditionally held to be, on various "levels" of being or analysis, that which will give us a comprehension of how things hold together. The cause gives us the "secret" of the happening of the thing and of the latter's connection to other things. But what assigns this value of "cause" to some particular thing or event? By what justification can we call anything or any event a cause and oppose to it the effects, which are held simply "to follow from" and "be dependent upon" the cause? These questions have their greatest importance when directed to proofs of the necessary existence of an ultimate first principle; for such a principle presupposes acceptance of the intelligibility of the category "cause" and of the legitimacy of the demand that there be, at the foundation of things, a first cause.

Hegel finds the following. On levels of reality other than that claimed to be the ultimate level, what is cause and what is not cause but effect is determined by the subjective interests of the individuals who seek an understanding of the events or the phenomena. Thus, what is "cause" in one framework of investigation may be either an "effect" in another framework, or even completely irrelevant in a third framework. Moreover, for anything to be a cause, it must (a) actually or potentially *be* a cause, and (b) therefore must be appropriate as a cause to the actual or potential effect. But this means that the effect (actual or potential) is itself a necessary condition for the cause being a cause, and therefore means that in this way (as "teleological" cause) the effect is the cause of the cause. One need not here intend any appeal to a teleological framework of any sort; what is meant is simply that the cause of anything is dependent upon being "the cause of the effect" in order to be cause. Thus, in a second way, subjective prejudgment is what determines that one is going to speak of causes in one particular way rather than in other ways, and hence there is nothing in the nature of cause-effect itself that determines one thing or event to be cause and another to be event.

However, on the ultimate level of reality or where a primordial reality is concerned, it would seem that the first or ultimate cause is purely objective and is fixed independently of subjective interests. As the classic argument goes, without an ultimate cause there would be no secondary causes or effects; but this is contrary to what experience teaches us—namely, that there is being and that things happen. Therefore, the argument concludes, logic (and in particular the principle of sufficient reason) demands that there be a first cause. But Hegel argues that the case is not in general different when we speak of ultimate cause; on the contrary, it is much like the true discussion of relative causes. He points out that (1) it is still true that in order that a cause be a cause, there must be an effect, whether this effect be the "sum total of all causes and effects" or only a particular effect; (2) the "in order that" transforms the effect into the highest type of cause for causes—namely, one that initiates and installs a cause as a cause; therefore (3) the so-called effect is in reality the cause of the very possibility of the so-called cause; for example, the creator god cannot possibly be a creator god without the creation, just as the craftsman cannot be the cause of the artifact unless there is an artifact caused by him; therefore (4) effect is cause and cause is effect and any hierarchy or priority can be shown to be arbitrary.

If one resorts to a possible/actual distinction, and claims that the cause prior to the actual effect is a possible cause and thus still a cause, there are two responses. First, the possible cause is possible cause only because there is a possible effect. Second, the transformation from possibility to actuality is due to the presence of the actual effect. Thus, effect remains determinative of cause.[13] The general conclusion to be drawn according to Hegel is that the essence of reality is a matter of reciprocity—that is, that what we found in the analysis of the measure of being is present now as the absolutely reciprocal determining of what-is by itself, as the completely internal self-determination of what-is by what-is. Each thing that exists is what it is and nothing else because other things are what they are.

The determination of actuality is thereby established, actuality being the fully and internally determined state of reality. The absolute and rigid opposition of necessity and contingency, of condition and conditioned, is effaced; for contingency is what constitutes necessity *in concreto*. Hegel shows that the traditional exclusion of contingency by necessity and of necessity by contingency is a pure abstraction, based on an arbitrarily fixed linear conception of what actuality must be like. Absolute and effective necessity is constituted not a priori, but post hoc as the result of what has contingently occurred.[14] All the conditions in force in a given situation are what make the situation *what it is*—that is, *what it has become*—that is what it *essentially* is. And, in turn, each of the conditions are themselves the conditions they are only due to the presence of the other conditions. But the configuration of conditions at any given time fixes what exists at that time as what it is, and thus necessity and contingency, as a slice of a theoretically instantaneous present, are identical.

It might seem that I have now established that closed universe of Hegel which I have said I was seeking to show as a misinterpretation; for we now have contingency and necessity conflated, and have established a completely and internally determined reality. But there are two issues here that make Hegel's analysis work in a radically different way, one having to do with levels of discourse or levels of being, the other having to do with time. As for the matter of levels of discourse and being, Hegel consistently insists that we speak only of one level at a time. The tradition was driven to the various notions of stability that made up essence because it illegitimately tried to fix the nature of a thing or event at one level of being by an appeal to a "higher" or more abstract level of being. So, for example, the essence of this chair supposedly could be fixed only by looking to the level of chair-in-general. Whatever was necessarily abstracted from this chair to get to the chair-in-general or to the form of the chair was simply accident or contingent appearance. The essence of a human being, the essence of a nation, and so forth, were all derived in the same way. It therefore became a doctrine in the tradition that essence could not be brought down to the level of particulars, and therefore that particulars (as opposed to universals) were incidental. So, according to the tradition, the essence of any particular given thing or event is just what that thing or event is not.

Contrary to this, Hegel argues that if we are truly to get to concrete essence, then we must stay at the same level of discourse or the same level of being in terms of which the thing about which we are talking exists. This is what I have called his radical doctrine of essence or his radical essentialism. We *can* get to the essence of a particular thing or event, even though that essence involves us with an inexhaustible richness of elements and conditions that co-constitute the world of that thing or event. We can generalize for one purpose or another, but we must remember that to generalize is to move to a position of inferiority, not one of superiority. The more we abstract or generalize, the more we lose the matter-at-hand or the real state of affairs.

When considered in terms of temporality, this doctrine of essence reveals its true radicality. Hegel made the famous pun in his *Encyclopedia:* "Wesen ist was gewesen ist."[15] We lose the pun in translation, but what the sentence means in English is that essence is what has been. Now, given the reciprocal, inner- and self-determining nature of what-is, if we capture the essence of anything, we have captured it only to the degree that the conditions have come to be what they are: not what they will be, but what they are. Thus we get Hegel's famous restriction for philosophy, not only in the *Philosophy of Right*, but in his system as well and especially in his conception of the history of philosophy: thought—that is, dialectical thought—that is, philosophy—cannot be employed to say *anything at all* about the future and can tell us *nothing at all* about that domain traditionally referred to as "eternity." Any talk of essence is restricted to a discussion of the happening of being *as it has happened*, and *not* as it will happen or as it eternally happens in the traditional sense of the term "eternity." Thus, any discussions of the future involve us in radical otherness. Philosophical science and all forms of *Wissenschaft* are limited to what-is as it has come to be, and thus there is radical otherness in respect to the future.

In keeping with his findings about necessity being constituted by contingency, all necessity is post hoc and we can comprehend only what has come to be and nothing a priori. Thus the future is open insofar as it has not yet been determined by the conditions that will determine it, and this is true, for those conditions do not yet exist. Therefore, we can neither speak of an end to history as an end *simpliciter*, nor can we deny such an end. End cannot be spoken of at all if it refers to the present—that is, to what is as it now is. What we can speak of is a qualified end, and that is the only way Hegel ever spoke of a temporal end. For example, he completes his lectures on the history of philosophy by telling his students that he has explained to them the way the history of philosophy has completed itself *up to the present time*. In fact, Hegel's lectures on the history of philosophy do not even contain an account of his own philosophy. Thus, the qualifying phrase "up to the present time" is all-important, and is present in the *Phenomenology*, the *Logic* and *Encyclopedia*, the *Philosophy of Right*, and the rest of Hegel's lectures.[16]

If we were now to look at the Doctrine of the Concept in his *Science of Logic*, we would find what I have just adumbrated as essence and necessity presented under the term "freedom," and it is this that finally removes the absolutist determinism said to belong to Hegel. The move from essence to concept is a move from necessity (at the end of essence) to freedom (at the beginning of the concept). How freedom comes out of necessity is simple to see at this point. What is free is what is internally self-determined. What is internally self-determining is limited and determined by nothing but itself, for all determinations are internal. Thus, if necessity is properly understood and not abstractly understood, freedom and necessity have a positive relation to each other. The difference is that freedom is not blind as was necessity—that is, one is not simply carried along with whatever happens. Freedom inheres in the domain of the concept because the concept or conceptualization is the grasping of the laws of the formation of reality—it is thought. Through analyses of concepts of different sorts, then through analysis of judgments and syllogisms of various sorts, Hegel shows just how the structure of being and essence are consciously to be grasped.

This comprehension is not something abstract for Hegel; for all thought, including philosophical thought, is embedded in human activity and its conditions, and thus is embodied thought.[17] Hegel knows (and shows clearly already in his *Phenomenology*) that people do not stand around saying things like "this is a tree" or "this rose is red" or "elephants are animals" or "beings are either living or nonliving." They do it in the midst of their actions, with intentions about the significance of the utterances or about the results that are to follow from the utterances. So to say to myself, for example, "these are beautiful red roses. So I am going to buy them, since Bonnie likes red roses," is not to utter an abstract syllogism, but to direct my action, and upon reflection to make sense of my action. The categories of the logic are also embedded in the purposive activity involved in my buying of the roses.

Hegel's claim about his categorial analysis is that its content is embedded in our activities in the world. A being is free insofar as that being can properly unpack or work its way through the conditions that make the situation of the moment just what it is and nothing else. Philosophy and philosophical thought are important for Hegel only because philosophy enables us intelligently to proceed through this multi-measured and multiconditioned cosmos. And as we do, we ourselves (1) become part of the conditions that reciprocally condition what else there is, and (2) are conditioned by what else there is.

Now one can clearly see how this would be paradoxical to traditional thought. On the one hand, Hegel makes claims for science (understood as *episteme*) and absolute knowledge, and on the other hand denies the very conditions under which, according to the tradition, such a science and absolute knowledge could be legitimately claimed. If, as I have argued, Hegel can neither predict the future nor speak of eternity in the traditional sense, then Hegel has only a perspective on reality and is thus a historicist in that sense. But it would follow that as a historicist, he is by definition incapable of generating a science or a standpoint from which one could have absolute knowledge, and thus his claim to absolute philosophy would be a sham. And yet Hegel *does* make these claims to absolute science. The Socratic anxiety (i.e., wanting to know "ahead of time" what a thing is so that one can always recognize it when one sees it) raises its ugly head when confronted with the ambiguity and contradiction here, and we are thrown into a fever.

Enter right-wing Hegelianism: we can clear up the problem by ridding ourselves of the very dialectic and radical otherness that constitutes the heart of Hegel's *Science of Logic*. And the left-wing, still essentially rationalistic and governed by the Platonic-Aristotelian tradition, either formulates its critique and sets out through ideological commitment to make the world into what Hegel's (stable) view of reality saw as reality, or with Marx postpones "the end," as eschatological end, for the coming of the perfection found lurking in what is seen as Hegel's as yet incomplete determination of the essence of history.

What Hegel's critical and constructive categorial analysis of the *Science of Logic* leads us to, however, is a confrontation with the quest for certainty and stability present in the Platonic-Aristotelian *therapeia* for the Socratic Anxiety. That therapy, as we have seen, consisted in granting to the "stable" side of the oppositions the truth of reality and to the "other" side the falsity of appearance and accident. Hegel's analysis shows that the granting is groundless and arbitrary. If we approach that openness of being to itself to which Hegel's system leads us, then the anxiety itself must disappear; for that anxiety is built in fact on the presupposition that such a therapy is needful.

In other words, the traditionalist argument is question-begging. It goes like this: (1) there must be an eternal truth or set of truths, since (2) without it there would only be change and inconstancy; (3) change and inconstancy are by themselves obviously unacceptable, because there is no eternal truth or set of truths by means of which we can stabilize them, and (4) they therefore must be stabilized so that there be an eternal truth or set of truths, since (5) without it there would only be change and inconstancy. All arguments like this, which I call "arguments from the truth," are question-begging; and thus all attacks on historicism, on relativism, and on positions that claim the absence of eternal truths are question-begging. They are, in a word, all unsound arguments; for only by presupposing that there must be eternal or lasting truths has it been established that there must be eternal or lasting truths. The main Platonic-Aristotelian tradition rests on this simple logical fallacy.

Merleau-Ponty's Existentialism

If we return to the four passages I chose from Merleau-Ponty's *Adventures of the Dialectic*, we will see now that a ground for Merleau-Ponty's existential position is to be found in Hegel. The place of the individual is the place of the contingent, but a contingent always already situated in the world and thus both constitutive of and constituted by what comes to be. After the fact, we can look back to the "necessity" of what happened; but that necessity is only post hoc and what we always face is radical otherness. However, that is not a limitation; for, as Hegel has shown, it is the *only* concrete sort of necessity there is. Furthermore, because only the doctrine of the concept and freedom completes the pure metaphysical system, it is only in a cosmos that includes human beings that this logic and its categories have a reality. As the consequent philosophical sciences of nature and spirit show, this contingency, in which humans are both dependent upon and constitutive of ongoing reality, has grounded an ambiguity that came, independently of Hegel of course, to haunt all of Merleau-Ponty's philosophy.

What we can now comprehend, and what Hegel could see only dimly, is that the space between philosophy and nonphilosophy, between thought about the nature of reality and that reality itself in the making (including the human beings who contribute to that making), between what can be known with certainty and what cannot, involves a radical separation, a radical otherness, necessitated by the very doctrine of essence and of the constitution of necessity by contingency that Hegel claimed for actuality. Just because the necessary is constantly being constituted and reconstituted by the contingent, and just because philosophy can grasp what-is only through reflection on what has come to be (i.e., on the already-constituted-necessary being), the reconstitution that carries us into the future must necessarily escape us in our philosophical reflections.

Hegel, on the one hand, insisted on this himself; for it clearly and literally constituted the essential part of his system. But on the other hand, he did not know how to handle it except by resorting to traditional ideas about the relation between philosophy and life. For example—and this shows us how he was in part responsible for the victory of the right over the left—at the end of his lectures on the philosophy of religion, repeated over many years, he cast the philosopher as one apart, who is a member of the priesthood charged with guarding the eternal truth and who cannot be bothered with the human problems that drag us into the future.[18] Or, in the *Philosophy of Right*, after making clear this point about the openness of the future, he leaves us with no idea of the relation between his analysis of the state (and of its eventual destructive fall into history, to be judged in the future) and the real political problems of the present. He rests on a distinction between "the actual" (*das Wirkliche*) and "the existing" (*das Daseiende*). This left him open to the moves of both the right and the left, the one settling for the perfection of the existent, the other launching a war against the existent.

On the other hand, Merleau-Ponty also leaves us without a proper philosophy of action. But I would suggest that the "new liberalism" and the "relativization of revolution" of which he speaks, for example, at the end of *Adventures of the Dialectic*, can have that nonabsolutist ground that Merleau-Ponty seeks. The model of essence and of intelligibility that Hegel gives us, but that he himself did not fully understand, is not a model that shows the fixed determination of all contingencies, but rather a model that presents us with the contingency of all fixed determinations. This does not throw us into the nothingness of a Sartrean freedom, nor does it cause us to fix the contingent by means of a party absolutism; rather it lets us accept, but also makes us responsible for, the future that comes out of our actions in conjunction with the rest of reality. At the same time it also fixes that reality, momentarily, in such a way that we are condemned to acting from the necessity we have just contingently fixed through our present and past actions.

Radical essentialism is present in both Hegel and Merleau-Ponty. It signifies a rejection of the position that essences stand apart from or exist at a higher level than that of which they are essences. It understands the term "essence" in a way that calls us back to the concreteness of individual life. It leads to a "dangerous" philosophy of ambiguity only for those who are still imprisoned in the Platonic-Aristotelian tradition and its question-begging position and cannot understand that *there is* a lived intelligibility without eternal essences. In fact, there *is* ambiguity here, the ambiguity constituting the "truth" of action and meaning "in the process of self-invention." Radical otherness is of the essence in philosophy because it is of the essence in our ordinary lived existence.

13

Situation and Suspicion in the Thought of Merleau-Ponty: The Question of Phenomenology and Politics

Merold Westphal

Writing in 1960, Merleau-Ponty begins the Introduction to *Signs* with a comment on the distance between philosophy and politics, his philosophy and his politics. "*How different—how downright incongruous*—the philosophical essays and the ad hoc, primarily political observations which make up this volume seem!" (S., 3).

He seems ambivalent about this. On the one hand there are the questions, "Is it not an incredible misunderstanding that all, or almost all, philosophers have felt obliged to have a politics, whereas politics arises from the 'practice of life' and escapes understanding? The politics of philosophers is what no one *practices*. Then is it politics?" (S., 5). Hearing these from Marxists and former Marxists who, "divided about everything else, seem to agree in *confirming* the separation of philosophy and politics," Merleau-Ponty understands the disillusionment of those whose efforts to unite philosophy and politics have been refuted by experience (S., 6). But he knows that there can be bad divorces as well as bad marriages, and so he also understands those who "know better than anyone that the Marxist link between philosophy and politics is broken" but who "act as if it were still *in principle* . . . what Marx said it was: philosophy simultaneously realized and destroyed in history, the saving negation and fulfilling destruction." Though clear that this "consolation is not an innocent one," he cannot hide his nostalgic sympathy (S., 8).

On the other hand we find a future-oriented nostalgia for an age that will take philosophy more seriously:

> Above all, we have not yet learned a philosophy which is all the less tied down by political responsibilities to the extent that it has its own, and all the more free to enter everywhere to the extent it does not take anyone's place (does not *play* at passions, politics, and life, or reconstruct them in imagination) but discloses exactly the Being we inhabit. [S., 13]

Merleau-Ponty turns immediately to a new section whose themes are being, flesh, language, and the relation of visible to invisible. Three sentences from the opening paragraphs of the new section give its flavor: "Even the action of thinking is caught up in the push and shove of being." "In the dark night of thought dwells a glimmering of Being." "Colors, sounds, and things—like Van Gogh's stars—are the focal points and radiance of being" (S., 14–15).

A disillusioned Marxist? A hopeful Heideggerian? Both, no doubt. But if so, that only poses the question, What is the relation between philosophy and politics in Merleau-Ponty's work? By his politics I mean his political writings, so this is not directly a question about the relation of theory to practice but about two modes of reflection. By his philosophy I shall mean the phenomenological ontology whose early version is *Phenomenology of Perception* (1945) and whose late version is adumbrated in *The Visible and the Invisible* (1961).[1] By his politics I shall mean his attempt to wrestle with Marxist theory and with contemporary political life in the light of Marxist theory. In this case early and late refer to *Humanism and Terror* (1947) and *The Adventures of the Dialectic* (1955), respectively.

My thesis is that the difference and even incongruity that Merleau-Ponty sees between philosophy and politics in *Signs* is characteristic of his work as a whole. Aristotle is perhaps a useful model. On the one hand is his *Organon* and such writings as *De Anima*, *Physics*, and *Metaphysics*, which together form a powerful union of method and ontology.

On the other hand are his *Nicomachean Ethics* and *Politics*, which have a tangential relation at best to the other works. *Episteme* and *phronesis* are different, and even incongruous for Aristotle. Similarly, it seems to me, Merleau-Ponty's phenomenology of perception, which in both its early and later forms is a powerful synthesis of method and ontology, has a minimal significance for his political writings. If this reading is sound and if, as I suspect, it points to a deficiency in Merleau-Ponty's thinking, that deficiency will concern his philosophy more than his politics, for reasons that will emerge in what follows.

Merleau-Ponty's Politics and the Hermeneutics of Suspicion

A clue to an important feature of his politics is found in his claim that, long before Husserl and Heidegger, Marx, Nietzsche, and Freud were practicing phenomenology (Ph.P., viii). Surely he does not mean that they were engaged in the transcendental idealism of *Ideas I* or *Cartesian Meditations*. Their phenomenology, like Merleau-Ponty's in *The Phenomenology of Perception* and Heidegger's in *Being and Time*, is an existential or hermeneutical phenomenology that emphasizes the situated character of an intentionality that occurs against the background of already given meanings.

But this is insufficient to characterize what unifies the method of Marx, Nietzsche, and Freud. Their thinking embodies not hermeneutics in general but the hermeneutics of suspicion, as Ricoeur has so helpfully pointed out by calling them the "masters" of the "school of suspicion."[2] With or without the concept of the unconscious, the hermeneutics of suspicion seeks to uncover (unmask, demystify) the self-deception (false consciousness, bad faith) born of ambivalence. An individual or group is aware of a thought, desire, motive, or behavior to which, on the one hand, it is committed, but which, on the other hand, it cannot acknowledge without guilt or shame; so it manages not to notice.[3] Freud's definition of a dream as *"a (disguised) fulfillment of a (suppressed or repressed) wish"* expresses succinctly this self-deception and the ambivalence that underlies it.[4]

Merleau-Ponty's politics is the sustained practice of the hermeneutics of suspicion. In *Humanism and Terror* he holds no brief for Soviet practice, but, as it turns out, briefly holds on to Marxist theory. Perhaps it cannot shape history and he finds himself "waiting for a fresh historical impulse which may allow us to engage in a popular movement without ambiguity" (H.T., 153, xxiii). But "it remains powerful enough to discredit other solutions" (H.T., 153). It does so precisely by helping "to dissipate the myths" that ground the propaganda of both communism and anticommunism, making it a duty not to choose between them (H.T., xxix).

The myths Merleau-Ponty mentions are not so much the memory of primordial time as forgetfulness of recent history and present structure. He has in mind the "active forgetfulness" of which Nietzsche speaks.[5] The first chapter of *Humanism and Terror* opens on the theme of forgetfulness:

> [The anticommunist] has forgotten that all regimes are criminal, that Western liberalism rests upon the forced labor of the colonies and twenty wars, that from an ethical standpoint the death of a Negro lynched in Louisiana, or of a native in Indonesia, Algeria, or Indochina is no less inexcusable than Rubashov's death; he forgets that communism does not invent violence but finds it already institutionalized, that for the moment the question is not to know whether one accepts or rejects violence, but whether the violence with which one is allied is "progressive" and tends toward its own suspension or toward self-perpetuation. [H.T., 1; translation of "aussi peu pardonnable" changed by the editors. See H.T., 41.]

The communist who gets excited about the revolutionary decisiveness of the Stalinist purges "has forgotten that violence—anguish, pain, and death—is only appealing in imagination, in art and written history . . . the screams of a single man condemned to death are unforgettable" (H.T., 2).

Neither forgetting is innocent. "The anticommunist *refuses* to see that violence is universal while the exalted sympathizer *refuses* to see that no one can look violence in the face" (H.T., 2, emphasis added). This self-deception may not be deliberate, but neither is it involuntary. "Consciousness is not a good judge of what we are *doing* since we are involved in the struggle of history and in this we achieve more, less, or something else than we thought we were doing." Because he remembers the role that active forgetting plays in producing this gap between what we do and what we think we do, Merleau-Ponty does not merely speak of the situational opacity of historical action but of "mystification" (H.T., 104). He is practicing the hermeneutics of suspicion.

So it is that during his trial Rubashov (Bukharin) is reminded of "all those considerations it was *necessary to neglect*" (H.T., 5, emphasis added). Similarly, "as soon as de Gaulle's government was established it sought every means of forgetting its own origins in insurrection and managed it quite well" (H.T., 38). And again, Trotsky's humanist critique of Stalinism is possible only by virtue of forgetting his own practice of violence and the writings in which he justified it (H.T., 85–88).

But Merleau-Ponty's real target is neither individuals nor national governments but the two superpower systems that make the cold war necessary and a third world war all too possible. While he can side with neither communism nor anticommunism, he can seek to "dissipate the myths" that fuel their violence by exposing their motivated forgetfulness. Because he lives in the West and because the occasion of his own book is a book that helps the West to forget what it most needs to remember (Koestler's *Darkness at Noon*), Merleau-Ponty's task becomes largely one of "depriving Western politics of that wonderfully clear conscience which is so remarkable in much of contemporary Anglo-Saxon writing" (H.T., 175).

His primary technique for this attempt to compel remembrance is to highlight the way in which lofty principles distract attention from realities they thereby help to disguise.[6] In the liberal, capitalist democracies of the West these realities include colonial exploitation, colonial and other wars, propaganda, wage labor, unemployment, the violent suppression of strikes, anti-Semitism, and racism (H.T., xiii, xxiii–xxiv, xliv–xlv, 103, 107, 169–70, 174–75, 186). The debate between the Western democracies and communism is not "between the Yogi and the Commissar but between one Commissar and another" (H.T., 175; cf. 109, 150–51, 177).

Merleau-Ponty insists, "Any defense of the West which *forgets* these truths is a mystification" (H.T., 177, emphasis added; cf. 179–80). This last sentence of the last chapter echoes the opening paragraph of the Preface:

> Communism is often discussed in terms of the contrast . . . between political realism and liberal values. Communists reply that in democracies cunning, violence, propaganda, and *realpolitik* in the guise of liberal principles are the substance of foreign or colonial politics and even of domestic politics. Respect for law and liberty has served to justify police suppression of strikes in America; today it serves even to justify military suppression in Indochina or in Palestine and the development of an American empire in the Middle East. The material and moral culture of England presupposes the exploitation of the colonies. The purity of principles not only tolerates but even requires violence. Thus there is a mystification in liberalism. Judging from history and by everyday events, liberal ideas be-

long to a system of violence of which, as Marx said, they are the "spiritual *point d'honneur,*" the "solemn complement" and the "general basis of consolation and justification." [H.T., xiii–xiv][7]

Merleau-Ponty's conclusion is that there are two quite distinct concepts of liberty, depending on their *use*:

> There is a liberty which is the insignia of a clan and already the slogan of a propaganda. . . . There is already a warlike attitude involved in democratic liberties taken as the sole criterion of judgment upon societies, or in democracies absolved of all the violence they perpetrate here and there because they recognize and at least internally practice the principles of liberty—in short, in liberty which has paradoxically become a principle of separation and pharisaism. [H.T., xliv–xlv]

Principles can function as alibis and liberty can function as an idol that legitimates oppression (H.T., xiv, xxiv).

The point is not to accuse the West in order to acquit communism. The difference is that whereas liberalism hides from itself behind its *lofty principles*, communism hides behind its own *good intentions*. Merleau-Ponty affirms those intentions as the one genuine humanism. But because Marxism itself rejects the notion that good intentions provide a justification for our actions (H.T., 28, 128), he insists that communists must give up "the alibi of good intentions" (H.T., 109; cf. 43, 62, 70). Revolutionary violence would be justified if in fact it tended to repress itself and to produce a classless society. But terror is not legitimized by the intention to produce the classless society, and the gap between communism's good intentions and its deeds becomes more and more conspicuous (H.T., xviii, xx–xxi). Just as Koestler keeps reminding his character, Rubashov, that his own theory will not let him plead the sincerity of his good intentions (H.T., 7, 9, 10, 33), so Merleau-Ponty keeps reminding contemporary communists that the Marxist is supposed to have "recognized the mystification involved in the inner life" and that "a policy cannot be justified by its good intentions" (H.T., 21, xxxiv). A terror that increases state power and militarism appeals to its good intentions in bad faith no less than a liberalism that appeals to its high principles to mask its institutionalized violence. Both pay attention to the abstractions that make them look good in order to forget the concrete experience of their victims.[8]

Merleau-Ponty practices the same ideology critique grounded in a hermeneutics of suspicion in his shorter, occasional essays. In 1947, for example (the year of *Humanism and Terror*), he responds to the "veritable stupor" into which François Mauriac says he was thrown by an editorial in *Les Temps Modernes* critical of French policy in Indochina (S., 323). In response to Mauriac's claim that the French had established a "beneficent civilization" out there, he asks why after eighty years they are still hated as enemies and accuses Mauriac of using morality as an alibi (S., 323–24). He finds it scandalous that

> a Christian should show himself so incapable of getting outside himself and his "ideas," and should refuse to see himself even for an instant through the eyes of others. The least revolutionary among us have understood once and for all through the Spanish Civil War and the German Occupation . . . what the great "ideas" of those in power mean for the oppressed. [S., 324]

Does Mauriac not see that his essay is "a moralizing cover for a violent solution . . . an article written to give us a good conscience and justify our power in Indochina . . . designed to put [people] to sleep" (S., 325)? He should listen to the Vietnamese, one of whom told Merleau-Ponty:

> Your system functions beautifully. You have your colonialists. And among your administrators, writers, and journalists, you have many men of good will. The former act, the latter speak and are the former's moral guarantee. Thus principles are saved—and colonization remains in fact just what it has always been. [S., 325]

In his 1949 essay on Machiavelli, Merleau-Ponty reminds us "that principles commit us to nothing, and that they may be adapted to any end" and that "principles applied in a suitable situation are instruments of oppression" (S., 219–20). Of course everyone is for freedom and justice. "What distinguishes them is the kind of men for whom liberty or justice is demanded, and with whom society is to be made—slaves or masters" (S., 220–21).

This means that there is a pure morality, an easy-going mood, a softness, even a humanism that can be catastrophically cruel (S., 211, 216). Machiavelli is right to insist that "values are necessary but not sufficient" for a humane politics; and Marx is wise to seek "a different base than the always equivocal one of principles" (S., 221–22). For there is a moralism that is "the pious dodge of those who turn their eyes and ours toward the heaven of principles in order to turn them away from what they are doing" (S., 223).

In his 1950 essay on the U.S.S.R. and the "labor camps," Merleau-Ponty bemoans "the ten million deported Soviet citizens, the stupidity, the panic of justifications. . . . We see very few men who let themselves be led by interest alone; they always provide themselves with convictions" (S., 265–66). So panicked are the justifications, in fact, that the Soviets are willing to borrow convictions from anywhere. There is, of course, their own humanist ideal, though in relation to today's communism these ideas "act more as its décor than its motive force" (S., 268). Then there are the nineteenth-century ideas that criminals are only blind and need enlightenment, reeducation rather than punishment, work therapy rather than righteous anger. "These innocent ideas become the height of cant and trickery when they adorn the camps where men are dying of work and hunger; when they conceal the repression of a harshly unequal society; when, under color of re-educating . . . it is a matter of breaking the opposition" (S., 267). Ultimately the panic leads to borrowing the capitalist idea that industrialization and increased productivity justify everything, so that "the best Communists are deaf to ten million prisoners" (S., 267–68).

Of course, it would be an equal but opposite bad faith for the West to use the legitimate critique of the camps to distract attention from its own "diffuse or concealed forms of slavery." Because a society is responsible for everything it produces, "Marx was right to reproach liberal thought, as for an accountable fraud, for the artifices by which it puts unemployment, colonial labor, and racial inequality beyond accountability" (S., 270–71). In such a context the self-righteous Western critique of the camps is just one more such artifice.[9]

By the time of *Adventures of the Dialectic* (1955), much has changed in Merleau-Ponty's politics. The "Marxist wait and see attitude" of *Humanism and Terror* has turned out to be a dream (A.D., 228–30). Now instead of challenging Soviet and liberal practice from the standpoint of Marxist theory, the latter itself is the subject of critique. Marxist theory cannot entirely wash its hands of Soviet practice. As he will write in 1960, Marxism retains "a real heuristic value, but it is certainly no longer true *in the sense it was believed to be true.*" It is "not simply the converse of truth but rather a truth that failed" (S., 9–10).

But Merleau-Ponty's politics retains its character as a hermeneutics of suspicion directed against both East and West. He bitterly complains about the false consciousness of both the "free world" (he uses italics) and communism. Their battle is not one between "free enterprise" and Marxism:

> Under the cover of philosophies that date back a century or
> two, the established politics are building something entirely dif-
> ferent. In the vices as in the virtues of the two systems there
> are so many geographical, historical, or political conditions
> which intervene that the philosophies they claim are clearly
> mere ornaments. If we want to abandon our daydreams, we
> must look at the *other thing* these ornaments are hiding and put
> ourselves in a state of methodical doubt in regard to them.
> [A.D., 225]

Thus on the right he finds liberalism disguising historically contingent choices as the very law or unalterable order of things themselves
(A.D., 9, 16: cf. 20–24, 32). This covering up of choices is not entirely
innocent. With reference to Weber's thesis about capitalism he writes:

> Ideology is never mystification completely unawares; it requires
> a great deal of complacency to justify the capitalistic world by
> means of Calvinistic principles; if these principles are fully ar-
> ticulated, they will expose the ruse of attempting to turn them
> to one's own purposes. The men of the past could not com-
> pletely hide the truth of their era from themselves; they did not
> need us in order to catch a glimpse of it. [A.D., 20]

But history outwits capitalism, which, by producing the proletariat
"makes evident *a contrario* the 'relations between persons' which are its
reality but which it is very careful to hide, even from itself" (A.D., 44).

Meanwhile on the left the communists do not see the mixture of
constraint and privilege in Soviet society "because their eyes are fixed on
the dialectic." Of course they place it in the future:

> It is the same thing to no longer believe in the dialectic and to
> put it in the future; but it is seen to be the same thing [only] by
> an external witness, who contents himself with the present, not
> by someone who commits the fraud and who lives already in his
> intended ends. The dialectic thus plays precisely the role of an
> ideology, helping communism to be something other than what
> it thinks it is. [A.D., 96][10]

Thus "communist ideology is deceitful, and we can ask the nature of the
regime which hides itself in the philosophy it teaches instead of expressing itself there" (A.D., 99).

Merleau-Ponty's Phenomenology of the Situated Subject

Merleau-Ponty's reluctant departure from Marxism drew him "increasingly away from the 'dream' of a homogeneous society" (Cooper, 133). His early political thought saw in the theory of the proletariat as the meaning of history "the humanist face of Marxism" (H.T., 118). History has not taken that turn, and perhaps it never will (H.T., 147, 155). Does that make Marxism utopian? No, "the Marxist attitude [remains] attractive, not only as moral criticism but also as an historical hypothesis" (H.T., 157). As moral criticism it provides an ongoing check against mystification and can discredit alternatives to the classless society even when it cannot shape history (H.T., 155, 153). And as a historical hypothesis it enables us to "preserve liberty while waiting for a fresh historical impulse which may allow us to engage in a popular movement without ambiguity" (H.T., xxiii).

The later politics of Merleau-Ponty sees this waiting to be wishful thinking, a hollow hope. The Marxist idea of a classless society must be relativized, because "there is no force in history which is destined to produce it" (S., 139). The very idea of a definitive end of history, of a revolution accomplished is a dangerous dream (A.D., 23–24, 39, 205–6). "Revolutions are true as movements and false as regimes" (A.D., 207). Nor is this an accident. For revolutions are useful only as long as they are self-critical, but violence is the end of self-criticism (A.D., 73, 90). A new political ideal grounded in a new philosophy becomes necessary. "The progress of socio-economic history, including its revolutions, is not so much a movement toward an homogenous or a classless society as the quest, through always atypical cultural devices, for a life which is not unlivable for the greatest number" (S., 131).

Given this backing off from the Marxist ideal and Merleau-Ponty's new appreciation for liberal institutions (by no means unqualified, as we have just seen), it is not surprising that Henri Lefebvre should complain, with reference to *Adventures of the Dialectic*, "The philosophy of ambiguity justifies the situation instead of denouncing it."[11] Because the concept of ambiguity is at least as characteristic of Merleau-Ponty's philosophy as of his politics, and because it is at least as characteristic of his early as of his later philosophy, Lefebvre's critique turns out to be a question directed less toward Merleau-Ponty's last political book than toward his philosophy as a whole. Is the philosophy of ambiguity, in either its early or its later version, a critical philosophy in any meaningful political sense? Yes, I want to suggest, but only minimally. Does it provide a coherent conceptual framework for the critical thrust of Merleau-Ponty's own (early and later) politics? No, at least not at its deepest level.

Merleau-Ponty's phenomenology of perception (later, vision) is a philosophy of ambiguity because of the way it treats traditional dualities. Here is a list, neither complete nor systematic, of those to which he gives considerable attention: soul or mind/body, spirit/matter, subject/object, self/world, consciousness/nature, for-itself/in-itself, *noesis/noema*, *naturans/naturata*, active/passive, self/other, sense/nonsense, personal/prepersonal or anonymous, visible/invisible, spoken/silent. Ambiguity results from the fact that, G. E. Moore to the contrary notwithstanding, none of these poles can be said to be what it is and not another thing. Just the opposite. Each of these moments turns out to be deeply implicated in its polar opposite, and vice versa. In a manner half Hegelian and half Derridean, Merleau-Ponty dialectically deconstructs each dichotomy so that opposites turn into one another and both pure identity and pure difference disappear. Nothing can be nailed down neatly. Ambiguity, thus defined, is common to *The Phenomenology of Perception* and *The Visible and the Invisible*. One can speak of a more radical ambiguity in the latter case insofar as the dualities are undermined more deeply. But as we turn from the body-subject to the narcissism of Being (V.I., 139–41; cf. 256), we do not leave ambiguity behind. We only intensify it.

It is as a philosophy of ambiguity that Merleau-Ponty's phenomenological ontology focuses on the situatedness of those who see and speak. From here, where I can see this side of the cube, I cannot see the other side. Of course I can move either the cube or myself so as to see the other side, but when I have seen all the sides the total "perception" I construct is just that, a construct never given in experience. Because the world is always around me and never simply before me (Ph.P., 395), my grasp of it is always perspectival and partial. At first this concept of situation as perceptual perspective seems innocent enough. But from Nietzsche to Gadamer to Thomas Nagel in *The View from Nowhere*, we have been reminded that this commonplace is not as philosophically innocent as it may at first seem.

We can distinguish three stages by which Merleau-Ponty radicalizes our reflection on perceiving a cube. First, there is the implication that there can be no pure and unconditioned acts of consciousness, for *prior* to any *Sinngebung*, any adoption of a thesis, the subject is *already* situated in and committed to a world of meanings it did not constitute (Ph.P., 355, 360, 423, 450, 453). Second, the world of meanings in which the subject is situated is both a natural and a cultural world (Ph.P., 84, 347, 358–65; Pr.P., 6). The perceiving self is both a body-subject and a social-subject, embedded in both biological and historical meanings. For Merleau-Ponty the point of existentialism is:

> To find a way of thinking about our condition. In the modern sense of the word, "existence" is the movement through which man is in the world and involves himself in a physical and social situation which then becomes his point of view on the world. . . . My involvement in nature and history is likewise a limitation of my view on the world and yet the only way for me to approach the world, know it, and do something in it. [S.N.S., 72; cf. 65][12]

The really decisive point, however, is the third one. Here we learn that the perceiving subject is not only to be unable to see all of the object; it is equally unable to see all of itself. For on Merleau-Ponty's account of situation, it is not just that the subject is in the world; it is equally true that the world is in the subject. "I am thrown into a nature, and that nature appears not only as outside me . . . but it is also discernible at the centre of subjectivity" (Ph.P., 346). Nature "finds its way to the core of my personal life" (Ph.P. 347). Sedimentation, habit, and the past fall on the subject side of the equation (Ph.P., 441–42). Geraets is right in saying that to the subjectifying of the world in Merleau-Ponty there corresponds a " 'mundanization' of the subject" (Madison, 282, Appendix I), which makes it possible for him to say, "Inside and outside are inseparable. The world is wholly inside and I am wholly outside myself" (Ph.P., 407).

This dialectical deconstruction of the dichotomy between subject and object is fatal to Cartesianism:

> [Its definitions] make matters perfectly clear both within and outside ourselves: we have the transparency of an object with no secret recesses, the transparency of a subject which is nothing but what it thinks it is. The object is an object through and through, and consciousness a consciousness through and through. [Ph.P., 198]

The inability neatly to distinguish subject from object means that, on the object side, we must abandon talk about "absolute being," "a world in itself," "a universe perfectly explicit in itself," "ready-made things," and "the world ready made" (Ph.P., 41, 96, 207–8).

On the other side of the not so great divide, the subject's inability to keep itself pure and unspotted from the world leads to the oft cited conclusion that "the most important lesson which the reduction teaches us is the impossibility of a complete reduction" (Ph.P., xiv). For the goal of the reduction is precisely to draw a clear boundary between subject and object. This project need not deny that "consciousness is *in the first place* not a matter of 'I think' but of 'I can' " (Ph.P., 137, emphasis added; cf. 147, 156–57). It needs only to affirm that in reflection consciousness can decontaminate itself, making possible a sharp distinction between transcendental ego as *naturans* or *noesis* and constituted object as *naturata* or *noema*. But the situatedness of consciousness means that the transcendental Ego is not only "not initially given" but also "never absolutely acquired" because "I can never say 'I' absolutely" and "every act of reflection, every voluntary taking up of a position is based on the ground and the proposition of a life of prepersonal consciousness" (Ph.P., 208; cf. 60–61). In dialogue with Hyppolite, Merleau-Ponty insists:

> Even though consciousness is able to detach itself from things
> to see itself, human consciousness never possesses itself in com-
> plete detachment. . . . There is not one of our ideas or one of
> our reflexions which does not carry a date, whose objective re-
> ality exhausts its formal reality, or which transcends time.
> [Pr.P., 40–41][13]

Thus the cogito, the transcendental unity of apperception, the coincidence of the "I think" and the "I am" are always a task and a promissory note, never something given or achieved (Ph.P., 344, 406). Just as we do not enter the world through judgment, so we do not escape it through reflection. We are, as it were, its Siamese twin.

Merleau-Ponty reaffirms the significance of situatedness in his later philosophy:

> Philosophy is not science, because science believes it can soar
> over its object and holds the correlation of knowledge with be-
> ing as established, whereas philosophy is the set of questions
> wherein he who questions is himself implicated by the ques-
> tion. But a physics that has learned to situate the physicist
> physically, a psychology that has learned to situate the psychol-
> ogist in the socio-historical world, have lost the illusion of the
> absolute view from above: they do not only tolerate, they en-
> join a radical examination of our belongingness to the world
> before all science. [V.I., 27; cf. 92, 117]

If it can be justly said that in his later philosophy he "recognizes that the notion of situation . . . is not, as a matter of fact, an ultimate notion" (Madison, 257), this does not mean that he abandons the notion but rather that he seeks to radicalize it. It is as if, having situated our perception and a fortiori our speech and thought in the world of nature and of culture, he now seeks to situate our situatedness itself within the horizon of Being or flesh (V.I., 127–28, 147–49, 153, 185).

This radicalizing occurs in two ways, by deepening the analysis of our situatedness and by broadening the conclusions drawn from this analysis. The deepening occurs primarily through detailed attention to two themes already present in *The Phenomenology of Perception*, the passivity that underlies the activities of experience and the anonymity or prepersonal horizon that surrounds and grounds personal experience.[14] First the primacy of Being is affirmed and with it the passive character of perception, language, and thought in general, illustrated by the musician, the poet, and the painter, and implicating above all the philosopher. Then this very passivity is seen to have as its flip side the anonymity at the heart of the personal (V.I., 139, 142, 155).

The broadening of conclusions concerns the impossibility of the Husserlian reduction. Inasmuch as perception and thought are the passive acts of anonymous persons in whom the world inheres, not only prephilosophical experience (V.I., 109–15, 153) but also philosophical reflection is destined to an ambiguity without neat distinctions (V.I., 33, 39, 43–44). This means that "the incompleteness of the reduction . . . is not an obstacle to the reduction, it is the reduction itself" (V.I., 178; cf. 172).[15]

We cannot read this as merely a repetition of the Husserlian revisionism and existential phenomenology of his famous 1945 Preface. The distinction between subject and object has been undermined so thoroughly (V.I., 22–23, 28–29, 130–31, 167, 174, 185) that the very concept of intentionality must be replaced with that of transcendence (V.I., 210, 244).[16] This is what he means when he writes, "The problems posed in [*The Phenomenology of Perception*] are insoluble because I start there from the 'consciousness'-'object' distinction" (V.I., 200; cf. 183 and P.H., 69–70), thereby agreeing, as often noted, with the 1946 charge of Beaufret:

> The only reproach I would make to the author is not that he
> has gone "too far," but rather that he has not been sufficiently
> radical. The phenomenological descriptions which he uses in
> fact maintain the vocabulary of idealism. . . . But the whole
> problem is precisely to know whether phenomenology, fully de-
> veloped, does not require the abandonment of subjectivity, and
> the vocabulary of subjective idealism as, beginning with Hus-
> serl, Heidegger has done. [Pr.P., 41–42]

The Political Significance of Merleau-Ponty's Philosophy

It is time to return to the question with which the previous section began, whether Merleau-Ponty's phenomenological ontology in either its early or later and more radical version can be the basis for a critical politics or whether, as Lefebvre suggests, his philosophy of ambiguity or experiential situatedness "justifies the [political] situation instead of denouncing it." We hear in this charge an echo of Marx's charge that in Hegel and Feuerbach idealism and materialism interpret the world differently but do not change it. There is perhaps more agreement than disagreement with Lefebvre (at least about Merleau-Ponty's philosophy) when Madison suggests that, as part of the skeptical, humanist countertradition in philosophy, it leads its author quite naturally to a final peace with liberalism (Madison, Appendix II).[17] My own thesis is that while Merleau-Ponty's philosophy has some political bite, it falls short of what is best in Merleau-Ponty's own early and late politics by failing to ground a hermeneutics of suspicion.

While reflecting on the possibility of subjectivity, Merleau-Ponty tells us there can be "no purely philosophical politics, for example, no philosophical rigorism, when it is a question of a Manifesto" (V.I., 266). What he here calls rigorism he usually designates as dogmatism. Just as his philosophy of the situated subject seeks to discredit the dogmatism of empiricism and intellectualism in *The Phenomenology of Perception*, so his politics employs the same concepts to undermine dogmatic Marxism and dogmatic liberalism. His stubborn refusal to accept either the either/or of empiricism/intellectualism or the either/or of communism/anticommunism has a common ground in his situational critique of dogmatism.

In *Humanism and Terror*, for example, he seeks to undercut the dogmatism of cold warriors on both sides by invoking a constant return from theory to the life-world of concrete experience. For theory becomes dogmatic precisely by abstracting from life as real people live it. The specific purpose is threefold: (1) to focus the discussion of violence on violence as experienced by its victims, (2) to point to the ambiguity of political decision, rarely if ever an absolute choice between good and evil, and (3) to highlight the openness of universal history, which leaves the facts not yet univocal and a total viewpoint always out of reach.[18] A similar battle between situation and dogma takes place in *Adventures of the Dialectic*.

The situational critique of political dogmatism, whether on the left or on the right, seems to me to be the extent of the political impact of Merleau-Ponty's philosophy. It is not unimportant but it does not seem to me to go very far. For, in the first place, it does nothing to illumine the dynamic of false consciousness and demystification, which we have already found to be the heart of both his early and late politics. In the second place, it does not even do justice to his critique of dogmatism. For the political dogmatisms of communism and anticommunism are *motivated* in a way in which the philosophical dogmatisms of empiricism and intellectualism are not. As the former move from the concrete to the abstract, their *forgetting* is *refusal* in a strong sense. For the purpose (subjective) and function (objective) of the theories in question is to hide the experience of each system's victims in order to justify the violence it uses to enforce domination and privilege.[19] Situational analysis shows why dogmatism is not viable. But it cannot show, as Merleau-Ponty himself does in his political writings, why it is such a vital part of political life—that is, why it is so badly needed and how it functions as willful truth in the service of the will to power.

For Merleau-Ponty the struggle to dedogmatize political discourse is but a moment in the more fundamental project of demystifying it. The critical element in his politics does not come from his philosophy of ambiguity, for its political significance requires a hermeneutics of suspicion to bring it to fruition. Nor does it come from the Marxist ideal of a classless society, for as both his early and his late political writings show, that ideal apart from the critique made possible by a hermeneutics of suspicion provides no reliable political guidance. As the initial analysis of the first section above indicates, the heart and soul of Merleau-Ponty's politics is the hermeneutics of suspicion.

The question of the relation of his philosophy to his politics can only be the question whether his phenomenology of perception and his ontology of vision provide a philosophical rationale for the hermeneutics of suspicion. My thesis is that they do not, and that the orientation to perception is the reason this is so.

Contemporary philosophy on both sides of the Atlantic has largely been:

> A critique of the *sovereign rational subject*—atomistic and autonomous, disengaged and disembodied, and, at least on some views [including Husserl's], potentially and ideally self-transparent. . . . In short, the epistemological and moral subject has been definitively decentered.[20]

That Merleau-Ponty has contributed significantly to this decentering is beyond question. But precisely how? With reference to Marx, Nietzsche, and Freud, along with Darwin, Wittgenstein, and Heidegger, the editors just quoted mention five elements of this decentering of the subject: (1) the unconscious, (2) the preconceptual, (3) the irrational in the mode of desire and the will to power, (4) the social, historical, and cultural shape of consciousness, and (5) the embodied and engaged mode of the subject's being in the world. It is worth noting that while the first and third of these have played the largest part in developing the hermeneutics of suspicion, it is the other three that figure most prominently in Merleau-Ponty.

We best see his relation to the hermeneutics of suspicion by examining his relation to psychoanalysis and the unconscious. His early writings describe the positive relation between phenomenology and psychoanalysis in terms of the triumph of meaning over causality in understanding human behavior (Ph.P., 158). This is important, but clearly not strong enough. In 1960 he describes a closer affinity: "It is by what phenomenology implies or unveils as its limits—by its *latent content* or its *unconscious*—that it is in consonance with psychoanalysis. . . . Phenomenology and psychoanalysis are not parallel; much better, they are both aiming toward the same *latency*" (P.H., 71). I think this claim is fundamentally mistaken. Merleau-Ponty shares with psychoanalysis only a generic critique of subjectivity. What is decisive for him is dependence and ambiguity; what is decisive for a Freudian hermeneutic is self-deception and ambivalence.[21] Dorothea Olkowski rightly senses a tendency in Merleau-Ponty to identify the unconscious with the ambiguous, and J. B. Pontalis rightly sees this tendency as reductive and regressive.[22] For what gets left out in such accounts is what is utterly crucial for Freud, repression and resistance, the *motivated activity* of the subject in hiding facets of itself from itself.

In *The Structure of Behavior* we read "that there is repression when integration has been achieved only in appearance and leaves certain relatively isolated systems subsisting in behavior which the subject refuses both to transform and to assume" (S.B., 177). Since this notion of refusal is important in Merleau-Ponty's political critique of false consciousness, we look for some account of it. But virtually in vain. We find only reference to "a fragmented life of consciousness which does not possess a unique significance at all times" and to "the ambivalence of immediate consciousness" (S.B., 178–79). So little is he interested in exploring the structure of this fragmentation and ambivalence that he leaves them entirely undeveloped and a bit later is content to write:

> It has been said that what is called unconsciousness is only an
> inapperceived signification: it may happen that we ourselves do
> not grasp the true meaning of our life, not because an uncon-

> scious personality is deep within us and governs our actions,
> but because we understand our lived states only through an
> idea which is not adequate for them. [S.B., 220–21]

Instead of exploring the earlier hints about the source of this inadequacy of self-knowledge, he drops the question of motivation entirely. In Merleau-Ponty's politics forgetting is an act of refusal. In his philosophy he forgets that he has mentioned refusal.

In *Phenomenology of Perception* we get no more help in developing a hermeneutics of suspicion. Objectivism is treated as a prejudice that permits consciousness "to forget its own phenomena" and as an obsession whose forgetfulness can be described as repression (Ph.P., 58, 70). But an analysis that would support this Nietzschean and Freudian language is not to be found. We are reminded of Stekel's understanding of frigidity as refusal, of Freudianism's concern with psychological motives in the realm of meanings rather than mechanical causes, of neurotic forgetfulness as an act in which "I keep the memory at arm's length, as I look past a person whom I do not wish to see," and of aphonia and anorexia as acts of refusal that can be described as hypocrisy, bad faith, or self-deception (Ph.P., 158–64). But if we look for a phenomenological account of these activities by which we hide ourselves from ourselves, we find only the denial that they are voluntary (which Merleau-Ponty strangely seems to identify with deliberate choice). Instead of a phenomenology of the will, which seems to be called for here, we hear only that such self-deception "is part of the human lot" (Ph.P., 162–63).

The famous footnote on historical materialism is equally disappointing (Ph.P., 171–73). With help from the base-superstructure metaphor, historical materialism calls attention to the role of theories of various sorts in legitimizing political and economic domination (cf. note 7 above). Merleau-Ponty's politics highlights the mystification (of self and of others, too) involved in the theorizing (propaganda) of both left and right. But his footnote talks only about the dialectical, holistic relation that the theory posits between economic and other factors of historical change. And the parallel with Freud is only that he "expands" the notion of sex in the same way that Marx expands the notion of economics. On the topic of motivated self-deception there is a curious silence.

Against this background, Merleau-Ponty's account of false love is not surprising, though it remains puzzling. He knows about a deceitful love in which "I conspired with myself to avoid asking the question in order to avoid receiving the reply which was already known to me" because "there was never even a semblance of love, and never for a moment did I believe that my life was committed to that feeling" (Ph.P.,

378). This conspiring with myself to avoid noticing something of which I am fully aware is just the kind of phenomenon whose careful analysis would throw great light on the key element of Merleau-Ponty's political criticism. But he mentions it only to distinguish it from another phenomenon to which he does give a subtle and powerful analysis. In false love I persuade myself, mistakenly, that I am in love, not in spite of knowing to the contrary, but precisely because I do not know that I am not in love. In my immaturity and inexperience I mistake a superficial excitement for the real thing:

> [Merleau-Ponty draws a parallel with] the criminal [who] fails
> to see his crime, and the traitor his betrayal for what they are,
> not because they exist deeply embedded within him as uncon-
> scious representations or tendencies, but because they are so
> many relatively closed worlds, so many situations. If we are in a
> situation, we are circumvented and cannot be transparent to
> ourselves, so that our contact with ourselves is necessarily
> achieved only in the sphere of ambiguity. [Ph.P., 381]

Clearly the parallel is badly drawn. What would illumine the false consciousness of the criminal and the traitor is the inner conspiracy (inner hypocrisy) of deceitful love, about which Merleau-Ponty has nothing to say.

What Merleau-Ponty tries to give us is a reinterpretation of the unconscious without repression. Either he leaves the latter out entirely or he deprives the idea of what gives it its Freudian force, as in the following passage:

> The lived is certainly lived by me, nor am I ignorant of the feel-
> ings which I repress, and in this sense there is no unconscious.
> But I can experience more things than I represent to myself,
> and my being is not reducible to what expressly appears to me
> concerning myself. That which is merely lived is ambivalent
> [does he not mean ambiguous?]; there are feelings in me which
> I do not name, and also spurious states of well-being to which I
> am not fully given over. [Ph.P., 296]

Here he speaks of repression and ambivalence, but the voice is Jacob's and not Esau's (Gen. 27:22). These terms add nothing identifiable to the notion that I experience more than I can represent to myself. Such a formula expresses admirably what *Phenomenology of Perception* has to say about Freud and the unconscious, but it fails to do justice either to Freud or to Merleau-Ponty's own politics.

We have seen that the late Merleau-Ponty radicalizes his philosophy of situated subjectivity to the point of questioning or at least relativizing the very concept of the subject. Now we can see that in doing so he moves even further away from the hermeneutics of suspicion called for by his politics. He does not think so. He talks as if moving away from Husserl's Cartesianism is automatically to move in Freud's direction, meaning that as his phenomenology becomes increasingly an archeology it moves closer to Freud. It is in this context that he makes the claim cited above that phenomenology and psychoanalysis seek the same latency (P.H., 70–71).

This would be true only if Freud's concept of the latent were but a generic name for anything that resists the Cartesian clarity of consciousness. But it is tied too tightly to specific notions of repression and ambivalence for this to be the case; and these notions are conspicuously absent from the late Merleau-Ponty. For him the latent is the invisible of a radicalized phenomenology of perception, the *fungierende* intentionality of a radicalized philosophy of situation (S., 20–21; V.I., 136, 244; cf. 238). Both of these themes belong to the analysis of the anonymity, passivity, and horizonal character of experience sketched above. As such they have their home in a philosophy of ambiguity, not one of ambivalence. Where the unconscious is reinterpreted as the invisible, it is reduced, from the Freudian standpoint, to signifying those sedimented meanings that are never themselves an object but make the experience of objects possible (V.I., 180).

That the archeological turn of the late Merleau-Ponty is a turn away from rather than toward Freud and the hermeneutics of suspicion is most clearly and decisively expressed in one of its most insistent themes. Merleau-Ponty repeats again and again that the invisible he seeks to elicit is not contingently invisible, not something that is not visible now but might be later. It is intrinsically invisible as the condition of the possibility of the visible (V.I., 150, 215–17, 227–29, 247–48, 251, 254, 257). To try to render the invisible visible would be as foolish as to try to look at the edge of my field of vision. But it is characteristic of every theory of false consciousness that what I hide from myself can be brought to light, recognized, and acknowledged. The unconscious is not the preconscious that can be brought to presence at will. There is resistance. But resistance is not necessity. It can be overcome. Freud can, for example, discover and acknowledge his hatred of his father, and the conservative can come to recognize the ideological character of economic "science."

I have argued that Merleau-Ponty's philosophy is one of situation and ambiguity, though his politics calls for a philosophy of suspicion and ambivalence. Why is this so? We might say that it is because he is insufficiently Hegelian. Hegel's *Phenomenology of Spirit* begins as a phenomenology of perception. But its first major transition (from Consciousness to Self-Consciousness) is not just a move from subjectivity to intersubjectivity, but simultaneously from pure cognition to desire. This generates a philosophy of spirit with a political significance lacking in Merleau-Ponty's philosophy of spirit (intersubjectivity, language, history, and so forth). If Merleau-Ponty's self-criticism that his early work was too tied to a consciousness-object framework had had a Hegelian rather than a Heideggerian thrust to it, his own development might well have more nearly recapitulated the former's transition from theory to practice, cognition to action, which puts philosophy in touch with the political.[23] By contrast, the philosophy that moves from being-in-the-world to Being as its ground (and abyss), first in Heidegger and then in Merleau-Ponty, is esthetically but not politically fruitful.

So we might say that Merleau-Ponty is insufficiently Hegelian to do justice to what is deepest in his own politics. But I think we will be closer to the heart of the matter if we say that he is insufficiently Kierkegaardian. We read in *The Sickness Unto Death* that "the self is a relation that relates itself to itself."[24] It is a relation because it is dialectically dipolar in terms of such categories as temporal/eternal, finite/infinite, necessity/freedom, outer/inner, body/soul, and so forth. Like Merleau-Ponty, Kierkegaard seeks to undercut any dualistic interpretation of these polarities that would give independent identity to one moment vis-à-vis the other.[25]

But the key to Kierkegaard's account is that the self that is constituted by these relations also relates itself to itself. Though the self is a grounded self and thus constituted before it does any constituting, by virtue of its relation to itself its activity possesses a freedom and responsibility that give it a genuinely ethical character. The same self-relation creates the possibility of ambivalence and self-deception, and it is in *The Sickness Unto Death* that Kierkegaard most fully develops the hermeneutics of suspicion, which is the key to his own politics.[26]

Kierkegaard seems to have Augustine in mind:

> But you, Lord, while [Ponticianus] was speaking, were turning me around so that I could see myself; you took me from behind my own back, which was where I had put myself during the time when I did not want to be observed by myself, and you set me in front of my own face, so that I could see how foul a sight I was. . . . I had nowhere to go to escape from myself. If I tried to look away from myself, Ponticianus still went

on with his story, and again you were setting me in front of
myself, forcing me to look into my own face, so that I might
see my sin and hate it. I did know it, but I pretended that I did
not. I had been pushing the whole idea away from me and forgetting it. [*Confessions*, VIII, 7, Warner translation]

In the Pine-Coffin translation two of the key sentences read as follows:
"For I had placed myself behind my own back, refusing to see myself.
. . . I had turned a blind eye and forgotten it."

It is just this kind of self-relation in bad faith that is crucial to
Kierkegaard's analysis. Here metaphors of perception are used, but the
provenance of this phenomenon is plainly not sense experience. There is
a blindness here, but it is not the inevitable blindness of the *punctum
caecum*, which expresses the invisible for Merleau-Ponty. The analysis of
self-deception requires that we surpass our phenomenology of perception with an equally sophisticated phenomenology of desire and of the
will.[27] But for Merleau-Ponty the primacy of perception is also the ulti-
macy of perception, and he never makes this move. In his flight from the
transparent self of Husserl's Cartesianism, he also leaves behind Kierkegaard's self-relating self, throwing out the baby with the bathwater.
From the point of view of his politics, his philosophy is not too much
given over to subjectivity, but insufficiently subjective (since not every
inwardness is Cartesian). His politics does not suffer. It simply helps itself to the kind of subjectivity it needs. But his philosophy, like Aristotle's, remains at a somewhat awkward distance from his politics.

Notes on Contributors

Co-Editors:

Galen A. Johnson is professor of philosophy at the University of Rhode Island and author of *Earth and Sky, History and Philosophy: Island Images Inspired by Husserl and Merleau-Ponty* (1989).

Michael B. Smith is associate professor of French at Berry College, Georgia, and author of articles on Merleau-Ponty's philosophy in *Les Etudes philosophiques* and *Phenomenology and Pedagogy*. His translation of Michel de Certeau's *La Fable mystique* will appear in 1991 (University of Chicago Press).

Contributors:

Robert Bernasconi is Moss Professor of Philosophy at Memphis State University and author of *The Question of Language in Heidegger's History of Being* (1985), as well as a number of essays on continental philosophy and the history of social thought. He is currently writing a book, *Between Levinas and Derrida*.

Patrick Burke is associate professor of philosophy at Seattle University and is author of a forthcoming volume entitled *Beyond Phenomenology, Toward an Ontology of Presence: Self-Critique and Transfiguration in the Thought of the Later Merleau-Ponty* (Phaenomenologica of the Husserl Archives).

M. C. Dillon is professor of philosophy at State University of New York at Binghamton, and author of *Merleau-Ponty's Ontology* (1988).

Joseph C. Flay is professor of philosophy at Pennsylvania State University and author of *Hegel's Quest for Certainty* (1984).

Wayne J. Froman is chairman of the Department of Philosophy and Religious Studies at George Mason University and author of *Merleau-Ponty: Language and the Act of Speech* (1982).

Monika Langer is associate professor of philosophy at the University of Victoria, British Columbia, and author of *Merleau-Ponty's Phenomenology of Perception: A Guide and Commentary* (1989).

Claude Lefort teaches at the Ecole des Hautes Etudes en Sciences Sociales, Centre d'Etudes Transdisciplinaires: Sociologie, Anthropologie, Politique, in Paris. In addition to editing Merleau-Ponty's posthumous *Le Visible et l'Invisible* (1964) and *La Prose du monde* (1969), among his most important books are *Le Travail de l'oeuvre: Machiavel* (1972), *Les Formes de l'histoire* (1978), *Sur une colonne absente: écrits autour de Merleau-Ponty* (1978), and *L'Invention démocratique: les limites de la domination totalitaire* (1981). An English translation of selected writings by Prof. Lefort has been edited by John B. Thompson, *The Political Forms of Modern Society* (1986).

David Michael Levin is professor of philosophy at Northwestern University and is author of *The Body's Recollection of Being* (1985), *The Opening of Vision* (1988), and *The Listening Self* (1989), as well as editor of *Pathologies of the Modern Self* (1987).

Emmanuel Levinas, born in Lithuania in 1906, studied philosophy in Strasbourg from 1923 to 1930 (with a stay in Fribourg 1928–29, at which time he studied under Husserl and Heidegger). Naturalized a French citizen in 1930, Levinas has taught philosophy at the University of Poitiers, Paris-Nanterre, and Paris-Sorbonne. Levinas's own, original metaphysics finds its fullest expression in his two major works, *Totalité et infini* (1961) and *Autrement qu'être ou au-delà de l'essence* (1974). He has devoted numerous other books and essays to aspects of phenomenology, ethics, and Judaism (e.g., *Difficile liberté* and *Quatre lectures talmudiques*). Alphonso Lingis has prepared an English translation of selected pieces, *Collected Philosophical Papers of Emmanuel Levinas* (1986).

Gary Brent Madison is professor of philosophy at McMaster University and University of Toronto and is author of *The Phenomenology of Merleau-Ponty* (1981), *Understanding: A Phenomenological-Pragmatic Analysis* (1982), and *The Hermeneutics of Postmodernity* (1988).

Hugh J. Silverman is professor of philosophy and comparative literature at State University of New York at Stony Brook and is author of *Inscriptions: Between Phenomenology and Structuralism* (1987), as well as translator of Merleau-Ponty's lecture courses *Consciousness and the Acquisition of Language* (1973) and "Philosophy and Non-Philosophy Since Hegel" (1976), and editor of numerous collections in continental philosophy including *Philosophy and Non-Philosophy Since Merleau-Ponty* (1988).

Stephen Watson is associate professor of philosophy at the University of Notre Dame and has published widely in recent French philosophy. He is especially interested in poststructuralist thought.

Merold Westphal is professor of philosophy at Fordham University and author of *History and Truth in Hegel's Phenomenology* (1979) and *Kierkegaard's Critique of Reason and Society* (1987).

Notes

Introduction
Galen A. Johnson, Alterity as a Reversibility

[1] See Mark C. Taylor, *Altarity* (Chicago: University of Chicago Press, 1987), pp. xxviii–xxix.

Chapter 1
Claude Lefort, Flesh and Otherness

[1] Prof. Lefort's paper was originally presented as a lecture before the Merleau-Ponty Circle on Friday, September 18, 1987, at the University of Rhode Island. It was subsequently transcribed, then edited and revised by Prof. Lefort.—Editor

[2] A mention of reversibility in relation to history occurs without elaboration in Merleau-Ponty's opening definition of dialectics in the epilogue to A.D., 203–4; *A.D.*, 297–98. It is striking that several of the descriptions of reversibility that occur in V.I. are foreshadowed in this text: reciprocal action, inside and outside, and perpetual genesis.—Editor

Chapter 2
M. C. Dillon, *Écart:* Reply to Claude Lefort's "Flesh and Otherness"

[1] Numbers in parentheses refer to pages of "Flesh and Otherness" by Claude Lefort, published as chapter 1 of the present book.

[2] This text (and the other one to which I shall refer shortly) should be read in the context of the chapter "Other People and the Human World" from *Phenomenology of Perception*.

[3] "Merleau-Ponty and the Psychogenesis of the Self," *Journal of Phenomenological Psychology*, 9/ 1–2 (Fall 1978).

4 " . . . The image in the mirror prepares me for another still more serious alienation, which will be the alienation by others" (C.R.O., 136). " . . . This alienation of the immediate *me*, its 'confiscation' for the benefit of the *me* that is visible in the mirror, already outlines what will be the 'confiscation' of the subject by the others who look at him" (C.R.O., 137).

5 " . . . The image I have of my body by means of the sense of touch or of cenesthesia . . . we shall call the 'introceptive image' of my own body" (C.R.O., 115). Merleau-Ponty describes cenesthesia (which is to be kept distinct from "synesthesia") as "the mass of sensations that would express to the subject the state of his different organs and different bodily functions" (C.R.O., 114). In introceptivity, the experience of the world is reduced to firsthand experience of states of one's own body; in other words, the transcendence of the world and others is not experienced as such. The idea is roughly equivalent to Husserl's notion of the *Eigensphäre* (or sphere of ownness) in which there is no sense of otherness.

6 "To the extent that [the infant] lacks [a] visual consciousness of his body, he cannot separate what he lives from what others live as well as what he sees them living. Thence comes the phenomenon of 'transitivism,' i.e., the absence of a division between myself and others that is the foundation of syncretic sociability" (C.R.O., 135). Syncretism may be understood as a quality of experience characterized by an indistinction of perspectives.

7 There are, however, some passages that are difficult to reconcile with Lefort's interpretation. Here is one that is given particular stress in the course notes: *"Within this whole analysis, we will emphasize that the perception of other people is the perception of a freedom which appears through a situation"* (T.E.O., 57). This might be taken as definitive because the one aspect of the otherness of the other that resists being subsumed under the heading of immanent projection is the other's freedom. The other's freedom is that which grounds his ability to surprise, disappoint, threaten, or otherwise contest my projections: the transcendence of the other is revealed above all in the freedom manifest in his behavior.

8 "Merleau-Ponty and the Reversibility Thesis," *Man and World*, vol. 16, 1983. I should note here that the structure of reversibility sustains a series of vicissitudes as it manifests itself in different domains. Thus, for example, the reversibility of one hand touching the other is different from the reversibility of self and other—the former occurs within the singularity of one body, and the latter occurs across separate bodies (but within the unity of a single world). Other instances of reversibility (e.g., the reversibility of world-language relations) differ from these two. The isomorphism of reversibility in all its vicissitudes forms a unity by analogy. In sum, the general structure of reversibility, flesh folding back upon itself, must be modified to account for the fact that flesh is an adverbial "manner of being" and not a substance. Merleau-Ponty's ontology should not be construed as a monism.

9 "We have to wonder whether the world that Merleau-Ponty explored was not an already tamed world rather than that wild experience to which he wanted to give expression" (Lefort, 11). Here is Merleau-Ponty's response to Lefort's question.

[10] "A baby of fifteen months opens its mouth if I playfully take one of its fingers between my teeth and pretend to bite it. . . . 'Biting' has immediately, for it, an intersubjective significance. It perceives its intentions in its body, and my body with its own, and thereby my intentions in its own body" (Ph.P., 352). As this well-known text shows, the infant—at least by fifteen months of age—is not hermetically closed within the domain of cenesthesia, but manifests the movements of reversibility.

[11] This phrase—"the self's own other"—is intended to refer, not only to the body's objectivity to itself, but also to the other aspects of individual existence that remain opaque to firsthand knowledge and are usually collected under the rubric of the unconscious: the archaisms of my individual and racial past, the ekstasis of prereflective experience, and so forth.

[12] " . . . Every reflection is after the model of the reflection of the hand touching by the hand touched" (V.I., 204).

[13] See my *Merleau-Ponty's Ontology* (Bloomington: Indiana University Press, 1988), II, 7 ("Intersubjectivity") and III, 10, iv ("Reference and Truth") for my account of the development of this thought.

[14] Be that transcendental subject conceived as consciousness, *Geist*, or Language as the blind agency of history.

Chapter 3
Gary Brent Madison, Flesh as Otherness

[Quotations from English translations of Merleau-Ponty are sometimes altered slightly, in order better to capture what I take to be the spirit of the original.]

[1] " . . . as upon two mirrors facing one another where two indefinite series of images set in one another arise which belong really to neither of the two surfaces, since each is only the rejoinder of the other, and which therefore form a couple, a couple more real than either of them" (V.I., 139).

[2] See Lefort, "Flesh and Otherness," esp. 3, 8.

[3] See Dillon, "Écart," 14–17. According to Dillon: "Lefort sees reversibility as a relationship of two terms—sensible and sentience, visibility and vision, outside and inside, etc.—that doubles back on itself, and he sees otherness as requiring a third term" (Dillon, 14). I agree 100 percent with Dillon when he says: "But the body, as flesh, is the inside of the outside; that is, the Flesh of the world is the same as the flesh of the body, it is the outside of the inside; the circuit is closed within Flesh, within the relation of Flesh to itself, within its self-sameness" (Dillon, 15).

[4] See Edmund Husserl, *Cartesian Meditations* (The Hague: Martinus Nijhoff, 1960), 157.

[5] Saint Augustine, *Confessions*, III, 6 (Pine-Coffin trans.).

[6] "French philosophy was born when Descartes undertook to reply, in French, to Montaigne's *Essays* with his *Discourse on Method*" (Vincent Descombes, *Modern French Philosophy* [Cambridge: Cambridge University Press, 1980], 1).

[7] As Merleau-Ponty observes, the "discovery" of subjectivity by modern phi-

losophy was more in the order of a *creation*: "And why 'discovery'? Are we to believe then that subjectivity existed before the philosophers, exactly as they were subsequently to understand it? Consciousness is either unaware of its origins or, if it wants to reach them, it can only project itself into them. In neither case should we speak of 'discovery.' Reflection has not only unveiled the unreflected, it has changed it, if only into its truth. Subjectivity was not waiting for philosophers as an unknown America waited for its explorers in the ocean's mists. They constructed, created it, and, in more than one way, and [Merleau-Ponty adds] what they have done ought perhaps to be undone." See "The Discovery of Subjectivity" in "Everywhere and Nowhere" in S., 152–53.

8 See "Merleau-Ponty and the Counter-Tradition," appendix to my study, *The Phenomenology of Merleau-Ponty* (Athens: Ohio University Press, 1981), as well as my essay "Merleau-Ponty and Postmodernity" in *The Hermeneutics of Postmodernity: Figures and Themes* (Bloomington: Indiana University Press, 1988).

9 As I have argued in my book, *The Phenomenology of Merleau-Ponty*, and as the book's subtitle ("A Search for the Limits of Consciousness") is meant to suggest.

10 Augustine does not describe his longtime friend, Nebridius, as *his* alter ego; he describes *himself* as Nebridius's "second self" (*Confessions*, IV, 6). What Augustine really is in himself is the other of his own self's other. Compare with Merleau-Ponty: "Why am I myself? How old am I really? Am I really alone to be me? Have I not somewhere a double, a twin? . . . Every question, even that of simple cognition, is part of the central question that is ourselves, of that appeal for totality to which no objective being answers" (V.I., 104).

11 In a paragraph in which he discusses the phenomenon of reversibility, Merleau-Ponty says: "my activity is equally passivity . . . so that seer and the seen reciprocate one another and we no longer know which sees and which is seen" (V.I., 139).

12 See Augustine, *Confessions*, X, 9, 16: "I cannot understand all that I am. This means, then, that the mind is too narrow to contain itself entirely. But where is that part of it which it does not itself contain? Is it somewhere outside itself and not within it? How, then, can it be part of it, if it is not contained in it? I am lost in wonder when I consider this problem. It bewilders me . . . O Lord, I am working hard in this field, and the field of my labours is my own self. I have become a problem to myself, like land which a farmer works only with difficulty and at the cost of much sweat."

Chapter 4
David Michael Levin, Justice in the Flesh

1 This paper is an abbreviated and revised version of the paper I read in September 1987 at the Merleau-Ponty Conference held on the campus of the University of Rhode Island. I want to thank Eugene Gendlin and Joel Kovel for their very helpful comments, making it a much better paper than it otherwise would be. The original paper was entitled "Visions of Narcissism: Descartes, Freud, Lacan, Merleau-Ponty." It has subsequently been rewritten and will soon appear

under the title "Visions of Narcissism . . . " in a collection of essays on Merleau-Ponty edited by Martin Dillon and published by the State University of New York Press.

[2] Readers skeptical about my interpretation of the "sense of justice" should see Pierre Bourdieu, *Outline of a Theory of Practice* (Cambridge University Press, 1977), p. 124. Although, curiously, Bourdieu does not explicitly mention the sense of justice, his concept of *habitus*, a concept he defines with rigor and uses to great effect, obviously can be understood to include it without any difficulty. *Habitus*, he says, is "a principle generating and unifying all practices, the system of inseparably cognitive and evaluative structures which organizes the vision of the world in accordance with the objective structures of a determinate state of the social world: with . . . all its *senses*, that is to say, not only the traditional five senses . . . but also the sense of necessity and the sense of duty, the sense of direction and the sense of reality, the sense of balance and the sense of beauty, common sense and the sense of the sacred, tactical sense and the sense of responsibility, business sense and the sense of propriety, the sense of humor and the sense of absurdity, moral sense and the sense of practicality, and so on."

[3] Walter Benjamin, "Surrealism," in *Reflections: Essays, Aphorisms, Autobiographical Writings*, Peter Demetz, ed. (New York: Schocken, 1986).

[4] I am making use, here, of Heidegger's etymological interpretation of *logos* (noun) and *legein* (verb), according to which the root meaning is: to lay out (or lay down) and gather.

[5] See Michel Foucault, "The Subject and Power," in *Michel Foucault: Beyond Structuralism and Hermeneutics*, H. Dreyfus and P. Rabinow, eds. (Chicago: University of Chicago Press, 1982).

[6] For more on reversibility as condition of the possibility of justice, see John Rawls, *A Theory of Justice* (Cambridge: Harvard University Press, 1971) and Lawrence Kohlberg, *Essays in Moral Development*, vol. 1: *The Philosophy of Moral Development* (New York: Harper & Row, 1981).

[7] For more elaboration on this subject, see the chapters on the "body politic" in my trilogy: *The Body's Recollection of Being* (London and Boston: Routledge & Kegan Paul, 1985); *The Opening of Vision* (London and New York: Routledge, 1988); and *The Listening Self* (London and New York: Routledge,1989). Also see Eugene Gendlin, "A Philosophical Critique of the Concept of Narcissism" in my collection of papers, *Pathologies of the Modern Self* (New York: New York University Press, 1987).

Chapter 5
Stephen Watson, On "How We Are to and How We Are not to Return to the Things Themselves"

[1] V.I., 125.

[2] For further discussion, see my "On the Agon of the Phenomenological: Intentional Idioms and Justification," *Philosophy of the Social Sciences*, 17 (1987).

³ Ibid., 176.

⁴ See Jacques Derrida, *Edmund Husserl's Origin of Geometry: An Introduction*, trans. John P. Leavey, Jr. (Stony Brook: Nicolas Hays, 1978), p. 136. While this confrontation, Derrida argued, is endemic to reading Levinas, it is first of all endemic to Levinas's reading of Husserl. See the conclusion to Levinas's 1930 *The Theory of Intuition in Husserl's Phenomenology*, trans. André Orianne (Evanston: Northwestern University Press, 1973), 153ff.

⁵ See Merleau-Ponty's discussion of *Wesenschau* in "Phenomenology and the Sciences of Man," trans. John Wild, in *The Primacy of Perception*, James M. Edie, ed. (Evanston: Northwestern University Press, 1964), 72ff.

⁶ I have further defended this thesis in my "Merleau-Ponty's Involvement with Saussure," *Continental Philosophy in America*, H. Silverman, J. Sallis, T. Seebohm, eds. (Pittsburgh: Dusquesne University Press, 1983).

⁷ Ph.P., 296.

⁸ A.D., 226.

Chapter 6
Michael B. Smith, Two Texts on Merleau-Ponty by Emmanuel Levinas

¹ Alphonso Lingis, "Translator's Introduction," O.B., xxxviii.

² See the study entitled "The Philosopher and His Shadow" in S. McCleary's translations have been slightly modified—Trans.

³ The French verb *signifier* has, besides its normal meaning, "to signify," a special usage in jurisprudence: "to announce with authority." It is this second meaning, of issuing a command, that Levinas intends here.—Trans.

⁴ See S., 159–81.

⁵ In paragraph 58 and in a note to paragraph 51 of *Ideen I*, a transcendence of God that would not defeat the idealist project is envisaged by Husserl: a possibility described negatively. The point is to see how that view is given more concrete form in the posthumous Husserliana.

⁶ That is, the reintroduction of sociality into esthetic touching.—Trans.

⁷ See, on the ambiguity of sensation and sentiment, our *Otherwise than being*, chapter 2: "Intentionality and Sensing." On the enigmatic, see our study, "Enigme et phénomène," in *En découvrant l'existence avec Husserl et Heidegger*.

Chapter 7
Robert Bernasconi, One-Way Traffic: The Ontology of Decolonization and its Ethics

¹ For an English translation of these two texts, see pp. 53–66, above.

² Derrida, *L'écriture et la différence* (Paris: Seuil, 1967), 229; trans. A. Bass, *Writing and Difference* (Chicago: University of Chicago Press, 1978), 148.

³ See "The Trace of Levinas in Derrida," *Derrida and Différance*, David Wood and Robert Bernasconi, eds. (Evanston: Northwestern University Press, 1988), 13–29. In this essay, originally published in 1985, I note Merleau-Ponty's contribution to Levinas's concept of the trace, but there is more to be said on this score.

⁴ The ambiguity of Husserl's position on these questions had already emerged from Merleau-Ponty's account in "The Philosopher and Sociology" of the former's letter to Lévy-Bruhl (S., 98–113; *S.*, 123–42). Merleau-Ponty's interpretation was vigorously contested by Derrida in his preface to his translations of Husserl's "Origin of Geometry." *Edmund Husserl's L'origine de la géometrie* (Paris: Presses Universitaires de France, 1962), 115–23; trans. John Leavey, *Edmund Husserl's Origin of Geometry: An Introduction* (New York: Nicholas Hays, 1978), 111–17.

⁵ The remarks quoted do not appear in the first version of "Signature" as found in the 1963 edition of *Difficile Liberté*. They were first introduced into the Dutch version of "Signature" in 1969: *Het menselijk gelaat*, A. Peperzak, ed. (Utrecht: Ambo, 1982), 30. They were subsequently incorporated into the revised French version of 1976: R.P., 179/*D.L.*, 374.

⁶ In *Between Levinas and Derrida* (Bloomington: Indiana University Press, forthcoming), I take up the difficult question of whether and to what extent the distinction between Greek wisdom and the Greek language represents a reintroduction of the distinction between thought and language that Levinas had earlier denied. That it is necessary to distinguish Greek wisdom from the Greek language is proposed by the Talmud. Levinas has commented upon it in "La traduction de l'écriture," *Israel, le judaïsme et l'europe* (Paris: Gallimard, 1984), 331–62. That the forms of the Greek language are not the forms of the meaning it represents and do not leave a trace in what has been shown, is clearly stated in an interview published in *The Provocation of Levinas*, R. Bernasconi and D. Wood, eds. (London: Routledge, 1988), 178.

⁷ These ideas would form the basis for defending Levinas against an accusation Merleau-Ponty levels against a certain kind of abstract humanism: "He who condemns all violence puts himself outside the domain to which justice and injustice belong. He puts a curse upon the world and humanity—a hypocritical curse, since he who utters it has already accepted the rules of the game from the moment he has begun to live" (H.T., 110; *H.T.*, 117–18). Some interpretations of Levinas would be more vulnerable to this attack. The question is whether it is simply the I that is put in question by the face of the Other or whether ethics does not come to question itself and its very tendency toward an absolutism in the all too familiar sense. This questioning would explain what Levinas means by making the face absolute: not turning it into a standard or criterion, but absolving it of absolutism. Absolutism would therefore arise precisely in an ethics that was not beyond culture and history.

⁸ One might be tempted to try to indicate the difference between Levinas's account in terms of sense and that of Merleau-Ponty in terms of access by describing the latter's approach as horizontal (C.P., 95/*H.H.*, 46) and the former's as vertical. The model of verticality might be justified on the basis of Levinas's

tendency to construe transcendence as height. However, the contrast between the two thinkers in terms of a horizontal and a vertical transcendence would have to negotiate the suspicion Merleau-Ponty casts on the distinction in "Indirect Language and the Voices of Silence" (S., 70–73; S., 88–91).

⁹ In another context Levinas's use of the term "the West" would need to undergo examination. This is not only because it distorts the complex relation between the "the occident" and "the orient," as was very clear to me when I presented some of the thoughts in this paper to a group of philosophers in Tokyo in November 1988, but also because Levinas uses the phrase "the West" to conceal the complex relation within his thought between Judaism and Hellenism. Although the Greek language provides the forms of thought that allow for a certain universalism, Greek wisdom is put in question. It is at this point that Levinas's understanding of the meaning of Jewish universalism must be interjected, however carefully he attempts to separate his philosophical essays from his so-called confessional writings. The clue is that Levinas says that the key to understanding Jewish universalism is the role played by ethics in the religious relation (D.L., 38). In this context, he qualifies the sense in which Judaism is open to all by introducing the concept of election, although it should not be forgotten that, at least since *Totality and Infinity*, "election" has also served him as a philosophical concept.

¹⁰ Another example of a case where Levinas expresses his enthusiasm for Western culture over its other is to be found in a recent interview in which Levinas was asked about structuralism. In his reply, Levinas introduced the name of Lévi-Strauss, Merleau-Ponty's friend and colleague at the Collège de France. Levinas says that he associates Lévi-Strauss with what he says is "from the moral point of view" called decolonization and the end of European dominance. But Levinas admits that his own primary reaction is the "worse than primitive" one of asking if there is any comparison to be drawn between the scientific mind of an Einstein and the savage mind (*La Pensée sauvage*). Levinas is not content simply to express his suspicion of decolonization as a moral attitude. He attempts to deflate its moral presumption by reducing the issue to a contrast between two kinds of intelligence. "Entretiens" in François Poirié, *Emmanuel Levinas. Qui êtes-vous?* (Lyon: La Manufacture, 1987), 131.

Chapter 8
Patrick Burke, Listening at the Abyss

¹ V.I., 179.
² S., 317.
³ V.I., 103.
⁴ Ibid., 129.
⁵ S., 21.
⁶ V.I., 46.
⁷ Ibid., 38–39.
⁸ Ibid., 39.

⁹ Ibid., 116.
¹⁰ Ibid., 128.
¹¹ Ibid., 92.
¹² Ibid., 94.
¹³ Ibid., 95.
¹⁴ Ibid., 128.
¹⁵ Ibid., 101.
¹⁶ Ibid., 129.
¹⁷ Ibid., 116.
¹⁸ Ibid., 250.
¹⁹ Ibid., 216.
²⁰ Ibid., 214.
²¹ T.L.C.F., 65.
²² Ibid., 65–66.
²³ Levinas, "Il y a," *D.C.P.*, 145.
²⁴ Ibid., 146.
²⁵ Ibid., 145.
²⁶ Ibid., 152.
²⁷ V.I., 101–2.
²⁸ Ph.P., xiii.
²⁹ V.I., 121.
³⁰ Ibid., 104.
³¹ Ibid.
³² "Il y a," *D.C.P.*, 146.
³³ V.I., 103–4.
³⁴ Ibid., 103.
³⁵ T.L.C.F., 90.
³⁶ V.I., 261.

Chapter 9
Wayne J. Froman, Alterity and the Paradox of Being

¹ *Writing and Difference*, trans. A. Bass (Chicago: University of Chicago Press, 1978), p. 124.
² C., 180.
³ *Dialectic and Difference: Finitude in Modern Thought*, ed. and trans. R. Crease and J. T. Decker (Atlantic Highlands, N.J.: Humanities Press, 1985), 128.
⁴ Ibid.
⁵ Ph.P., 57.
⁶ V.I., 4–5.
⁷ Ibid., 7.
⁸ Ibid., 8.
⁹ Ibid., 93.
¹⁰ Ibid., 94.

[11] Ibid., emphasis added.

[12] Ibid., 9.

[13] Ibid., 11.

[14] *Writing and Difference*, 125.

[15] *Merleau-Ponty: Language and the Act of Speech* (Lewisburg, Pa.: Bucknell University Press, 1982).

[16] V.I., 79.

[17] *Writing and Difference*, 124.

[18] S., 180.

[19] V.I., 269.

[20] Ibid., 144–45.

[21] E.M., 164.

[22] V.I., 135. (The sign "[?]" is inserted by Claude Lefort in order to mark terms that are illegible in the original manuscript.)

[23] S., 181.

[24] V.I., 136.

[25] Ibid., 144.

[26] Ibid., 80.

[27] Ibid., 84.

[28] *Writing and Difference*, 102.

[29] Ibid.

[30] V.I., 84.

[31] Ibid., 84–85.

Chapter 10
Monika Langer, Merleau-Ponty and Deep Ecology

[1] See, for example, newspaper articles such as those dealing with the Brundtland Report: *The Globe and Mail*, Monday, April 27, 1987, A1, A10, A11: "Environmental disaster looming, global study warns." Note that the problem-solving approach has been severely criticized by ecophilosophers such as Lorne Leslie Neil Evernden, who points out that thinking "in terms of problems and solutions . . . characterizes our conventional worldview and condemns us to continue in this path of existence" (*The Natural Alien: Humankind and Environment* [Toronto: University of Toronto Press, 1985], 140).

[2] See, for example, Evernden, *The Natural Alien*; Morris Berman, *The Re-enchantment of the World* (Ithaca: Cornell University Press, 1981); Alan Drengson, *Shifting Paradigms: From Technocrat to Planetary Person* (Victoria: Light Star, 1983).

[3] See, for example, Jung and Jung, "To Save the Earth," *Philosophy Today*, vol. 19, no. 2/4 (Summer 1975), 108–17; Michael Zimmerman, "Toward a Heideggerian Ethos for Radical Environmentalism," *Environmental Ethics: An Interdisciplinary Journal Dedicated to the Philosophical Aspects of Environmental Problems*, vol. 5, no. 2 (Summer 1983); and Evernden, *The Natural Alien*, 60–76, 119ff.

Evernden has the most extensive presentation of Merleau-Ponty's position (in the *Phenomenology of Perception*) of any deep ecology author I found in researching my topic. Nonetheless Evernden, too, puts the emphasis on Heidegger. Erazim Kohák draws mostly on Husserl; but he also focuses more on Heidegger than on Merleau-Ponty. In fact, Kohák mentions the latter only in two footnotes in his *The Embers and the Stars: A Philosophical Inquiry into the Moral Sense of Nature* (Chicago: University of Chicago Press, 1984).

⁴ Alan Drengson, "Developing Concepts of Environmental Relationships," *Philosophical Inquiry*, vol. 8, no. 1–2 (1986), 61–62; Arne Naess, "The Shallow and the Deep, Long-Range Ecology Movement. A Summary," *Inquiry*, 16 (1973), 95–100. Naess notes: "The difference between the shallow and deep ecological movement has been made using many words. It would obviously be a risky undertaking to condense such descriptions using only one or two (anti-anthropocentrism, radical egalitarianism, . . .), or even a couple of hundred" (Naess, "Deep Ecology in Good Conceptual Health," *The Trumpeter: Voices from the Canadian Ecophilosophy Net Work*, vol. 3, no. 4 [Fall 1986], 20. See also Drengson, "Fundamental Concepts of Environmental Philosophy: A Summary," *The Trumpeter*, vol. 2, no. 4 [Fall 1985], 23–25. *The Trumpeter* Fall 1986 issue focuses on deep ecology).

⁵ Arne Naess says: "Within the deep ecology movement it is fairly common to use the term 'deep ecologist,' whereas 'shallow ecologist,' I am glad to say, is rather uncommon. Both terms may be considered arrogant and slightly misleading. I prefer to use . . . 'supporter of the deep (or shallow) ecology movement,' avoiding personification" (Naess, "The Deep Ecological Movement: Some Philosophical Aspects," *Philosophical Inquiry*, vol. 8, no. 1–2 [1986], p. 30, n. 5).

⁶ Drengson, "Developing Concepts of Environmental Relationships," *Philosophical Inquiry*, vol. 8, no. 1–2, 1986, 62. See also Michael Zimmerman, "Philosophical Reflections on Reform vs. Deep Environmentalism," *The Trumpeter*, vol. 3, no. 4 [Fall 1986], 12-13. The reader may find the following dictionary definitions (*Webster's New World Dictionary*) useful too: *biosphere*—"1. the zone of the earth, extending from its crust out into the surrounding atmosphere, which contains living organisms. 2. all the living organisms of the earth"; *eco*—"*a combining form meaning* environment or habitat"; *ecology*—"1. a) the branch of biology that deals with the relations between living organisms and their environment b) the complex of relations between a specific organism and its environment. 2. Sociology . . . "; *ecosystem*—"a system made up of a community of animals, plants, and bacteria and the physical and chemical environment with which it is inter-related."

⁷ Drengson provides a useful summary of what he considers to be the four main aspects of deep ecology (critical, analytical, creative, and practical) in Drengson, "Fundamental Concepts of Environmental Philosophy: A Summary," *The Trumpeter*, vol. 2, no. 4 [Fall 1985], 24. See also Warwick Fox, "A Sketch Map of Deep Ecological Territory," in his article "An Overview of My Response to Richard Sylvan's Critique of Deep Ecology," *The Trumpeter*, vol. 2, no. 4 [Fall 1985], 19. An excellent introduction to deep ecology is Bill Devall and George Sessions, *Deep Ecology: Living as if Nature Mattered* (Salt Lake City: Gibbs M.

Smith, Inc., Peregrine Smith Books, 1985). This book also provides a very useful annotated bibliography.

⁸ David Bennett and Richard Sylvan, "Deep Ecology and Green Politics," *The Trumpeter*, vol. 4, no. 2 (Spring 1987), 16. See also Devall and Sessions, *Deep Ecology*, 18–19,69.

⁹ See such works as Martin Heidegger, "Memorial Address," *Discourse on Thinking* (New York: Harper and Row, 1966); Karl Jaspers, *Man in the Modern Age* (Garden City, N.Y.: Doubleday, 1957); Morris Berman, *The Reenchantment of the World*; Lorne Leslie Neil Evernden, *The Natural Alien*; Devall and Sessions, *Deep Ecology*; Erazim Kohák, *The Embers and the Stars*.

¹⁰ Kohák, *The Embers and the Stars*, 12–13.

¹¹ Ibid., 22–25.

¹² Evernden, *The Natural Alien*, 5, 6, 14, 18ff., 124–28, 133–44.

¹³ Ibid., 125–26.

¹⁴ Ibid., 126.

¹⁵ Ibid., 49, 50, 84–86.

¹⁶ Ibid., 134.

¹⁷ See Naess, "The Deep Ecological Movement: Some Philosophical Aspects," *Philosophical Inquiry*, vol. 8, no. 1–2 (1986), 10–13; Evernden, *The Natural Alien*, 6–29.

¹⁸ Evernden, *The Natural Alien*, 5; Drengson, *The Trumpeter*, vol. 1, no. 1 (Fall 1983), 2; Drengson, "Developing Concepts of Environmental Relationships," 62.

¹⁹ Evernden, *The Natural Alien*, 7, 19–23. Note that the issue is not by any means clear-cut. In his article "Reply to Skolimowski" Devall notes that he and Sessions "have written extensively on strategies for natural resources management from a deep ecology perspective and contrasted these strategies with those advocated by supporters of a stewardship position" (*The Trumpeter*, vol. 3, no. 4 [Fall 1986], 15). See also chapter 8 of Devall and Sessions, *Deep Ecology*, and note that they say in Appendix D (241) that "some field ecologists may, on occasion, rise above their professionally scientific approach to Nature."

²⁰ Devall and Sessions, *Deep Ecology*, 65. See also Kohák, *The Embers and the Stars*, pp. xi, 9, 10; and Evernden, *The Natural Alien*, 60-62.

²¹ Warwick Fox, "Post-Skolimowski Reflections on Deep Ecology," *The Trumpeter*, vol. 3, no. 4 (Fall 1986), 16–18; Naess, "A Defence of the Deep Ecology Movement," *Environmental Ethics*, vol. 6, no. 3 (Fall 1984), 269–70; Drengson, "Developing Concepts of Environmental Relationships," 62–63; *The Trumpeter*, vol. 1, no. 1 (Fall 1983), 2; vol. 1, no. 2 (Winter 1984), 1–2; vol. 1, no. 3 (Spring 1984), 1–6 (includes useful bibliography); vol. 2, no. 4 (Fall 1985), 3. Like Naess, Sessions, and Kohák, Drengson is a professional philosopher.

²² Fox, "Post-Skolimowski Reflections on Deep Ecology," 16. Note that the notion of intrinsic value has been very controversial in ecophilosophical discussions, and its consideration has occupied much of the literature. See, for example, Anthony Weston, "Beyond Intrinsic Value: Pragmatism in Environmental Ethics," *Environmental Ethics*, vol. 7, no. 4 (Winter 1985), 323, 330. See also Kohák, *The Embers and the Stars* (the whole book seems to me to hinge on the

notion of intrinsic value). Note that Andrew McLaughlin points out some significant difficulties involved in the debate:

> Disputes over whether or not nature has or has not "intrinsic value" may not be the central question. After all, how can such questions be answered? . . . There are widely divergent intuitions about the "value" of nature, and . . . these differences rest on yet deeper questions. What should be taken as "nature"? Can such deeper divergences be resolved by the appeal to "intuition"? If so, whose counts? Perhaps there is the necessity for character development *before* one's "intuitions" can be trusted. *But* this risks becoming a dogmatic assertion of moral superiority. ["The Critique of Humanity and Nature: Three Recent Philosophical Reflections," *The Trumpeter* (Fall 1987), 2–3.]

For representative articles on the issue of intrinsic value, see those cited by Weston in "Beyond Intrinsic Value." See also Naess's criticism of Weston in Naess, "Deep Ecology in Good Conceptual Health," *The Trumpeter*, vol. 3, no. 4 (Fall 1986), 21. Further, see Henry Skolimowski, "In Defense of Ecophilosophy and of Intrinsic Value: A Call for Conceptual Clarity," *The Trumpeter*, vol. 3, no. 4 (Fall 1986), 9. See also Naess, "Self-realization: An Ecological Approach to Being in the World," Keith Roby lecture in community science, Murdoch University, 12 March 1986. (Published as MSBN 86905-101-6; and published also in *The Trumpeter* [Summer 1987], 35–42.) Naess emphasizes there that the "concept of *ecological self*" is not to be interpreted as that of the ego or "narrow" self. Rather, as Gandhi emphasized, it is a question of reducing "the dominance of the narrow self or the ego" and recognizing that we are "in, of, and for nature from our very beginning. Society and human relations are important, but our self is richer in its constitutive relations." Naess goes on to say:

> Through the wider Self every living being is connected intimately, and from this intimacy follows the capacity of *identification* and as its natural consequence, practice of non-violence. No moralizing is needed. . . . We need to cultivate our insight. . . . The Australian ecological feminist Patsy Hallen uses a formula close to that of the Buddha: We are here to embrace rather than conquer the world. . . . I suspect that our thinking need not proceed from the notion of living being to that of the world, but we will conceive reality or the world we live in as alive in a wide, not easily defined sense."

In short, Self-realization is "a term for widening and deepening your self so it embraces all life forms." Naess adds: "Academically speaking what I suggest is the supremacy of environmental ontology and realism over environmental ethics as a means of invigorating the environmental movement in the years to come" (2, 15, 17, 18, 20).

23 Fox, "Post-Skolimowski Reflections on Deep Ecology," 16. See also Naess, "A Defence of the Deep Ecology Movement," and Drengson, "Developing Concepts of Environmental Relationships."

24 Merleau-Ponty, "Eye and Mind," Pr.P., 159.

25 Ibid., 160.

26 Pr.P., 34, 160. See also S., 98, 197.

27 V.I., 105–6, 183.

28 Ibid., 106–9.

29 Ibid., 117.

30 S.B., 3.

31 Ibid., 4.

32 Ibid., 3, 9, 10, 65, 124–27, 130, 161, 181–84, 199, 201, 216–24.

33 Ibid., 184, 199, 224.

34 Ibid. and Ph.P., 456.

35 "An Unpublished Text," Pr.P., 3.

36 Merleau-Ponty, T.L.C.F., 63–69, 99; translation of "dérivation" altered by editors. See R.C.C.F., 95.

37 Ibid., 83. See also 79-82.

38 Ibid., 84–98, 124–31; and V.I., 14–27.

39 T.L.C.F., 93. Note that I have corrected the translation in keeping with the original French text: R.C.C.F., 131. Note also that Merleau-Ponty says: "The notions of Nature and Reason, for instance, far from explaining the metamorphoses which we have observed from perception up to the more complex modes of human exchange, make them incomprehensible. For by relating them to separated principles, these notions mask a constantly experienced moment, the moment when an existence becomes aware of itself, grasps itself, and expresses its own meaning" ("An Unpublished Text," Pr.P., 10–11).

40 T.L.C.F., 97.

41 Ibid., 98, 128, 129, 131 (and see French text, 137, 177). Note that Merleau-Ponty says in a working note of May 1960: "World and Being: their relation is that of the visible with the invisible (latency) the invisible is not another visible ('possible' in the logical sense) a positive only *absent*" (V.I., 251).

42 V.I., 27, 123, 138, 146, 153; and E.M., 187-88.

43 E.M., 166; V.I., 136–46, 153.

44 S.B., 176.

45 V.I., 102, 271. Note that Merleau-Ponty says this with reference to perception in speaking of philosophy; however, the same can be said of vision and painting. See also E.M., 186.

46 V.I., 139; and E.M., 167.

47 Ibid., 177.

48 Herbert Marcuse, *The Aesthetic Dimension: Toward a Critique of Marxist Aesthetics* (Boston: Beacon Press, 1978), 72.

49 Kohák, *The Embers and the Stars*, xii-xiii. See also David Gross, "On Writing Cultural Criticism," *Telos*, no. 16 (Summer 1973), 45–48.

⁵⁰ E.M., 170–88; and Evernden, *The Natural Alien*, 94–102. See also V.I., 88ff., 135.

⁵¹ V.I., 274. See also 253, 267, 269; and "An Unpublished Text," Pr.P., 6–10.

Chapter 11
Hugh J. Silverman, Merleau-Ponty and Derrida: Writing on Writing

¹ Maurice Merleau-Ponty, P.W., 58.

² See Michel Foucault, *The Order of Things* (New York: Vintage, 1970).

³ See Hugh J. Silverman, *Inscriptions: Between Phenomenology and Structuralism* (London and New York: Routledge & Kegan Paul, 1987), esp. chap. 5.

⁴ See V.I., chap. 4.

⁵ Jacques Derrida, *Margins of Philosophy*, trans. Alan Bass (Chicago: University of Chicago Press, 1982), 296. Hereafter cited as *Martins*.

⁶ See Jacques Derrida, *Spurs: Nietzsche's Styles*, trans. Barbara Harlow (Chicago: University of Chicago Press, 1979).

⁷ See Derrida, *Margins*, 307–30.

⁸ Derrida, *Spurs*, 39.

⁹ Ibid., 41.

Chapter 12
Joseph C. Flay, Hegel and Merleau-Ponty: Radical Essentialism

¹ Maurice Merleau-Ponty, "Hegel's Existentialism," in S.N.S., 63–70. The original, "L'Existentialisme chez Hegel," appeared in *Les Temps Modernes*, 7 (April 1946), 1311–19.

² G. W. F. Hegel, *Phenomenology of Spirit*, trans. A. V. Miller (Oxford: Clarendon Press, 1977). The original, *Phänomenologie des Geistes*, was published in 1807. For a modern edition, see *Phänomenologie des Geistes* (Hamburg: Felix Meiner Verlag, 1952). Citations below will be from the pagination of the English translation.

³ G. W. F. Hegel, *The Science of Logic*, trans. A. V. Miller (London: George Allen & Unwin, and New York: Humanities Press, 1969). *Wissenschaft der Logik* was first published in 1812–13. For a modern German edition, see *Wissenschaft der Logik* (Hamburg: Felix Meiner Verlag, 1963). Citations below will be to the pagination of the English translation. A point to be noted here is that this so-called radical change supposedly took place in a mere five years, which seems to me to be highly unlikely. There is what is probably an irresolvable controversy over the "early" versus the "late" Hegel. I do not recognize any such radical difference. For some arguments for this, see my *Hegel's Quest for Certainty* (Albany: State University of New York Press, 1984) and "The History of Philosophy

and the *Phenomenology of Spirit*," in *Hegel and the History of Philosophy*, Joseph O'Malley et al., eds. (The Hague: Martinus Nijhoff, 1974), 47–61. For a history of the dispute, see Otto Pöggeler, "Zur Deutung der *Phänomenologie des Geistes*," *Hegel-Studien*, 1 (1961), 255–94.

⁴ G. W. F. Hegel, *The Philosophy of Right*, trans. T. M. Knox (Oxford: Clarendon Press, 1945). Originally published in 1820. For a modern edition in German, see *Grundlinien der Philosophie des Rechts* (Hamburg: Felix Meiner Verlag, 1955). Citations below will be to the pagination in the English translation.

⁵ G. W. F. Hegel, *Enzyklopädie der philosophischen Wissenschaften im Grundrisse* (Hamburg: Felix Meiner Verlag, 1959). This is the edition of 1830. There is no single volume in English, but there are three volumes, one for each of the major sections of the Encyclopedia. See *Hegel's Logic*, trans. William Wallace (Oxford: Clarendon Press, 1975); *Hegel's Philosophy of Nature*, trans. A. V. Miller (Oxford: Clarendon Press, 1970); and *Hegel's Philosophy of Spirit*, trans. A. V. Miller (Oxford: Clarendon Press, 1971).

⁶ Alexandre Kojève, *Introduction à la lecture de Hegel* (Paris: Gallimard, 1947). There has been an English translation (*Introduction to the Reading of Hegel*) by James H. Nichols, Jr. (New York: Basic Books, 1969), but only a few essays from the end of the original have been included, and the editing by Allan Bloom has left the bulk of the lectures inaccessible in English. The real test of Kojève's reading of Hegel, however, must remain with the original lectures. Kojève's view has come under severe attack in the last decade, and deservingly so. For citations of some of the critiques, see the discussion in my *Hegel's Quest for Certainty*, 81–112, and the relevant notes on pp. 299 and 306.

⁷ In many ways Herbert Marcuse's *Reason and Revolution* (New York: Oxford University Press, 1941) is still the best explanation of the various movements and machinations involved in the original "forging" of the historical Hegel.

⁸ For some of my own arguments and some from others in support of my rather violent attack on Kojève, see note 6, above.

⁹ For Hegel's own remarks on this, see for example his *Phenomenology of Spirit*, 6–8, and his *Lectures on the History of Philosophy*, trans. E. S. Haldane (London: Routledge and Kegan Paul; New York: Humanities Press, 1956), 3:548-54. The latter pages should be read in conjunction with the discussion, in volume 1, Introduction, concerning development and the relationship between philosophy and time. These lectures cover the years from 1805 until his death in 1831. There is not yet a definitive edition, and therefore these lectures suffer from the "editing" of his "students"; for they were first put together in 1833–36, never having been approved by Hegel. One must therefore take care when citing from these lectures. My rule is that it is relatively safe to quote from the lectures if and only if there is support for the position in Hegel's own published writings. Citations below will be to the pagination in the English translation.

¹⁰ I follow here a method I have attributed to Hegel and which I call "reconstructive retrieval." For further discussion of this, see my "Hegel's *Logic*: The Ironies of the Understanding," in a forthcoming volume from SUNY Press containing the proceedings of the 1988 meeting of Hegel Society of America.

¹¹ I would propose that the problem that Richard Bernstein calls "the Carte-

sian anxiety" has its roots in Plato's philosophy, and so I call the problem the Socratic anxiety. See Richard Bernstein, *Beyond Objectivism and Relativism* (Oxford: Basil Blackwell, 1983).

¹² For a more complete discussion of this, see my "Hegel's *Logic*: The Ironies of the Understanding." There is nothing mysterious or illogical about Hegel's discussion of the category "being." Nor does Hegel think that this abstract "being" is a category that can stand on its own. Hegel begins with this abstraction only to show that it is an abstraction that had been embraced by the tradition.

¹³ From this dialectical reasoning alone we can derive the profundity that Hegel saw in the Christian doctrine of the Trinity. See my remark below, note 15, on Merold Westphal.

¹⁴ A crucial paper on necessity and contingency was published by Dieter Henrich. See "Hegels Theorie über den Zufall," *Kantstudien*, 50 (1958–59), 131–48. In English see also, for example, John Burbidge *On Hegel's Logic* (Atlantic Highlands, N.J.: Humanities Press, 1981). Burbidge also has a smaller study on this specific problem: "The Necessity of Contingency," in *Art and Logic in Hegel's Philosophy* (Atlantic Highlands: Humanities Press; Sussex: Harvester Press, 1980), 201–17. See also George di Giovanni, "The Category of Contingency in the Hegelian Logic," ibid., 179–200. There is a good full-length study in French, André Léonard, *Commentaire littéral de la logique de Hegel* (Paris: J. Vrin, 1974).

¹⁵ See Hegel's discussion of this in his *Science of Logic*, 389. He distinguishes here an ordinary sense of past, where something is past and gone, and the sense he wants to employ, which is put in terms of "timelessness." This term "timelessness" must be understood in the context of his theory of eternity and his denial of the abstract conception of eternity, which belonged to the tradition. It is this critical view of temporality (to be found, fundamentally, in his critique of the separation of the finite from the infinite) that is derivative from his categorial critique. Merold Westphal has made the distinction clear in his *History and Truth in Hegel's Phenomenology* (Atlantic Highlands: Humanities Press, 1979), where in the final chapter he clarifies Hegel's conception of the emergence of eternity in time, a conception that reverses the usual notion of a transcendence of time in order to reach eternity. See also my discussion of this in *Hegel's Quest for Certainty*, 244ff.

¹⁶ For example, Hegel ends his lectures of 1830 on the history of philosophy with the following remark: "This then is the standpoint *of the present day*, and the series of spiritual forms is with it *for the present* concluded" (3:52; italics mine). He then makes very clear that philosophy is to continue and even utters the hope that "this history of philosophy should contain for you [the students] a summons to grasp the spirit of the time, which is present in us by nature, and—each in his own place—consciously to bring it from its natural condition, i.e. from its lifeless seclusion, into the light of day" (ibid., 553). No "end" is to be seen here, either. Compare also his discussion, in the *Lectures on the Philosophy of History*, trans. J. Sibree (New York: Dover Publications, 1956), 452, where he talks of the problem of liberalism "with which history is now occupied, and whose solution it has to work out in the future," and pp. 86–88, his discussion of the new epoch in history to be initiated in the New World. For a modern German edition, see *G. W. F.*

Hegel Werke in zwanzig Bänden, Bd. 12, *Vorlesungen über die Philosophie der Geschichte* (Frankfurt am Main: Suhrkamp Verlag, 1970). Citations below will be to the pagination in the English translation. Finally, there is the warning in the *Philosophy of Right* that *no* philosopher, Hegel included, can leap beyond his own time. See *Philosophy of Right*, 11–12.

[17] On the embeddedness of language and thought, see, for example, *Science of Logic*, 37ff. This view must inform any analysis of the passages on language in the *Encyclopedia*, a fact ignored by most who comment on Hegel and language. See also my review of Daniel Cook, *Language in the Philosophy of Hegel* (The Hague/ Paris: Mouton, 1973) in *Studies in Language*, 2 (1978), 116–19, and my discussion of language in the first two chapters of *Hegel's Quest for Certainty*.

[18] The actual passage is the following: "But this reconciliation [which I have just shown philosophically] is itself only a partial reconciliation, without external universality, and philosophy is, in this connection, a sanctuary apart, and its servants form an isolated order of priests, who must not mix with the world and who have to care for the possession of Truth. How the temporal, empirical present finds its way out of this discord and schism, how it will form itself, is to be left to it and is not the immediate practical affair and concern of philosophy" (*Lectures on the Philosophy of Religion*, trans. E. B. Spiers and J. Burdon Sanderson [New York: Humanities Press, 1962], 3:151. The ambiguity is all here, and to take this passage by itself and make a case for Hegel's position as falling on one side or the other is just what cannot be done. This passage, in addition to showing the ambiguity, also shows Hegel's own inability to handle the full consequences of his own position.

Chapter 13
Merold Westphal, Situation and Suspicion in the Thought of Merleau-Ponty: The Question of Phenomenology and Politics

[1] I give the date of his death, for he was working on V.I. at that time. The partial manuscript and working notes were published in 1964. If I give short shrift to S.B., it is because I am persuaded by Joseph Kockelmans that, under the influence of Heidegger and the late Husserl, Merleau-Ponty works with a significantly different understanding of phenomenology in Ph.P. from that of S.B. See "Psychology in Merleau-Ponty's Early Works," R.E.P.P., 119–42. It is also because I am persuaded by Gary Brent Madison that the primary target of S.B. is empiricism, while the primary target of Ph.P. is intellectualism. See *The Phenomenology of Merleau-Ponty: A Search for the Limits of Consciousness* (Athens: Ohio University Press, 1981), 51. (Hereafter cited as Madison.) Both of these points emphasize the break with Cartesianism presupposed by the emphasis on the situated character of the perceiving subject, a theme central to my thesis.

[2] Paul Ricoeur, *Freud and Philosophy; An Essay on Interpretation*, trans. Denis Savage (New Haven: Yale University Press, 1970), 32. See also Roslyn Wallach

Bologh, *Dialectical Phenomenology: Marx's Method* (Boston: Routledge & Kegan Paul, 1979), and Merold Westphal, "Nietzsche and the Phenomenological Ideal," *The Monist*, 60 (April 1977), 278–88. Merleau-Ponty mentions Kierkegaard (along with Hegel) in the passage under consideration. On the hermeneutics of suspicion in Kierkegaard, see Merold Westphal, *Kierkegaard's Critique of Reason and Society* (Macon: Mercer University Press, 1987), especially chapters 2, 6, and 7, and "Kierkegaard's Psychology and Unconscious Despair," *International Kierkegaard Commentary: The Sickness Unto Death*, Robert L. Perkins, ed. (Mercer University Press, 1987). Merleau-Ponty was himself taking the hermeneutics of suspicion seriously as early as his favorable review of Scheler's *Ressentiment* (1935), in which he critiques the neo-Kantianism of Ramon Fernandez and calls for a philosophy that would take seriously "the life of sentiments and emotions and render the complaisances of M. Fernandez less secret." These words are from Barry Cooper's summary of the review in *Merleau-Ponty and Marxism: From Terror to Reform* (Toronto: University of Toronto Press, 1979), 4–5.

³ The reference to guilt or shame is important here. For the target of suspicion is not a generic evasion of self-acknowledgment but specifically the form that seeks to hide what is morally suspect. Mike W. Martin refers to this mode of self-deception as "inner hypocrisy," in *Self-Deception and Morality* (Lawrence: University of Kansas Press, 1986), chap. 3. This is why I challenge the suggestion of Hubert L. Dreyfus that there is a hermeneutics of suspicion to be found in division 2 of *Being and Time*. See "Socrates Between Jeremiah and Descartes: The Dialectic of Self-Consciousness and Self-Knowledge," *Philosophy and Theology*, 2, 3 (Spring 1988), 199–219.

⁴ Sigmund Freud, *The Complete Psychological Works: Standard Edition*, James Strachey, ed. (New York: Norton, 1953–74), 4:160.

⁵ *Genealogy of Morals*, second essay, section 1. "Forgetting is no mere *vis inertiae* as the superficial imagine; it is rather an active and in the strictest sense positive faculty of repression, that is responsible for the fact that what we experience and absorb enters our consciousness as little while we are digesting it . . . as does the thousandfold process, involved in physical nourishment" (Kaufmann translation).

⁶ Merleau-Ponty recognizes the possibility of disguising the institutional violence of liberal democracy by appeals to the concepts of providence or misfortune (H.T., 16, 107). But his focus is on the role played by principles and ideals.

⁷ The Marx quotation is from the earliest published statement of the theory of ideology critique, the 1843 Introduction to an anticipated *Contribution to the Critique of Hegel's Philosophy of Right*. Merleau-Ponty continues: "In refusing to judge liberalism in terms of the ideas it espouses and inscribes in constitutions and in demanding that these ideas be compared with the prevailing relations between men in a liberal state, Marx is not simply speaking in the name of a debatable materialist philosophy—he is providing a formula for the concrete study of society which cannot be refuted by idealist arguments. Whatever one's philosophical or even theological position, a society is not the temple of value-idols that figure on the front of its monuments or in its constitutional scrolls; the value of a society is the value it places upon man's relation to man. It is not just a

question of knowing what the liberals have in mind but what in reality is done by the liberal state within and beyond its frontiers" (H.T., xiv).

⁸ It is clear that while Merleau-Ponty argues that Stalinist violence could have been justified, he also concludes that it is in fact without justification. What he writes in 1960 is already his view in 1947, that "the U.S.S.R. and its recent adversaries are perhaps on the same side, the side of the old world" (S., 4).

⁹ Merleau-Ponty is regularly suspicious of the self-satisfaction gained by distracting attention from one's own sins through shouting loudly about those of the enemy. Compare Cooper, 97, with 77–78 and 145.

¹⁰ With help from Weber, Merleau-Ponty repeats his earlier critique of hiding reality behind virtuous feelings and pure motives (A.D., 27–28).

¹¹ Quoted by Martin Jay in *Marxism and Totality: The Adventures of a Concept from Lukács to Habermas* (Berkeley: University of California Press, 1984), 382.

¹² The temporality in which the subject is situated is especially important here (Ph.P., 347, 365, 398, 423). Along with speech as gesture, it serves as a bridge between the natural and cultural worlds, which cannot be clearly distinguished from the subject who is already "in" and "of" them while being the one "for whom" they are phenomena.

¹³ See note 12 and Madison, 157–59.

¹⁴ For the passivity motif, compare Ph.P., 347, 358, 404, 427, 448; Pr.P., 6, 8, with V.I., 42–43, 118, 129, 139, 151, 155, 176, 181, 185, 197, 221, 264-66, 274; E.M., 167 (Ernst and Klee). For the theme of anonymity, compare Ph.P., 216, 240, 331, 347, 404, 448, with V.I., 139, 142, 155, 201, 246.

¹⁵ In other words, we find the transcendental subject we are looking for when and only when we realize the *Ineinander* relationship between the self and its world (cf. V.I., 172), the impossibility of clearly and distinctly distinguishing between them.

¹⁶ At this stage of the game Merleau-Ponty would agree with this assessment of his earlier work: "Although Merleau-Ponty refuses to recognize Husserl's transcendental Ego, substituting for it instead the lived body as the first subject of perception, his position basically does not differ in any radical way from Husserl's; for, like Husserl, Merleau-Ponty postulates that the only meaning of being is being-for-the-subject and maintains immanence as the first requirement of philosophical method" (Madison, 226).

¹⁷ The link between the countertradition and liberalism seems to me looser in both directions than this would suggest. It is hard to imagine placing such key figures as Protagoras, Gorgias, Kierkegaard, and Nietzsche in the liberal camp. Nor is liberalism essentially linked to a skeptical humanism. In Locke and Jefferson, for example, it grounds itself in a rationalist theory of natural rights. It is true, as Allan Bloom has pointed out, that a relativism that might be placed in the countertradition has increasingly come to be the popular rationale for liberalism. See *The Closing of the American Mind* (New York: Simon & Schuster, 1987), 25–30.

¹⁸ I think it is fair to say that the philosophy of ambiguity or the hermeneutics of finitude as developed especially by Heidegger, Gadamer, and Merleau-Ponty provides the best *philosophical* framework for interpreting the demise of the concept of totality narrated by Martin Jay in *Marxism and Totality*. Neither theoreti-

cians nor practitioners are very good at grasping the whole insofar as they are situated in, surrounded by, and even invaded by the world they seek to understand and change.

[19] Here again Martin's notion of "inner hypocrisy" is helpful. See note 3 above. For the motivation that makes this mystification self-deception and not just limited vision is a moral motivation. As a device for overriding conscience, it presupposes the presence of conscience.

[20] From the General Introduction to *After Philosophy: End or Transformation?*, Kenneth Baynes, James Bohman, and Thomas McCarthy, eds. (Cambridge: MIT Press, 1987), 4.

[21] Similarly, I find the following interpretation dubious: "With a certain affinity to the work of Marx and Freud, the *Phenomenology* [*of Perception*] attempts to accomplish a 'letting-go' of the thinking subject and show him to be a dependent subject—dependent in regard to a life or current of existence which properly possesses a meaning of its own. The personal subject merely continues on in a tradition which he did not initiate but received as an inheritance" (Madison, 69; for a quite different reading, see 164). This is good as far as it goes, and there surely is "a certain affinity" with Marx and Freud. But again, dependence on the impersonal is not the same as false consciousness for the sake of overriding conscience. See note 19 above.

[22] Dorothea Olkowski, "Merleau-Ponty's Freudianism: From the Body of Consciousness to the Body of Flesh," R.E.P.P., 102, 105, and J. B. Pontalis, "The Problem of the Unconscious in Merleau-Ponty's Thought," R.E.P.P., 85, 88–89.

[23] I do not mean to suggest that Hegel embodies the Marxist overcoming of philosophy in its realization, only that practice and action clearly emerge as themes of philosophical reflection, giving that reflection a political significance lacking in Merleau-Ponty's.

[24] Søren Kierkegaard, *The Sickness Unto Death*, trans. Howard V. Hong and Edna H. Hong (Princeton: Princeton University Press, 1980), 13.

[25] Kierkegaard's dialectical analysis is more Hegelian than Derridean, designed to preclude a dualistic interpretation, but not to undermine the dipolar categories as such. For more detailed analysis, see John Elrod, *Being and Existence in Kierkegaard's Pseudonymous Works* (Princeton: Princeton University Press, 1975), chap. 2.

[26] Compare "Kierkegaard's Psychology and Unconscious Despair" with *Kierkegaard's Critique of Reason and Society*, especially chapters 3 and 7. My overall argument about the relation of phenomenology to critical social theory is in harmony with that of Paul Piccone and James L. Marsh. Piccone argues that critical theory requires a phenomenological foundation. "From Tragedy to Farce; The Return of Critical Theory," *New German Critique*, 7 (Winter 1976), 91–104. And Marsh argues that phenomenology can become politically critical only as a hermeneutics of suspicion. "Dialectical Phenomenology: From Suspension to Suspicion," *Man and World*, 17 (1984), 121–41, and "Dialectical Phenomenology as Critical Social Theory," *Journal of the British Society for Phenomenology*, 16 (May 1985), 177–93.

[27] Part of what "equally sophisticated" means here is that such a phenomenol-

ogy need not assume that in its desire the self is transparent to itself nor that in its willing it is the ground of itself. Kierkegaard explicitly refuses both these assumptions in *The Sickness Unto Death*. It is because Paul Ricoeur's reading of Freud in both *Freud and Philosophy* and *The Conflict of Interpretations* is a semantics of desire rooted in a phenomenology of the will that it is more fruitful for a critical theory of culture than Merleau-Ponty's reinterpretations of Freud. The possibility of the transition from fallibility to fault is crucial for Ricoeur. See *The Symbolism of Evil*, trans. Emerson Buchanan (New York: Harper & Row, 1967), 3. It corresponds closely to the movement from ambiguity to ambivalence and from situation to suspicion.

Index